Horses in the
British Army
1750–1950

Horses in the British Army 1750–1950

Janet Macdonald

Pen & Sword
MILITARY

First published in Great Britain in 2017 by
PEN & SWORD MILITARY
An imprint of
Pen & Sword Books Ltd
47 Church Street
Barnsley
South Yorkshire
S70 2AS

ISBN 978-1-47386-371-2

Typeset by Concept, Huddersfield HD4 5JL.
Printed and bound in England by TJ International Ltd, Padstow, PL28 8RW.

Pen & Sword Books Ltd incorporates the imprints of Pen & Sword Archaeology,
Atlas, Aviation, Battleground, Discovery, Family History, History, Maritime,
Military, Naval, Politics, Railways, Select, Social History, Transport, True Crime,
and Claymore Press, Frontline Books, Leo Cooper, Praetorian Press,
Remember When, Seaforth Publishing and Wharncliffe.

For a complete list of Pen & Sword titles please contact
PEN & SWORD BOOKS LIMITED
47 Church Street, Barnsley, South Yorkshire, S70 2AS, England
E-mail: enquiries@pen-and-sword.co.uk
Website: www.pen-and-sword.co.uk

Dedication

In memory of Jasper and Oscar,
the most beloved two of all my horses.

Contents

List of Plates

Author's Note

- For simplicity, I have referred to all animals as 'he', except when specifically referring to mares.
- Although not strictly the British Army, I have included the army in India as though it was.
- Although he did not become the Viscount and then Duke of Wellington until 1809 and 1814 respectively, I have referred to Sir Arthur Wellesley by that name throughout.

Acknowledgements

I am grateful to all who have assisted with researching this book, especially the staff at The National Archives, Kew (especially William Spencer), at the Royal Army Veterinary Corps Museum, at the Royal Logistics Corps Museum, at the Hartley Library at the University of Southampton, and at The King's Troop, Woolwich, and Mick Crumplin, Len Barnett, Joyce Dudeney and the Sussex Yeomanry, Kim Blackburn for photographs, Sharon Cregier, Andy Spatcher, Dick Tennant, Mark Thompson, and as always my husband Ken Maxwell-Jones, still performing additional research, photography, chauffering and coffee-making duties.

Glossary

Abyssinia – now Ethiopia.

Action – the way a horse moves, ideally with all legs moving up and down in a straight line.

Aids – the signals given by a rider to a horse with hands, legs and heels.

Araba – a bullock wagon used in Crimea.

Bail – a pole separating horses in a stable.

Bearing rein – a tight fixed rein designed to keep the horse's head at a desirable level; considered cruel if too tight.

Breaking in – the process of teaching a horse to accept a rider or harness.

Cacolet – a sort of chair for carrying wounded on either side of a horse or other animal.

Casting – sold alive when no longer useful for army service through age, recurrent illness or injury.

Cavalry – mounted soldiers who fight from horseback.

Class – type of horse by use: charger, troop horse, draught, etc.

Cob – a short sturdy horse.

Common – a poorly bred horse, with lumpy limbs and a coarse head.

Coronet – the line of flesh and hair immediately above the hoof.

Crush – a tight enclosure, or one which can be tightened, to handle unruly animals.

Dragoons – a type of mounted infantryman who rode to battle but fought dismounted. The word derives from their flintlock carbines, called 'dragon-fire spouters'.

Entire – a male horse which has not been gelded; a stallion.

Epizootic – veterinary term for an epidemic, such as rinderpest.

Fascines – bundles of withies and brush, used to fill ditches or provide a protective shield from enemy fire.

Feather – hair on the legs/heels of a horse, of varied length and thickness.

Flat – an ignorant person who could easily be persuaded to buy something useless.

Flat-catcher – a weedy horse, the sort often bought by a flat because it was showy.

Forage – horse feed, a generic term which could mean all feed, or the long grasses and other vegetation cut by the troops.

Forging/clicking – a noise made by the horse's shoes clicking together.

Frog – the V-shaped spongy part on the underside of a horse's foot, important for absorbing percussion.

Fuller – the groove in a horse shoe.

Gabions – wickerwork or wire baskets filled with stones or earth, used to build embankments or provide a protective shield from enemy fire.

Hairy heels – not very well-bred (can also be applied to humans).

Halter – a headstall made of leather, webbing or rope used to tie horses up; sometimes used as the headpiece of a bridle.

'Hard' feed – corn, often crushed, served dry.

hh – 'hands high', a measurement taken at the wither. A hand is 4in.

Highlow – an ankle length shoe fastening at the front.

Hogging – cutting off all the hair of the mane and forelock.

Horse – this term includes mules or other beasts used for riding, draught or burden, under the Army Act 1912, Section 190.

Horse Guards – cavalry regiments dedicated to protecting the sovereign.

Horsemastership – the art of caring for horses by feeding, grooming, watering and good exercise.

Hussars – a type of light cavalry, often armed with carbines as well as swords.

Lancers – a type of light cavalry, armed with lances as well as swords.

Leggy – a horse whose legs are disproportionately long.

Mesopotamia – now Iraq.

Mucking out – cleaning out droppings and wet bedding from a stable.

Notifiable – an infectious disease which must be reported to the authorities.

Points of the horse – parts of the equine body, such as the withers, hocks, etc.

Porte (also the Grand Porte) – the governing body of Turkey.

Remount – a horse bought for the army before issue to a particular unit, or to replace a casualty.

Rising trot – the movement of a rider up and down in the saddle in time with the horse's movement in trot.

Sap – a type of trench, either covered or dug in a zigzag, to approach an enemy position.

Sapper – the engineer who digs a sap.

Shabraque – a saddle-cloth, usually ornate.

Sheath – the male horse's penis cover.

Sitting trot – the opposite of rising trot, when the rider absorbs the motion through his back, waist and hips.

Snead – the curved handle of a scythe.

Spruit – a small deep watercourse, dry except after heavy rain.

Squadron – a unit of cavalry.

Staling – equine urination.

Surcingle – a belt, shaped to fit at the withers, which goes right round the horse to keep rugs in place.

Thrush – a bad-smelling fungal infection of the underside of the feet.

Treads – an injury caused to the back of the forefeet by a strike from the front of the hind feet.

Withers – the highest part of a horse's shoulder, immediately under the pommel of the saddle.

Introduction

Suddenly I heard the gallop of horses, and turning, saw Moore. He came at speed, and pulled up so sharp and close, he seemed to have alighted from the air; man and horse looking at the approaching foe with an intenseness that seemed to concentrate all feeling in their eyes. The sudden stop of the animal, a cream-coloured one with black tail and mane, had cast the latter streaming forwards, its ears were pushed out like horns, while its eyes flashed fire, and it snorted loudly with expanded nostrils, expressing terror, astonishment and muscular exertion. My first thought was, it will be away like the wind! But then I looked at its rider and the horse was forgotten. Thrown on its haunches, the animal came sliding and dashing the dirt up with its fore feet, thus bending the General forward almost to its neck; but his head was thrown back, and his look more keenly piercing than I ever before saw it. He glanced to the right and left, and then fixed his eyes intently on the enemy's advancing column, at the same time grasping the reins with both his hands, and pressing the horse firmly with his knees. His body thus seemed to deal with the animal while his mind was intent on the enemy, and his aspect was one of searching intenseness beyond the power of words to express. For a while he looked, and then galloped to the left, without uttering a word.[1]

This description, by Charles Napier, of Sir John Moore's movements at the battle of Corunna in 1809, together with numerous artistic depictions of cavalrymen in action, and even more numerous books on cavalry, explains why, when one mentions horses in the army, most people say 'Ah yes, cavalry'. But there is far more to military horses than those carrying gallant soldiers in battle, be they cavalry, dragoons or lancers. The two wars which used vast numbers of horses were the Boer War (1899–1902) and the First World War (1914–1918). Although we do have some figures for the Boer War, they are by no means complete, but for the First World War we do have good numbers.[2] From these, we can see that at the end of August 1918, when the total number of horses and mules was 828,360, the number designated as riding horses was 193,747 (23.4 per cent). And that is riding horses, not cavalry horses; we don't have a number that splits it up, but one estimate for the 1880s for a force of eight infantry regiments, three cavalry regiments, two artillery batteries, officers for all those and a general and his staff gives 1,200 cavalry horses (three regiments at 400 per regiment) and other riding horses at 363 (30.25 per cent). And these are figures for a fighting force; add horses for all the officers and non-coms of other units, such as the Commissariat, the Royal Engineers (RE), and the medical and veterinary services, and the percentage of cavalry horses drops further.

In the Napoleonic Wars, where we do have some figures, the percentage is even lower. Of all the British Army soldiers in 1794 (85,097), only 17 per cent (14,527) were cavalry. When war was resumed after the Peace of Amiens in 1805, it was 12.5 per cent and in 1813 it was 11.3 per cent.[3] There were a mere 5,137 cavalrymen at Waterloo.

So if only a smallish percentage of the horses in the British Army were cavalry, we have to consider what all the others did. And going on from there, how they were acquired, trained and cared for, and when no longer needed at the end of each war, what happened to them.

Chapter One

The Nature of the Beast

To a predator, horses represent mobile meat, and being instinctively aware of that, they are always ready to take flight when alarmed. They are not equipped to fight off a predator, only being able to kick (with either or both hind feet together) at things behind or buck to dislodge things on their backs. Although they do have formidable front teeth, it is a rare horse who uses them on a human, and then it is more likely to be a sly nip than a full high-speed open-mouthed attack. Stallions do use their teeth when fighting other stallions over mares, but even they are unlikely to bite humans.

Given all of this, it should not be surprising that young equines who have not grown accustomed to new surroundings and the objects and noises they meet are more likely to shy or try to run away when they encounter something new, or on a windy day when moving vegetation or flags might conceal a lion or a dragon.

The simple answer to this is to make sure that youngsters are accompanied by an older sober horse until they have accepted that the world is not going to bite them. However, even mature horses can take fright and stampede.

Thunderstorms and hailstorms (these are prevalent in the centre of France, in the area known as Berry) are the main causes of stampedes. They are less likely to happen if each man is at his horse's head, talking to him and stroking him. But sometimes a stampede will start for no reason discernible to humans, and if not stopped, can do serious damage to the horses and whatever they encounter. In the Crimea, Temple Goodman reported that on their first night in camp, because the ropes and picket poles were rotten the horses got loose and galloped all over the camp, knocking down tents.[1]

The Countess of Ranfurly, who accompanied her husband and the Sherwood Rangers in Palestine in March 1940, told of a day when, having paused for lunch and watering in a narrow lane with houses on one side and a hedge on the other,

> suddenly, without the slightest warning, two squadrons of horses ... charged down the track at full gallop. They swept by like an avalanche, some of them crashed headlong into two army trucks which were parked in the lane, others hit the telegraph poles which fell like nine-pins and, as they passed, Dan's troop broke loose and went with them. When the dust

cleared [there was] an incredible scene of destruction – injured men, dead horses and a tangle of equipment lay everywhere and, far away, a moving trail of dust showed the horses were still racing madly on. ... [it took ages to find the horses] some had gone back to Latrun [the previous day's base] some are still lost. Dan found his chestnut mare covered with blood – all the skin torn off her shoulders and flanks. She had galloped through a barbed-wire fence. But many other horses were worse and several had to be shot. [It happened again in the night] one horse crashed into the cook-house and sent it up in flames. The poor cook had both his legs broken.

... no one knows what caused these stampedes. Some think that there may be a mad horse which is the ring-leader. But the fact is that at some indefinable signal a hundred horses will move as one, and nothing will stop them. The Cheshire Yeomanry who are up at Acre in the north have had the same trouble; some of their horses stampeded and plunged over a cliff into the sea.[2]

Stampedes occurred elsewhere. In the depot at East Alton, USA, in June 1915 some 3,000 horses from two large paddocks stampeded during a severe thunderstorm. Several horses got onto the railway line, where thirteen were killed by a train; twelve others were killed, and ten were never found, being thought to have got onto islands caused by the flooding of the Mississippi river and drowned. Some of the horses from the first storm were found 30 miles away from the depot. A further storm three days later hit the same depot, without a stampede, but three horses were killed by lightning.

Part of the stampede situation is that horses are herd animals, and each will follow the others in frightening circumstances. Even without frights, they prefer to be with their usual companions, and can be difficult when asked to leave them, which is not a problem if they are trained to work alone, but this can take some time, especially with artillery or cavalry horses. For this reason, staff officers carrying despatches used their own horse.

One, fortunately rare, example of equine panic is their reaction to fire. They can be taught to ignore small fires out of doors, even jumping over them on displays, but they cannot cope with fire in their stables. Opening doors does not, as one might suppose, encourage them to run out, and the only way to get them out is to cover their heads with a coat or blanket and lead them out, but even this does not always work.

As a general rule, horses grow calmer as they mature, becoming less nervous as they become used to what is going on around them and more trusting of humans. That herd instinct means that like all animals which live in social groups, horses grow up learning to obey the group leader. In a domestic situation, it is humans who fill that role. As is normal in nature, mature animals will sometimes challenge that role and need to be put in their place. This occasionally happens with older mares, who are the leaders in the wild (except in the mating season), but most frequently with stallions, especially in summer when in-season mares are around, and hardly ever with geldings, which is, of course, the reason for gelding. Mares can sometimes be uneven tempered, while geldings are generally more even tempered and calmer all round.

As well as becoming generally calmer, older horses (usually after about twelve years old) are likely to show signs of age in their legs, with such issues as splints and side-bones. With good care and gentler work after his mid-teens, a horse can live to about thirty-two or thirty-three. That gentler work could be as a 'schoolmaster', teaching people to ride, as a calmer mount for a nervous rider, or, in Victorian thinking, for a lady.

Modern police horses and ceremonial military horses are given 'nuisance' training so they become used to sudden and potentially frightening events: children's balloons, opening umbrellas, cheering crowds and even gunshots and artillery fire. As with all things equine, a wiser older horse who takes such things in his stride will help youngsters learn to tolerate all sort of 'dragons', even skateboards!

The other side of this coin is that horses will grow very attached to their human if treated kindly (carrots and peppermints help). There are numerous stories of horses staying with their injured masters in frightening circumstances, or following them; for instance the officer's horse at Corunna, who swam after the boat which was taking his officer master to a ship for evacuation. Alas, that horse could not be taken aboard and had to be left behind. Whether he drowned or swam back to shore is not known, but the outcome cannot have been happy.

Work Capacity

A horse in good condition, when forming part of a large body of cavalry, should be able to cover 20–25 miles a day. Most of this would be done at a walk, at an average pace of about 4mph. A distance of 40–45 miles a day would constitute a forced march and might have to be done at 5–6mph, necessitating the occasional use of the trot, a pace averaging 8mph. The smaller the body of cavalry involved, the quicker would be the rate of marching, and at the strength of a regiment a march of 30 miles might be done at the rate of 6mph, thus giving the horse more time for rest. Whatever distance had to be covered, the cavalry had to be prepared to go into action at once and deliver a charge at the rate of 12mph, perhaps followed by a fast pursuit of a broken enemy. Modern hunters may do as much as 40–50 miles a day, but would only do this twice a week at most. The RHA harness horse could do about the same, when pulling guns and their wagons; in other words, the vehicles should be capable of keeping up with cavalry. Draught horses pulling heavy loads would be much slower.

Condition

One of the most important factors for a horse's ability to perform properly is his condition. Horses are considered to be in good condition when they feel firm when stroked and are neither thin nor over-fat and flabby. Both tire quickly and then move unevenly in walk and trot, or sweat and have difficulty breathing properly. They often stumble and may fall and break their knees. If pushed to make an extra effort, they may sprain a tendon. The obvious response to such indications is for the rider to dismount, if the situation allows, and lead his horse, or even stop for a while before going on. Such out-of-condition horses need to be worked gently at the walk twice a day for several days, and their daily work gradually increased.

Conformation

A horse's (and mule's) ability to work properly and for many years, both essentials for the military horse, arises from his shape and good conformation. The two essentials, from which everything else devolves, are heart and lung capacity, which basically means a broad chest and well-sprung ribs, and good legs. If you ignore the head and neck, a horse is basically like a rectangular table, with a leg at each corner, and like a table, if one leg is not straight, it will not stand properly. If the non-straightness is due to a joint, so that the weight does not pass properly down the limb, that joint will wear unevenly. Looking from the side, one might point out that the hind legs are not straight up and down as are the front legs, but as long as the bend at the hocks is not extreme, there will be no problems. It is from the rear that hock deviations can best be seen, the worst of these being 'cow hocks', where the legs slope in and the hocks are too close together.

The worst of the front leg faults is known as 'over at the knee', where there is a bend forwards at the knee. This, together with knock knees, can be corrected over time with remedial shoeing. The front legs should be well spaced at the top and a good width should carry on through and behind the girth. The back, equally, should be broad and, apart from the dip behind the wither, comparatively level. Too much bend downwards is called 'sway-backed' and is a weakness; too much bend upwards is called 'roach-backed' and makes for difficult saddle fitting. If not extreme, this shape is normal in mules and donkeys, and acceptable in a pack horse.

The pasterns, the length of bone between the hoof and the fetlock, should slope at about 45 degrees; more than this involves excessive flexion of that joint, while less, especially if the pastern is almost perpendicular, gives a jolting ride and excessive percussion up through the legs. The shoulders should also have a slope of about 45 degrees in a riding horse but be more upright in a draught horse, where much of the power comes from the front. Upright shoulders in a riding horse, like the upright pasterns, gives a jolting ride, which is uncomfortable and tiring for the rider on a long march; it also passes excessive concussion up from the feet to the joints.

There are numerous other faults of conformation, but those listed above are most likely to indicate weakness or discomfort to the rider. There remains only the neck and head and the faults to be found there are more related to beauty than function. The neck should not be too long or too short, nor look as though it has been put on upside-down; this is known as a 'ewe-neck', but is not a major fault. The head should not appear over-clumsy or heavy. In general, the British prefer a straight or slightly dished face (which comes from the Arabian blood in the thoroughbred) rather than a Roman nose. A very few horses have lop ears, which they cannot prick up, but hear perfectly well. At the end of the day, handsome is as handsome does.

Like all other animals (and humans), intelligence in horses varies from beast to beast. In general, it is something that acquaintance with the animal will determine, but a horse with an alert expression that watches what is going on about him will be intelligent, while one that has a dull eye and is not interested in the world is likely to be dim. Temperament also varies: the default is that any given horse, once he has got over youthful nervousness, will be calm and happy; one which is nervy and starts at sudden noises or movement may never get over it. This is common in poorly bred thoroughbreds, and such a horse is potentially dangerous to his rider. However, sometimes this nervyness is due to over rich feeding, and can be controlled by reducing the amount of 'heating' food in his diet. Heating food can include beans or oats, and only experimentation will show how much should be given.

Captain Hayes, a prolific author of practical books on horses and riding, and an army veterinarian, remarked that a cruel habit was indulged in by the 'kaffirs' at Port Elizabeth, who would strike the horses on the muzzle in an attempt to prevent the animals treading on their feet. It would, he said, be better to provide these men with stout boots to protect their feet, which would also prevent the horses becoming 'head shy' from expecting a blow when anyone went near their heads.

Some horses get bored when they spend long periods in the stable, often associated with an injury. Some weave (constantly shifting their weight from one front foot to the other and often swinging their head in the same rhythm) and others crib-bite and wind-suck (taking hold of a surface with their teeth and sucking in a gulp of air, which they swallow). The weaving tires them out, crib-biting wears out their front teeth, often so much that they can no longer graze, and wind-sucking interferes with their digestion. These stable vices are incurable, and unfortunately are often copied by other horses. They were considered serious enough to be a cause for rejection when buying.

Other vices, which are not dependant on a stable, are kicking and biting. For horses who kick at the walls of their stable (usually through boredom, although if it is only occasional they may be kicking at a rat), hanging a prickly bush on the walls may be a deterrent. The modern way to deal with kicking out-of-doors is to tie a red ribbon in the kicker's tail to warn others to keep clear. Biting can be dealt with by fitting a muzzle, or a tight noseband.

Mules

There are two types of mule. The cross between a male donkey and a female horse is the most valuable sort, and can be distinguished by its voice, which is like that of the donkey. The other is a cross between a male horse and a female donkey, and neighs like a horse. Both are sterile, but can still get the urge to reproduce, so the males are usually gelded. Mules are not fully grown until five and should not be worked hard before that age; they can then go on until twenty-five. (Wellington preferred them to be over six.) The larger ones tend to be weak in the lower part of the leg, from the knee down.

The mule is more capable of bearing fatigue than the horse, and is less restive under heavy loads. Males (horse mule or john mule) can carry larger loads than females (hinnies). The average load for a pack mule is a little over 200lb, with all but 160lb of this being the pack saddle; larger mules can carry up to 320lb total, smaller ones 120lb. They move at 2½ to 3½mph and can cover some 15–20 miles a day on good surfaces; a day's journey in a mountainous country with bad roads was 10–12 miles loaded, 15 or 16 unloaded.

Mules can pick their way easily on bad tracks or steep slopes but move faster going uphill than down. However, they do not take kindly to sudden loud noises, such as gunfire or thunder. They will happily follow a leader (usually a mare wearing a bell), and do not need to be tied together head to tail. Some believe they prefer a grey mare to follow. This loose configuration cannot be used in a baggage train or as part of a mixed convoy, when they have to be tied head to tail and led by a human.

Mules proved to be far more resistant to adverse circumstances than horses: deaths from disease or during transportation on land and sea were less than half of those among horses, and they could be kept in good condition on 75 per cent of the food ration allotted to horses. They were less liable to disease (including mange) and thus formed a smaller proportion of the patients in veterinary hospitals, although there was an outbreak of surra in Lucknow in the Second World War. Their skin is harder and less sensitive to rain and sun, and their hooves are harder than horses' hooves; for this reason they are better able to tolerate going unshod.

The reputation of mules for being stubborn is more a myth than reality. They can dig their heels in and refuse to move, but this is usually in a situation where the mule believes danger is waiting. In such a situation they can neither be forced nor frightened into moving. Those bought by the army were usually already broken-in, but when they had to be broken-in from scratch, this needed to be done gently and calmly, taking care to establish confidence.

In the Peninsula, as well as food for the men and forage for the animals, mules were allocated, one per regiment, to carry camp-kettles. Three more were allocated to a battalion of infantry to carry the regimental surgeon's chest, the paymaster's books, and tools for the armourer and entrenching. Cavalry regiments had two mules each for the armourer's panniers, the sergeant saddler and the veterinary surgeon. However, the mules which carried the items for the armourer, saddler, veterinary surgeon and entrenching tools were the only 'public' mules (i.e. supplied by the army); the others, known as regimental mules, had to be provided by the officers of the regiment from the allowance they received for 'bât, baggage and forage'. This caused some difficulties when a regimental mule was killed, lost or became ill; since there was no specific allowance to replace it, the officer to whom it belonged would try to get his hands on a mule which was captured or stolen; these theoretically belonged to the Commissariat.

When mules were used by the artillery, the numbers needed were calculated by Alexander Dickson, after consultation with Beresford, as being 555 per battery and 215 for baggage, making a total of 770 per brigade. This figure had originally been stated at 670 for the battery, 329 for baggage and a reserve of 302, making a total of 1,301. In his journal, John Edgecombe Daniel reckoned some 12,000 mules followed the army in the offensive of spring 1811. In May 1813 a figure of 18,300 was given, of which all but 100 were for the cavalry, infantry and artillery. The other 100 were for the engineers and headquarters staff.[3]

For the Second Boer War, numbers of mules purchased in India, Africa and Europe are unknown, but 80,525 were shipped from North America. Much the same applies to the First World War, with total numbers unknown, but 213,321 were shipped from North America.

Donkeys

Donkeys are much smaller than mules, although Spanish donkeys can be larger than those familiar in Britain. There are four large breeds: the Catalonian, which is black and stands up to 16hh; the Andalucian Cor de Bise which is grey, very large, and thought to be especially elegant; the Zamorra, which is heavily built and suited to farm work; and the Muscat Burro, which is white and large. There is also the French Âne Berrichon, which is black with brown points and a dainty face. The larger donkeys could carry as much as a mule of the same size, but the smaller ones could only carry about 100lb and did not fit standard-sized army pack saddles. However, over 10,000 were sent from South Africa to India and Burma between 1942 and 1945. Their appetite is commensurate with their size, and they thrive on coarser food than mules.

Chapter Two

Getting the Horses

Before the formation of the Remount department in 1887, it was up to the colonels of each mounted regiment to buy the horses for the rank and file. This was done either through the regiment's agent, by using trusted dealers, or by sending an officer to the local horse fair. Although the main requirement at that time was for a riding horse (as opposed to a draught horse), each regiment had its own thoughts on size, colour and tail length. The earliest army horses were, whenever possible, black, as are those of the Household Cavalry today. Officers had to supply their own horses.

Horses used by the British Army were of three sorts. The tall (over 15hh), fast animals for the cavalry were, and still are, known as the 'hunter' type, which come in three sizes: lightweight, mediumweight and heavyweight. These 'weights' refer to the substance of the horse itself and the size and weight of the rider it is intended for, being able to carry these riders at speed across country and over fences and other obstacles. The cavalry has always tended towards the showy thoroughbred type of horse, whether those which belonged to the officers or those bought for the troopers. Smaller animals, known as cobs, were preferred for dragoons and mounted infantry, and as 'ride and drive' gun horses for the artillery. Finally, draught horses, either heavy or light, were used for various types of supply wagon, and to pull the guns of the Royal Artillery.

By 1750 the practice of docking the tails of both civilian and military horses was common, and the length of the docked tail was also laid down. The Duke of Cumberland's regiments required horses to have a 'swish' or nicked tail, and a painting of 1751 shows a horse with a short docked tail (but not as short as the Cadogan tail). By 1753 the sergeants' horses of the Greys had hunters' tails, as did the Royal Dragoons.

In 1755 the Duke of Cumberland, then Captain General of Dragoons, wrote in his general orders that he did not like '. . . the large footed, hairy leg'd Cart Horses that are too commonly bought for the Dragoons'. These might be suitable for pulling heavy guns, but were too slow for cavalry purposes; what was needed was 'nimble active animals' able to gallop and thus capable of going rapidly into action after a long march to the battlefield. They should have clean legs, without excess hair on their heels, light feet, sloping shoulders and backs which were short but broad, so they could carry a good bundle of forage. And to keep the heights down and prevent the excuse of their having grown since purchase, none was to be bought any younger than rising five, or, if for immediate use, rising six.

The heavy cavalry had traditionally ridden large horses, the so-called 'Great' or 'Black' horse, standing at over 16hh. A Board of General Officers reported in 1796 that suitable large horses were hard to come by, and officers, who were expected to provide their own horses, were consequently allowed to ride horses that stood not under 15hh. During the French Revolutionary and Napoleonic Wars (1793–1815), Britain sent numerous troops abroad. Although they did try to obtain horses and mules in the theatre, many of these had to be sent from Britain, especially where the enemy (usually French) had already invaded and bought or requisitioned all the available animals.

In his 1889 report on the annual return of sick and lame horses, George Fleming, principal Veterinary Surgeon to the Forces, remarked on the factor of age in relation to health and mortality. The highest number of admissions to treatment were at four years of age, at 17.66 per cent of the total; at five it was 13.4 per cent, at six it was 10.63 per cent and at seven it was 9.08 per cent. Between eight and thirteen it averaged 6 per cent, while for those over thirteen it was 'trifling'. Much the same applied to mortality rates: 16.56 per cent at age four, about half that at age five, and then decreasing as age advanced.

Fleming pointed out (not for the first time) that buying young remounts entailed heavier risks: in 1888, 413 of the 1,676 remounts bought were only three years old and 1,025 at four years. 'Regiments and corps', he said, 'are anxious to have their remounts in the ranks doing duty as soon as possible,' with the result that a large proportion were undergoing the exertion of adult horses before they had reached anything like maturity. He went on to remark that 'the presence of so many immature horses in regiments is also a source of embarrassment and expense, as they require so much attention, medical and otherwise, and hamper troops in their movements'.

What he did not mention, but is worth commenting on, is that such young horses have not developed their full bone growth, and working too much or under heavy weights will damage their bone structure and develop various problems, especially in the legs, which will shorten their useful working life. Young horses also tend to be somewhat scatty and nervous, which is a great nuisance to those around them.

The first incidence of difficulty in obtaining suitable horses in the French Revolutionary and Napoleonic Wars was in General Abercromby's Egyptian Campaign in 1801. His force was originally sent out to seize Cadiz and parts of southern Spain, but after a nonsense over landing troops in which Admiral Keith, who commanded the naval fleet and the troop transports, dithered about the safety of the landing on a rocky shore in dubious weather, this had to be given up. The force moved down the Mediterranean to Minorca, where they were able to restock their food supplies and have some necessary ship repairs done at the Naval yard, then sailed on to Malta and finally to Marmaris, on the southern shore of Turkey just north of Rhodes, where they remained for some months, waiting for information on the support the Turks would give them, practising for their landing on the Egyptian coast of Aboukir Bay, and waiting for horses which Lord Elgin, the British Minister at Constantinople, had purchased for them.

Elgin had reported that Syrian horses were not up to the work required of them, and that while there were plenty of Arabian riding horses, they were stallions and not trained for cavalry work, as the Turks were not accustomed to the formal discipline used by the British cavalry. There were no draught horses at all as wheeled vehicles were rare and normally drawn by oxen; pack animals were donkeys, mules or camels. Spurred on by Abercromby's quartermaster general Colonel Robert Anstruther's messages of urgency, which said speed was more important than quality, Elgin bought 200 horses and had them sent overland to Smyrna, and contracted for 500 more. In all, 400 actually arrived, and despite Elgin having seen the first batch of horses himself, what arrived was clearly not what he had seen; he had to conclude that they had been changed en route. Many had sore backs or were lame, and many of these had to be shot, or at best sold. Despite additional cavalry troops having been added to Abercromby's force, bringing the total up to just short of 1,200, none of Elgin's purchases were usable. Some 120 weedy specimens were considered to be just about usable for artillery, but they were so small and weak that the artillery harness had to be reconfigured to reduce the weight, and it required ten or twelve of these horses to pull each gun instead of the usual team of six. A purchasing party was sent inland from Marmaris and came back with 450 horses. These were very small, barely more than ponies, and while they would be usable for patrol work or for the mounted sentries known as vedettes, they were useless for cavalry charges. Meanwhile the Turkish Grand Vizier had sent 1,000 horses, but again these were poor specimens and only 750 were deemed fit for service.

The next difficulty was getting the horses ashore. The sea around Aboukir Bay was too shallow for the British fleet, and they had to stand off several miles. The troops and their essential supplies were got onshore in ships' boats and the horses had to go the same way. The boats were flat-bottomed, and matting or brushwood was put into them to give the horses a reasonable footing; accompanied by their riders or grooms, they were rowed ashore. At this stage 486 cavalry horses, 186 artillery horses and 120 chargers for staff officers and field officers were landed, but even these few were delayed by weather and heavy surf.[1]

The next problem occurred during Sir James Craig's expedition to Naples in 1805; told he would also have to 'undertake defensive operations in the mountainous areas of Sicily', he embarked with 300 dismounted men but with no horses for his artillery or transport. He thought he would be able to buy them locally but could not. While en route he was put under the Russian commander needing instant use of cavalry, artillery and other vehicles. He had to rely on Neapolitan government agents to buy dragoon horses; they were unsuccessful, despite requisitioning the carriage horses of the nobility.

A few years later General Whitelocke's expedition to Brazil also found it difficult to get suitable horses. Those intended for cavalry work were not fit for it and were passed on to the Commissariat for use as pack horses. When the supplies they carried had been eaten, they were used to carry the non-walking wounded. Most of the horses were so wild they were deemed not fit for harness, and such few as had not been driven off by the enemy had all been left out at grass and were not used to eating dry forage or corn and so refused it. Whitelocke's army finally had to abandon them.

The 'stocks' of horses in other theatres of war had also constantly to be replenished: at the Battle of Talavera (27–28 July 1809) 211 horses were killed, 71 were wounded and 159 went missing. Wellington remarked later, 'The Peninsula is the grave of horses; I have lost no less than twelve for my own riding.' He didn't mention the period over which he lost these horses, nor suggest that this was an abnormal number; it was not unusual for officers to take at least two to ride themselves and more for their baggage and their grooms. In October 1808 twenty-seven officers took seventy personal horses; six cavalry regiments and two troops of horse artillery took almost 4,000 in total. There are no available overall statistics for horse losses (or purchases) during the Peninsular War, but given that it went on for over six years, with continual replacements of personnel, the numbers must have been significant. It is known, however, that in December 1805 over 24,000 horses went out to Austria (the battle of Austerlitz) and in late 1809 some 17,000 went to Holland for the Walcheren campaign.

Wellington did try to buy horses locally when he arrived in Portugal in August 1808, but failed to find the quality or the numbers he needed; the available animals were generally small and just not up to the job. After Wellington had gone home to attend the hearing on the infamous Convention of Cintra and Sir John Moore was appointed Commander-in-Chief for the army in Spain, his subordinate Sir David Baird, despite having brought horses from England, had only a few cavalry horses when he landed at Corunna, and found it impossible to buy others. There was a big horse fair at Leon in November 1808, and Commissariat officers were sent there to buy horses and mules but were unable to do so on any useful scale, partly because they lacked proper funds (a continual problem in the Peninsular War) and partly because suitable animals just were not available. They ended up hiring mules for Spanish $1 a day, to include their forage, plus rations for the driver. When the hire fee was paid irregularly, 5lb of corn per animal was issued.

Later, in April 1813, Wellington wrote to a friend about the lack of horses coming from England, complaining that there were not enough for the artillery and that they would have to take to the field with less artillery than the French, and would have no spare horses. What he needed was horses over five years old, but he warned against letting the home regiments send their old and worn out horses, as they had done in July 1809 when some sixty-one horses were sent, these having already been rejected by the Commissariat as not fit for service in Ireland.

After Waterloo, as is almost always the case at the end of a long war, the government was keen to economise, and did this by what is now known as a 'Reduction in Force'. The Royal Horse Artillery and the field batteries of the Royal Artillery were both reduced to skeleton forces, and the cavalry was allowed to deteriorate so that in 1836 it was reported that most of their troop horses were not fit for a campaign.

In 1844 the Queen's Regulations included the following comment on the matter of remounts:

> The number of British Cavalry in the British Army being small ... it is of the utmost importance that this portion of the Army should be of the best description. That is that both Heavy and Light Cavalry should be equal to the Charge in Line as well as the Duties of Outposts. The horses which are selected and trained for the Cavalry should therefore be of sufficient height and strength to be capable of performing the duties of that branch of the Service with the greatest efficiency.

Major G. Tylden, in his book *Horses and Saddlery*, remarks that, 'how heavy cavalry were to be equal to the duties of outposts if they were to ride the heavy weight remounts which needed so much feed and rest to keep them really fit is difficult to see'. Captain L.E. Nolan (of Charge of the Light Brigade fame) agreed. In his book *Cavalry, Its History and Tactics*, published in 1853, he remarked that 'the power of heavy cavalry lies in the strength and breeding of the horse, and the courage and activity of the rider', given that the combined weight of the rider and his equipment detract from the speed and lasting qualities of the horse.

Crimea

When the Crimean War came in 1854, there was what should have been a predictable shortage of suitable horses and it was necessary to import them from other European countries. In the two years of 1853–1854 some 13,000 horses were imported into Britain while 2,200 were exported; these figures are probably low, as they were derived from Customs House returns which did not require all horses to be registered. Most of the riding horses used in the Crimea were sent there from England, although that was probably not their country of origin. Some also went from India, via the Red Sea.

As is well known, the bad management of the British Army in the Crimea caused a major fuss and resulted in a formal enquiry. This included matters involving the horses and other animals, although most of the questions asked related to the shortage of fodder for them; however, it did also cover the difficulties involved in obtaining enough animals for moving supplies and other materiel. Since these animals were the responsibility of the Commissariat, members of the Commissariat Department were amongst those giving evidence.[2]

Commissary General Filder reported that he had thought the Commissariat should have animals equivalent to 14,000 pack animals before the army left Varna for the Crimea. In fact, when they moved he was able to take no more than seventy mules (and seventy carts); by January 1855 they had only 333 pack horses and mules, and twelve camels. He was able to buy a total of 5,300 animals, either through contracts he made, or by sending military officers out to make purchases, although the latter were unable to find more than 150. He was able to obtain 1,500 bullock carts from Omar Pacha, and imported 247 mules from Spain, but these were immediately commandeered by Lord Raglan to carry huts. Others had to carry fuel to the troops instead of human and animal food. Many of these mules and some horses were stolen, due either to deliberate neglect by their drivers, or to the difficulty of keeping them together on the appalling roads; many of the drivers themselves deserted. None of this was helped by the fact that one load of horses was not branded during the general muddle when they were unloaded from their transport ship. Between the landing of the army in the Crimea in September 1854 and February 1855, when the Committee of Enquiry started taking evidence, 2,329 horses and mules had been imported into the Crimea, but after 1 January 1855 some 889 had either been shot or died as the result of the bad weather, exposure and fatigue.

Later, Sir Richard (later General) Airey also sent out officers to see what they could collect in the way of animals and other useful items. Captain Sankey came back with 105 wagons and their draught animals, and Captain Hamilton got 67 camels, 253 horses, 45 carts full of barley, poultry and other supplies, and more than 1,000 cattle and sheep. Captain Nolan was sent to find water but came back with a convoy of Turkish government wagons full of flour. In all, 350 wagons with their teams and Tartar drivers were acquired.

The principal method of buying horses was by appointing British consuls to act as agents, paying them a percentage of the cost of the animals. These agents soon found that the task was time-consuming, keeping them from their other work and away from their posts. Some appointed sub-agents, and the government also appointed military officers as special agents, sending accountants with them to pay for the purchased animals, check expense accounts, and pay the necessary salaries using bills of exchange. Animals were bought from a large area, as far away as Trebizond, Baghdad, Bucharest and Spain. Depots were set up to collect these animals, one in the Dardanelles for purchases from Spain, Piedmont, Sicily and the Archipelago, and another at Sinope for those coming from Asia Minor, many of which were Arabs. During 1856 some 28,000 horses, mules and camels had been purchased by these agents. When the 10th Hussars left the Crimea for home, to their great regret all their Arab horses had to be handed over to the Turkish government.

As always, officers could buy their own horses locally if they could find them. Temple Goodman remarked in a letter that there were good little ponies there for sale, which made good baggage carriers for officers once tamed. Until then, they kicked their loads off as soon as they were put on.

During 1867–1868 the British Army was engaged on an expedition to Abyssinia (Ethiopia). The country was comparatively unknown but the transport arrangements were large enough to rank with those of the Crimea. The troops faced a 380-mile march to Magdala over country which totally lacked provisions and good roads so all supplies had to be carried by pack animals. There were not enough mules in India to fill the need, so a buying commission was sent to obtain 8,000 from Spain, Italy, Turkey and Syria. They were delivered initially to depots in Alexandria and Suez (going from Alexandria to Suez by train), then transported to Zula on seven steam ships chartered by the Bombay government. Some 2,640 were purchased in the Punjab.

For the Afghan War of 1878–1879, some 3,700 horses and 4,510 mules were bought.

During the second half of the nineteenth century the major European countries entered into enormous rearmament programmes, as a result of which the British government also had to review its ability to mobilise in a hurry, especially for the defence of the United Kingdom. Not surprisingly, the supply of remounts was deemed a matter of importance (but not sufficiently so to accept the increased costs of maintaining this supply). There was, in fact, no specific scheme for mobilising the army until 1886, and even then it took nearly five years to mature and then the regulations issued were based on what was available, not on what might be needed.

By 1873 civilian use of horses had decreased with the rapid spread of railways, both as saddle horses and as coach horses and roadsters. This led to concern over the potential reserves of horses for the army, and a Committee under Lord Rosebery was appointed 'to Enquire into the Condition of the Country with regard to Horses, and its Capabilities of Supplying Present or

Future demands for them'. This found that while there were plenty of thoroughbreds (used for racing and in the hunting field), there had been a marked decrease in other breeds.[3] The popular Cleveland Bay and the old-fashioned Hackney, the most valuable harness horses for the army, were almost unobtainable. There was an enormous demand on the continent for Hackneys, and one firm of buyers said that they sent forty or fifty Hackney stallions each year to France, Italy and other countries. Another agent said that he had bought twenty or thirty Hackney stallions each year for twenty-three years, and that they were used for breeding artillery horses because 'they did not want to canter, and they improve the courage of the native mares'. All of this meant that horses for home use were actually being imported into England: some 29,000 in 1883, and as many as 200,000 in 1893.

In 1883 the War Office set up a committee, with Lieutenant General Sir Frederick Fitz-Wygram in the chair, to investigate the availability of horses needed for the mobilisation of two army corps. The active service requirement for these was about 12,000 horses each, but the peacetime establishments of the two combined were less than 14,000, so they needed a further 10,000, which would have to be purchased during the first three months of mobilisation. The committee also considered that a further 40 per cent would be needed as replacements, but noted that in the first year of the Crimean War losses were closer to 80 per cent.

In 1881 official statistics showed some 3 million horses in England used for agriculture, trade and private use, about 70,000 of which were suitable for army use. The question was how many of these would actually be available when the time came, and whether they would have to be compulsorily purchased. To this end, in 1887 a horse registration scheme was set up, owners being encouraged to register a proportion of their horses, and the newly formed Remount Department had the option of buying these at a fixed price in times of emergency. The owners of these animals were paid an annual 10s per horse to retain them.

As the 1890s progressed, the number of effective horses in the British Army slowly increased, from just over 15,000 in 1891 to just under 17,000 in 1898; the number of horses registered under the scheme was 14,550, of which some 10,000 were draught animals, many of them having come from Canada. These were thought to be ideal for field artillery; others were bought for the London omnibus companies. Horses were imported from other countries as well, over 14,000 annually, as the supply of British-bred horses diminished; most of the 'English' remounts were not English at all. The Horse Registration Scheme, although showing where horses could be had, did not specify that they should be kept in peak condition (i.e. not fat and with muscle developed from regular work) or that they should be suitable for mounted troops. Even if they were, it did not mean that they would be trained for military work.

All this came to crisis point with the Second Boer War. Because there were not enough horses available in the United Kingdom, they had to be bought on a grand scale from elsewhere: North and South America, Australia, Canada, India and parts of Europe, as well as what was available in South Africa itself. Over the thirty-two months of that war just short of 632,000 horses and mules were purchased for the army. Over 377,000 of these died before the war ended, from disease, lack of sufficient food and ignorance of how to care for them. This terrible loss was blamed on the Remount Department, and after a report from Colonel William Birkbeck, at that time Assistant Inspector of Remounts in Cape Town, questions were raised in Parliament, throwing the blame on Major General Truman, who was then running the Remount Department. An attempt was made to force him to resign, and when he refused, a court of enquiry was set up to investigate his competence; one claim was that he lacked the resourcefulness to handle an exceptionally difficult situation and was slow-witted even for peacetime activity.

The report following the enquiry did include some comments on horse purchasing in North America. There had been no need to advertise, as the arrival of the purchasing officers very quickly became well-known and they had many applications from dealers. They merely had to select which were the most suitable to be given contracts. There were horse auctions in the USA, which the purchasing officers attended, but at these it was impossible to examine the animals before the sale began. Once started, as many as seventy horses per hour were sold, often in what were called 'bunches' of several horses together. The dealers would not let the officers buy direct at auctions. They tried to buy horses from the Native American tribes, but with the exception of the Crow, few suitable horses were offered. They also investigated the possibility of buying at Chicago, but the largest market there dealt only in the heavier sort of draught horse.[4]

One matter which came into question was the suitability of the horses bought in different countries. At the end of the war, in July 1902, Lieutenant General Lyttelton, commander of the Transvaal and Orange River colonies, sent the Quartermaster General to the Forces a report consisting of the opinions of the commanding officers of various units on horses from different countries.[5] The opinions on these varied, on both type and temperament, but none of the five reports on Hungarian horses approved of them. Comments included: 'I've seen Hungarian horse studs and these animals are only the refuse of the country'; '... essentially a flat-catching stamp of horse which no hunting or polo playing man would buy'; and 'Evidently a bad class purchased'.

In 1911 another committee, chaired by F.D. Acland MP, was formed to consider the best way to solve the problem of a shortage of cavalry horses. After investigation, it recommended that the Cavalry Division should have immediate access to trained and seasoned horses which they could call on to meet their increased requirements at mobilisation. The system adopted was one copied from the Austrian Army, which took and trained young horses, then boarded them out to farmers and other civilians who agreed to produce them in good condition when required for war. If, when called for, they were found not to be in adequate condition, the allottee was fined and had to pay the costs of sending them back.

The horses used to draw buses in London were suitable for army draught work, but numbers of these were dropping dramatically after the turn of the century as mechanised buses and electrified trams took over. In 1907 there were some 2,500 horse buses, but by 1912 this figure had dropped to 376 and soon after there were none at all. There were a few still in other cities. A London traffic census conducted in 1911 found that only 13 per cent of all passenger vehicles (buses, trams and cabs) were horse drawn, and by 1913 this number had fallen to 6 per cent, but 89 per cent of goods vans were still using horses, particularly heavy horses for the larger and heavier vehicles such as coal wagons and brewers' drays. A general Horse Census made in 1912–1913 showed just under 900,000 horses suitable for regular and territorial armies – more than sufficient for the army's immediate needs.

The First World War

Several years before war was actually declared in August 1914, it was beginning to be obvious that it could not be avoided, and schemes for rapid mobilisation were set up. As far as the Remount Department (now referred to as a service rather than a department) was concerned, this would mean obtaining a large number of horses at short notice, bringing the peacetime establishment of 25,000 animals to 165,000. When the time came, they achieved this in twelve days, purchasing these animals from the lists of the Registration Scheme. The horses called in were taken to collection stations in each district, then moved on by train to remount depots. After this episode of urgent buying, few horses were taken from the lists of the Registration Scheme.

There were heavy casualties in the first ten days of the war: the Remount Service received an urgent request for 300 cavalry, 200 artillery and 200 transport horses per week, plus 1,000 riding horses. By mid-September 1,200 horses were being sent to France, with an additional request for 1,500 light and heavy draught horses and mules to carry ammunition. The Indian Army asked for 1,000 cavalry horses and more draught horses. On 20 September the weekly number of horses sent was increased to 3,000, but by the end of

November the British Expeditionary Force had nearly full depots and wanted no more horses for a while.

As well as animals required for the British Army, the British Remount Service supplied them for other countries, including the Belgian Army from March 1916; the following year they asked for their monthly supply of light draught horses to be increased from 300 to 600. This request was refused, but they did receive a one-off shipment of 150 additional animals. In December 1917 the Portuguese Army asked for 600 light draught animals; this was also refused but the War Office told the Remount Service that if they had to clear their depots, they could let the Portuguese have some mules.

Horses and mules for India and Mesopotamia were purchased in India, Australia and China under the aegis of the Indian government. Few mules were available in India and China and these had to be supplemented by animals bought in South America. Arrangements for shipping these animals to India from the various countries were made by the War Office direct with the Ministry of Shipping. Those from the southern hemisphere needed a long time in India for acclimatisation; shipment was impossible during the summer months, so India had to estimate her requirements many months in advance.

It is difficult to pin down accurate figures of animals from the various sources but something well in excess of 120,000 went from England to Egypt, Italy, Salonika, Sinai, Palestine and the Dardanelles. A total of almost 470,000 were bought in Great Britain, and further animals came from India, Australia and South America, but the greatest number came from North America. Of those bought in Britain, almost 175,000 were riding horses, many of them for non-combatant riders such as senior officers, their staff, medical and veterinary officers, and clerics; each divisional commander could have, on loan, four cobs and saddlery for chaplains.[6]

In 1916 the minutes of the Army Council reported that recent demands for remounts had been for wastage replacement only. They estimated that 10,000 would be needed monthly for six months to make up for wastage, plus 30,000 to complete the establishment of new units overseas, and about 40,000 for future demands.[7]

Buying in the USA and Canada
It was first thought that the neutrality of the USA might prevent buying in that country, so the British Remount Commission began its work by sending an officer to commence buying in Kansas City. When no difficulty was experienced there, operations were extended to other American horse centres, including St Louis, Chicago, Fort Worth and Denver.

Over four and a half years the British Remount Commission bought 449,615 horses and 287,533 mules in the USA and Canada. Britain was not the only country to buy horses in North America; France, Belgium and Italy bought some 500,000. When these buying activities were reported in March 1915, the report commented laconically that they were not considered to be a serious threat to the British buying operation, as their standards were lower, and 'it gave the dealers an opportunity of disposing of rejects'. By far the largest number of these animals came from the USA; Canada's supply of horses was limited and it only produced 31,402 for the British Remount Commission and about 10,000 for the French Army.

There were several occasions when the Commission had to stop buying. The first was in December 1914, when the Canadian government started purchasing horses for its own army and asked to be given a free field for about eight weeks; the purchasing officers in Canada were withdrawn and sent to the States instead. This caused complaints from Canadian breeders and farmers, followed by questions in the House of Commons at Ottawa. The Canadian government gave permission to recommence buying in March 1915, but this only lasted until May. In November 1915 all purchasing ceased again, this time because of reduced demands and because the Commission had a fair reserve in hand, and did not start again until mid-March 1916. By the end of that year, the demand increased again. This yo-yo situation continued throughout the war; although buying was not officially stopped it was reduced or increased several times, sometimes in particular locations rather than country-wide.

There were some difficulties with the seasonally cold weather in Canada and the northern States. The winter of 1916/17 was particularly hard and snowy, with disrupted rail services and delayed shipping from ports which were iced up. The Montreal and Southern Counties Railway experienced particularly heavy snowfalls, with up to sixteen feet of snow in places. This proved difficult for the train snowploughs to shift and in some cases actually damaged the ploughs. This severe weather continued into April, when it began to rain heavily, which turned the depots into quagmires; that autumn there was again abnormal rain. This may have been the primary cause of the gangrenous dermatitis which affected the hooves of many horses. After three and a half years of use, the depots were contaminated with this disease, and there was much other sickness, leading to more careful veterinary examinations of animals on arrival.

Another very bad winter occurred in 1918/19, said by older inhabitants to be the worst in their memory. Heavy snowfalls occurred as far south as the southern States, but Chicago and the Mid-West were the worst affected. Several depots were cut off and some trains which had already departed were halted en route, causing suffering to the animals. This also affected the amounts of coal reaching the ports, which prevented the departure of ships waiting for fuel. Several ships en route to Montreal were considerably delayed by the exceptional amounts of ice in the Gulf of St Lawrence. Shipping at the ports of Halifax and St John was also held up.

After the Armistice, a cable was received with instructions to shut down the Commission; no more purchases were to be made and animals in stock were to be disposed of. Neither the American nor the Canadian government wanted them, so they were sold at public auction at nine locations in the United States and one at Montreal; the various depots were closed and the officers returned home as soon as their duties were complete.

During the course of the four and a half years that the Commission operated, totals of 484,636 horses, 287,564 mules and 175 stallion donkeys (for India) were purchased, giving a grand total of 772,375. Of the horses purchased, less than 30 per cent were for riding. The rest, and all the mules, were for draught purposes.

There was a general lack of information at the beginning of proceedings on the conditions in the United States relating to the market, climate, railways and the price of forage and labour. The vastness of the country was only appreciated when it became necessary to move animals from their purchase point to the ports of embarkation. They had to use numerous railway companies because the main lines did not always go exactly where the Commission would have liked them to go. For instance, there was no simple route from Boise (Idaho) to New Orleans; anyone wishing to send animals would have to go via Chicago, and then either Covington, Newport News and Memphis, or Kansas City and Little Rock, and finally to New Orleans. Kansas City to Newport News had to be done via Covington. A further problem with the vastness of the country was that it was difficult for dealers to get in touch with their buyers when a change of type of animals was required.

Buying Mules

Mules could be purchased almost anywhere (Britain being the exception). There were eleven principal mule-producing states in America, with the best markets being St Louis and Kansas City. In the trade mules were divided into two types: cotton mules and sugar mules. The cotton mules tended to be built on thoroughbred lines and light boned and their weight varied from 850 to 1,100lb and their height from 14.2 to 16hh. The sugar mules were of the same type, but generally heavier and bigger. The carter and pack mules were smaller, the carters being between 14.3 and 15.1hh, and the pack mules 14.1hh or less.

On 1 March 1916 an arrangement was made with the Guyton and Harrington Mule Company of Kansas City for the purchase of mules, and a set of instructions was issued to the four purchasing officers who inspected possible purchases, each accompanied by a veterinary officer. All mules would be subjected to the mallein test to detect glanders. Purchased mules should not be shod and their feet should be neatly trimmed. Their tails were to be left long. A daily report on purchases should be sent to headquarters, which would periodically send instructions on despatching the mules to embarkation ports. Until that time, the mules were to receive a daily ration of 8lb of oats and 20lb of dry fodder, together with a liberal allowance of salt and plenty of water. An inspection of their yard at St Louis in 1916 found that the facilities were well constructed. Around 1,000 mules were kept there, and the arrangements for their care was reported to be good.

However, in early 1917 allegations were made by one of the Mule Company's employees that 'reflected on the integrity of some of the members of the Commission'. These were so serious that a firm of solicitors was engaged to conduct a thorough investigation. They reported that there were no grounds for the allegations, but that there had been an 'injudicious act' by one of the Commission's members.

Notification of the time of departure and number of animals being sent to depots should be wired to the officer in charge of the depot. Entrainment should be overseen by the purchasing officer or veterinary officer. Messrs Guyton and Harrington were responsible for supplying a competent travelling foreman to each train to see to watering and feeding; he should be supplied with a form to fill in listing all events on the journey and should not be paid until this was received.

It was pointed out that mules did not automatically become a year older on 1 January, but on 1 May. Dealers were to be informed of this, and expected to adhere to it, even though some mules may have abnormally advanced dentition.

Shortly after this, the part of the Commission which had been responsible for the purchase of mules was amalgamated into the main horse commission.

By the beginning of August 1917 there was an increased demand for mules, and one of the dealers in St Louis, Messrs Howard, agreed to handle mules at Atlanta; this was followed by an inspection point at Nashville. Later that year the US government required that in future no mares should be purchased. This caused a 40 per cent reduction in the number of animals brought forward for inspection by the dealers. The requirement continued at 2,500 heavy artillery horses, 2,000 artillery horses, 1,500 cavalry horses and 6,000 mules per month. At the end of September a further 3,000 heavy mules were requested. At about the same time the US government intimated that the British buying was seriously interfering with their own, and asked for a time restriction, if not a complete cessation, of British buying. After some high-level discussions at Washington, it was agreed that purchasing might be continued provided that British prices matched those of America, that no new dealers would be appointed without American sanction, and that all purchases were reported to them. This did not interfere with the purchase of heavy or artillery horses, as the American requirement was for lighter animals, but it did affect the mule buying as the American requirements were much the same, although their 'types' were slightly different, being 'wheelers' of 1,250lb and upwards, 'leaders' of 1,000–1,150lb, and pack mules of 950–1,150lb. With this clash of requirements, and high prices being paid for mules for the booming cotton trade, it proved almost impossible to obtain more than half of what was required.

When the Commission first arrived in Canada, it found that mules were not available, so despite the possible difficulties of buying in the USA, a separate unit known as the Mule Commission was sent to Kansas City. Headed by Colonel C.H. Bridge, there were five buyers and a paymaster.

By the end of the First World War the mules being bought had been reduced to two main classes: gunner or artillery mules and heavy mules. There were three other classes: carters, special carters and pack. The gunners were required to be between five and twelve years old, not less than 15.1hh and weighing not less than 1,100lb, allowing for condition and allowing a little more weight for taller animals. They should be weighed and the weights entered in the purchasing book. The scales should be tested regularly. The mules should be compact, short-backed, deep-ribbed, deep-chested and wide (not narrow), with good legs (not leggy or badly cow-hocked) and well-developed feet. They should be sound in wind, eyes and limb and should not be light-coloured. Only dark greys would be accepted. They were to be branded on the quarters as were the gunners, and on the near side jaw a small letter H.

The heavy mules were to weigh not less than 1,200lb and their height was to be 15.3hh and upwards. They should be quiet to handle, not touchy or timid, and good staunch workers. The rest of their physical attributes should be the same as for the gunners. They were to be branded on the near quarter with a broad arrow and the buyer's brand, and on the off-quarter with a letter U.

Towards the end of the Second World War an order for the requisition of mules was issued in Sicily. There, mule breeding was under strict government supervision which produced a high standard of animal. There were government studs in several places on the island, and each mule had its own 'passport' showing its breeding and changes of owner. They were branded with a number which related to their village, to which was added the broad arrow when purchased by the No. 3 Remount Purchasing Commission. They were sent to mainland Italy in batches of 200–300, having been tethered at overnight stops in groups of twelve in a circle with a soldier in the middle. However, the locals, being skilled thieves, often managed to extract one.

Banking/Paying for Purchases

In Canada the Commission used the Imperial Bank of Canada from August 1914 to March 1915, then the Bank of Montreal to February 1919. In America the First National Bank in New York was used from January 1915 to February 1915, then J.P. Morgan and Company from March 1915 to February 1919. Funds were requisitioned from the War Office by a weekly cable, going into the American banks, and then, if needed, transferred from there to a Canadian bank. At the beginning of the Commission's activities, purchases of animals were paid for by Letters of Credit made out by the purchasing officer. This turned out to be unwieldy and subsequently payments were made direct to the dealers from the Paymaster of the Commission, certified by the purchasing officer and the General Officer Commanding.

Purchases outside the USA/Canada were made by Letters of Credit or under arrangements with national banks.

After the end of the First World War, and the British involvement in the Bolshevik revolution in Russia, the numbers of horses in Britain returned to a peacetime norm, except that the numbers of mounted troops shrank as their functions were increasingly converted to mechanised units. Staff officers no longer rode, except for ceremonial purposes, and the medical and veterinary officers also used cars and vans. Interestingly, many of the motor vans were used to transport forage for the army's horses.

In 1924 the War Office issued an updated version of instructions for impressment of horse-drawn vehicles[8] and in 1937 there was another updated manual, this time on Remounts.[9] Much smaller than the 1906 version, at a mere sixteen pages (as opposed to 102), it had no specimen forms and nothing on transporting horses by sea or rail. There were some new, brief sections on the necessity of providing rest depots for horses after long-distance travel, on sending untrained animals to the base remount depot (they should have been trained before despatch), and the need to send animals newly purchased in the field or captured from the enemy to the nearest veterinary depot for inspection and possibly quarantine. There was also a section on the 'kraal' system of depot layout, which was to be used at all depots.[10]

The Second World War

The annual requirement for the regular army in peacetime was estimated to be no more than 3,000 horses, about half for riding and the others for artillery. By 1939 numerous equines were still used in India for cavalry and transport purposes, but elsewhere the establishment stood at 2,600 horses. Such as there were, and the few that were purchased during the Second World War, were mainly used for transport, particularly for pack or light draught work in countries where the terrain did not allow motorised transport. The Remount Department had to hurry to find the 9,000 horses needed for mobilisation at the start of the Second World War. Most of the animals they found had been at grass or living in good stables; they now had to stand in the open on breast lines; on the whole they needed hard standing and shelter from the wind rather than overhead cover, but in very inclement areas large circus tents were used.

Between 1941 and 1943 numbers of army horses and mules in Britain increased to 5,450, partly to train for a possible campaign in Norway and partly for transport use at home, to save on motor vehicles, petrol and tyres. The Quartermaster General ordered that all army animals should be used for this purpose but there was a shortage of wagons and drivers. Only 400 wagons and 600 horses were used, on barracks fatigues and short haul deliveries.

However, it was decided to send a mounted cavalry division of 9,000 horses to Palestine. These had to be purchased by the Remount Corps, which was by then amalgamated with the Veterinary Corps. This was done in some haste, and not all the purchases were successful, some mares turning out to be carrying foals which they delivered on arrival. And all of them had to be acclimatized to the conditions in Palestine.

There were a few mules with the British Expeditionary Force in 1939–1940. Six mule transport corps totalling 2,700 animals were sent from the Middle East and India to carry ammunition. They served well, despite the cold weather, but as there were few farriers available to fit their shoes with 'frost nails', they did suffer from the slippery frozen pavements. One of these companies was captured by the enemy; the others reached Dunkirk but had to be left behind as there was no room on the ships for them.

From 1940 the Remount Department (using its old name again) was buying animals in India: mules for East Africa, the Middle East and Burma, and camels for the Aden garrison. Mules were also bought in South Africa, Argentina and the USA for use in India. The USA supplied almost 2,000 mountain mules and over 1,500 'Class II Equipment' mules, probably for pack work. Over 22,000 mules and over 10,000 donkeys were sent to India from South Africa during the period 1942–1945.

In 1941 the British Army took over 1,200 horses and 3,200 mules from Vichy France. The Light Draught animals were good specimens, but the Syrian horses and Barbs of the French cavalry were not. Mules were also used in Sicily, where these animals were in common use, and in the Italy campaign that autumn, in both cases for pack transport. By 1944 there were two Royal Artillery regiments using Walers and mules, and about a thousand captured horses were used in transport companies.

The method of branding for mules had to be changed in 1944. Branding on the hoof, which had been the standard procedure, was ineffective in the long term as the hooves grew and were trimmed for shoeing, and heavy accumulations of mud made the brands impossible to see. Instead they were branded on the right side of the neck (the US Army used the left side), using the broad arrow and the initial of the buyer's surname.

Disposal

After each war ended, there was the problem of what to do with the horses in foreign theatres. Even at the beginning of the Peninsular War, when Sir John Moore's force arrived at Corunna to return home, there were far too many fit horses for the numbers of transports available, and rather than let them fall into the hands of the pursuing French Army, these, and those which were terminally lame or sick, were either shot or driven over the nearby cliffs.

After the Boer War ended in May 1902, priority was given to disposing of all animals surplus to peacetime requirements. The actual number still in service and under veterinary care cannot be stated with any accuracy as there are several versions, but after deducting those required for the use of the Army of Occupation, a figure of about 215,000 serviceable horses and mules is arrived at, with another 28,700 sick animals. The war had drastically reduced the local horse population and a Regeneration Department was set up and funded by the British government. This purchased just short of 100,000 horses, mules, donkeys and oxen for the Cape Colony and Natal by the end of February 1903. During this period just under 20,000 horses and mules were destroyed, about one-third of them suffering from glanders. Over the course of this war somewhere in the region of 325,000 horses and 50,000 mules were 'wasted'.[11]

At the beginning of the First World War the policy was to allow contractors to remove carcasses for free, although some would pay a small amount for them; otherwise they were buried by AVC personnel. Towards the end of the war special buildings for the disposal of carcasses were erected, allowing substantial amounts of money to be obtained for them. The French were experiencing a civilian horse shortage after their requisitioning programme, and asked if animals no longer suitable for military use by the British Army could be made available. This was agreed, and cast horses were branded with an inverted broad arrow before being sold by auction. Most of these were older horses, but were still useful for civilian work.

These cast horses and mules were grouped into categories:

A – practically sound, 5–8 years
B – ditto, 9–12 years
C – unsound but fit for work, or over 12 years
D – unfit for work, to be destroyed.

Units retained in the Armies of Occupation and at home were completed with first choice horses from groups A and B. In the UK surplus animals were sold as they became available.

The process of landing artillery at Gallipoli led to many horse fatalities from shelling. It was not possible to burn the bodies so large graves were dug near the beach with great difficulty as the sandy soil fell back in as they dug. On one occasion a rough sea washed all the sand away, leaving the carcasses exposed. Some were towed out into the current; a few of these were carried out to sea but most drifted back and littered the beaches. Finally, after numerous deaths on the transports, a naval ship took them further into the current, tied them together, cut the bodies open and weighted them down before releasing them, all under great threat from submarines.

In France over 28,000 equines were sent from hospitals and evacuation centres to a central abattoir in Paris, where they were slaughtered and dressed for human food. Others went to local butchers in towns near veterinary hospitals. Those which were unfit for human consumption, and the by-products of most of the others, were sold to various trades. Seven installations known as 'Horse Carcass Economisers' were set up along lines of communication. Each of these had fourteen workers who dealt with up to thirty carcasses per day. Hides were cured, and flesh was dried and went into pig, poultry and dog food. Bones were crushed and degreased and ground into bone-meal. Oil from carcasses (up to 5 gallons per animal) went to soap manufacturers, and the hooves became glue. Many of these products were sent to England. The Army Veterinary Service produced figures for animal disposal work; in the four months from November 1918 to March 1920 some 61,232 went for human consumption, either by sale or by issue to prisoners of war.

War Office official statistics give some figures on these disposals and also of numbers of equines in the army at various times. For example, 225,856 horses and mules were killed, died, destroyed or went missing and 30,348 were cast in France and England by October 1917. Losses were particularly high in June 1917, due to a very cold spring. At the end of the war 499,161 animals were sold for work.[12]

The Board of Agriculture strongly objected to the repatriation of animals from anywhere except France, partly due to the risk of importing disease, and partly because of the cost. However, there was a scandal, with questions asked in Parliament, over the practice of selling animals in the open market, particularly in Egypt and the way these unfortunate beasts were treated by their new owners. It was this situation that led to Mrs Dorothy Brooke's founding of the charity 'The Brooke Hospital for Animals' in 1930 when she moved to Egypt and saw the state of old war horses. The charity continues its work today in eleven countries. An undertaking was given in Parliament that this situation would not happen again. In accordance with this agreement, such horses and mules as could not be used in Britain or France for civilian work after the Second World War were destroyed.

After the Second World War
In 1944 the RAVS began collecting captured horses from the liberated parts of France, many of which were seriously wounded. If fit when recovered, these were donated to local farmers until it was discovered that many were being passed on to black market butchers. This coincided with a need for horse transport companies, which were horsed entirely from captured animals; passed on to the RASC, they did valuable work in the docks and rear maintenance areas. About 1,000 horses were used in this way until the supply of captured fodder ran low, when numbers were reduced.

Many of the horses and mules abroad were brought back to England after health checks, and sold in small batches at auction. Any showing high anti-body levels went to medical supply companies such as the Wellcome Foundation, for the production of serums against diphtheria, gas gangrene and tetanus. The RAVS also worked on the repatriation of dogs, both those loaned by the public for war work and the pets of returning servicemen. A particular concern with the latter was the risk of rabies, but this did not materialise, despite some 1,000 dogs and cats which were known to have been smuggled in during the Dunkirk evacuation.

The Commander-in-Chief India arranged the demobilisation of the troops in Mesopotamia by withdrawing certain units to India completely horsed, and disposing of animals surplus to the Army of Occupation to meet the needs of the inhabitants.

Animals in East Africa were disposed of locally, as fear of infectious diseases debarred them from entry to other countries.

At the end of the Second World War a Civil Affairs veterinary service and the veterinary panel of the Allied Post-War Requirements Panel were set up. As well as conserving and replenishing flocks and herds, the RAVS worked on the replacement of draught animals which had been seized, especially by Germany, which, contrary to the popular impression that it was highly mechanised, was dependant on an establishment of over a million horses. Many of these were available for distribution to civilians and within three months over 44,000 were branded, tested for disease and distributed. Healthy but other-wise unservicable animals were slaughtered to feed surrendered troops and displaced civilians. As well as captured animals, those surplus to military requirements were also distributed. This situation pertained in South-east Asia as well as the Middle East and Europe; there were few private vets in Burma or Malaya even before the Japanese invasion. The Civil Affairs Service sent vets to Burma until the Civil Veterinary department was reinstated. There were serious outbreaks of rinderpest in both countries. Already suffering from a rice famine, the loss of over 50,000 buffaloes used to work the rice paddies exacerbated this until the RAVS brought the situation under control.[13]

Chapter Three

Remount Department Administration

The idea of putting the army remount function into a single service was first suggested in the 1850s but not effected until 1887. Prior to this, the purchase of horses was the responsibility of individual regimental colonels (for cavalry) and agents acting for the Royal Artillery and engineers. This worked well enough in peacetime but broke down rapidly in war time when demand exceeded supply, prices rose and the price set by the government was low, so regiments ended up with inferior animals. So the Remount Department was set up to ensure the uniformity and suitability of animals bought for the army, and then to train them.

At this time the Army Remount Department was part of the Quartermaster General's department, reporting to him through the Royal Army Service Corps; it remained there until 1941, when it was put under the Royal Army Veterinary Corps.

Colonel Ravenhill, who had been instrumental in both the Horse Registration Scheme and the formation of the Department itself, was appointed its first Inspector General of Remounts. He had three assistant inspectors, one of whom was Major General Truman, who succeeded him as Inspector General in January 1899.

Although there were several small wars, mainly in Africa, between those and 1899 when the Second Boer War started, there was no desperate need for additional army horses. The annual requirement was between 1,400 and 2,500 remounts. Two remount depots were set up, at Woolwich and Dublin, each commanded by a staff-captain and manned by soldiers from the cavalry and artillery. A remount squadron consisted of approximately 200 soldiers, who obtained and trained 500 horses. They were generally older, more experienced soldiers.

The depots, each under the control of an assistant inspector, were responsible for buying and training horses in England and Ireland, the English horses for the artillery and the Irish for the cavalry. The third assistant inspector was tasked with operating the Horse Registration Scheme. In July 1892 the responsibility for personnel at the remount depots was transferred to the Army Service Corps (ASC), which formed a remount company at each depot. This consisted of sixty-six men, including a company sergeant-major, a quartermaster and a farrier sergeant, plus sergeants, lance-corporals, corporals and privates.

In various ways the Second Boer War was not seen as a success, one of the problems being the difficulty met in obtaining and keeping the necessary number of equines in South Africa. An enquiry into the workings of the Remount Department was called for and duly organised.[1] This enquiry ran for forty-seven days, after which a report of the enquiry's findings was produced. It concluded that Truman was not to blame for the Department's shortcomings, but, on reading through the minutes of the evidence given, this author gained the impression that while Truman might have been capable of running the department in peacetime, when fewer than 2,000 new horses were required each year, he was not capable of dealing with the vastly increased numbers needed during this war, nor with the complications of organising what turned out to be twenty-four depots in South Africa, and arranging for transport for all the new purchases. Certainly he does come across as being slow-witted, as some of his contemporaries claimed. To a certain extent he was hampered by his physical environment (small offices in Victoria Street a mile away from the rest of the War Office in Pall Mall) and his procedural environment, in that he could make no decisions on his own. He had to make suggestions to his immediate superior, the Quartermaster General, who passed them on to the Secretary of State, who made a decision (often after consulting the rest of the Cabinet) and passed it back down the same way. Obviously this took several days at best, often more.

One area which showed up Truman's lack of ability to think administratively was in acquiring new staff. The need for staff was well known, and applications arrived from retired or reserve officers. These accumulated until Truman needed someone, when he picked out a likely candidate and sent off for his personal record from the War Department, a process which took many days. Once this had returned and was deemed satisfactory, he was able to go up the line for a decision accepting or refusing the applicant. At the enquiry, Truman was asked if it had not occurred to him that they could have saved that time by calling for the files as soon as an application was made, in order to weed out the unsuitable. His response was that it had not occurred, but that yes, it could be done. This 'oh gosh, I didn't think of that' reaction was his response to several questions during the enquiry, and to many others he replied either that he had no recollection of the issue, or that he no longer had the relevant paperwork: hardly the efficient responses that a person in his position should have made. He did, however, comment that there were some officers appointed whom he had not recommended but who had been put forward by what he referred to as 'a higher authority'.

Some facts which did emerge from the enquiry were that buyers in other countries should have started by visiting the British embassy, but did not always do so, it being felt that it was best to use dealers abroad, or those at home with contacts abroad, considering the many different languages and selling practices involved. For buying in Ireland, there was a list of government-contracted dealers, who had to deliver the horses at their own risk; there, and at other places, it was the practice of dealers at fairs and other sales to use 'blockers' who prevented other buyers from seeing the horses. Eventually, the Remount Department had eighteen officers purchasing abroad. Only one of these (in America) was unsatisfactory and had to be sent home. The system was that dealers brought batches of horses and mules to an agreed location, and the local officers inspected them and selected those they thought suitable. Usually they had a vet in attendance, but this was not always possible. Once approved, the horses were sent by train to the embarkation port to be sent off to South Africa by sea.

At about the same time there was an enquiry into purchases in Austro-Hungary, instigated after allegations by Sir Blundell Maple MP of bribes accepted by British officers for horse purchases. He raised this in Parliament in mid-1901, stating that he 'wished to know whether government was still buying horses from abroad. There was no doubt whatever that during the last eighteen months or two years, a great deal of rubbish had been bought from Austro-Hungary', and he mentioned 'swindles which had been taking place in South Africa relating to horses from Buda-Pesht [sic] and Vienna'. There was a difference of between £10 and £20 per horse in the prices paid by dealers and those paid by the government, which was divided amongst those who bought them. This was 'nothing less than a wicked robbery, for the horses sent to South Africa were of the most inferior class, and the use of such inferior horses had, no doubt, resulted in the deaths of hundreds and thousands of our men'. He went further, giving an interview to the *Daily Mail* in which he said 'I have no doubt that the war would have ended six months ago had the horses supplied been up to standard.' Commenting, 'it is a matter of honesty or dishonesty on the part of those selected for purchasing agents', he went on to allege that a profit of £50 per horse was made. He was, he ended, 'quite certain that a searching enquiry will be made'. The comments on the speedier termination of the war and the numbers of men killed for the lack of good horses were both complete nonsense uttered by a person who had little or no knowledge of warfare or the conditions in South Africa. Maple soon had to back down, as the committee of enquiry expressed their deep regret that he had committed himself to public statements which, despite his plea that he was activated by a desire to serve the public interest, were universally understood to be direct attacks on the honour and integrity of British officers.

The only specific case which seemed initially to require explanation arose from a misapprehension on the position of Captain Hartington. But in justice to that gentleman, and because that misapprehension seemed to be the origin of widespread suspicion, the committee thought it best to give a full explanation. Captain Hartington was an Army Veterinary Officer who retired from the service in 1881. In December 1899, at that time being completely unconnected with the public service, he introduced to Colonel St Quintin, the remount officer of the Imperial Yeomanry Committee, a Mr Lewison, who was subsequently given a contract to supply Hungarian cobs to the Imperial Yeomanry. He undertook to give Captain Hartington a 2.5 per cent commission on his contracts, which amounted in total to some £111,000, thus giving Hartington £2,775. Hartington was then employed on a fixed salary by Mr Lewison, to go with him to Hungary and assist in selecting suitable cobs. Hartington terminated his employment with Lewison when Colonel St Quintin employed him to examine and pass horses for purchase. This may have been an error of judgement but was not the criminal act which Maple imagined.

Apart from this one case, the allegations that officers were taking bribes seemed to rest on two assumptions: that the contractors had over-large profits and that they supplied very cheap and 'very bad' horses which were not fit for military service and should not have passed the inspectors. There were in fact two entirely separate transactions involved: purchases for the Imperial Yeomanry and purchases for the Remount Department. It transpired that Mr Lewison was not personally in a position to carry out any horse buying in Hungary so he signed the contract over to a Mr Hauser, a large horse dealer in Vienna, at a price which did indeed leave Mr Lewison with a large balance of profit. The urgency of demand did not allow St Quintin to take more steps to ascertain what was a reasonable price nor to check the capacity of the contractors to undertake a large contract without having to resort to middlemen. The poor quality of the animals bought – if indeed they were poor quality, as the evidence for this was very conflicting – was probably due to haste of need to meet a sudden emergency.

The Remount Department had made a contract directly with Mr Hauser, after receiving numerous applications from dealers hoping for an order from the government. Among these was a Mr Waugh from Newmarket, who was introduced by Sir Blundell Maple but did not receive any contracts. After complaints that Hauser had been allowed a monopoly, a contract for a few hundred cobs was given to a Mr von Fogler of Buda-Pesht, who was also introduced to the War Office by Maple.

The committee's final comment was that its members were surprised that before the decision to buy from Hungary was made, no steps had been taken since 1884 to ascertain the best sources of supply there, or the most reliable people to employ in the task. They also stated that they thought that even in peacetime the Remount Department should make it its business to carry out systematic studies of other countries as sources of horses in wartime, and that they should be held responsible for obtaining such information and keeping it up to date.[2]

One idea proposed in 1909 was to conduct a sort of census of the number and type of horses in the UK, as well as horse-drawn vehicles and mechanical vehicles which might be available when the time came. This was done in secret by the police. Opinions varied on the usefulness of this, as it did not cover the whole country, but it gave a rough idea of the number of horses in the country, and showed that a high proportion of them were very heavy horses, especially in some parts of Scotland. A further census, this time conducted by the Territorial Army, was undertaken in 1911, and was followed by the setting up of twelve county associations to conduct classifications; despite a large number of officers being seconded to the associations, this met with difficulties, so the task was handed over to the general of the home commands. The Assistant Director of the Remount Service was shown the results, which confirmed his suspicion that there was a general shortage of horses suitable for army work, especially those needed for the artillery. The outbreak of war in 1914 found the British Army with only 1,200 horses; within twelve days this number had increased to 165,000 animals, mainly by impressment, and a year later to 534,971 horses and mules, most of them purchased.

Initially there were three remount depots: Woolwich, which provided horses for the Royal Artillery, Royal Engineers (RE) and ASC; and two in Dublin for the cavalry, with a total establishment of 12,500 horses and mules. The Second Boer War showed this to be inadequate, with 326,000 horses and 51,000 mules lost, mainly through disease, so the establishment was increased to 25,000 animals and two more remount depots were started at Arborfield and Melton Mowbray. In 1911 a further depot at Pilckard's Farm at Chiddingfold near Godalming was given to the War Office by its owners for a period of twenty-one years. Just before war was declared in August 1914, the Remount Service had five depots in Britain, at Dublin, Woolwich, Melton Mowbray, Arborfield and Witley, each of which had a superintendant. It also had three Inspectors of Remounts, one each for artillery, cavalry and draught horses. It also had a depot at Pretoria.

After buying commenced in North America, three further depots were opened: at Shirehampton for horses received at Avonmouth; at Romsey for those received at Southampton; and at Ormskirk for those received at Liverpool. The depot at Ormskirk had a regimental headquarters and ten 500-strong remount squadrons, each with one superintendant, two assistants, six foremen, 150 grooms and riders and a number of smiths. Each squadron was subdivided into troops of 100 horses, with separate stables and a hut for a foreman and twenty-five men. This was one of the depots that dealt with horses imported from America. Horses from America that needed veterinary attention were moved to veterinary hospitals, and daily inspections were made at the depots and ailing horses also moved to a hospital.

Personnel at these depots included quartermaster sergeants, farrier sergeants, corporal shoeing smiths, saddlers and saddle tree makers, with numerous grooms and horse-trainers, mounted on bicycles. At its highest point, personnel at these depots numbered 423 officers and 6,731 men. These depots were originally manned by civilian grooms and stable lads, with military officers in charge, but many of these civilians were drafted for military service and had to be replaced by inexperienced men who had to be trained in horse care. Another solution to this problem was to use experienced horse-women. There was an all-female remount depot at Russley Park (near Baydon, Wiltshire). There were about a hundred horses there, and as it was mainly used for rehabilitation of officers' horses, they were good quality animals. It was started in 1916 and managed by Mrs Mabel Birkbeck; the head groom was Mrs Ironside. The premises, which had been a racing stables, were bought by the War Office in 1916, intended to be a breeding place for war horses.

Collecting centres were established at Swaythling and Shirehampton for horses trained at the other three depots for onward shipment overseas. As the army expanded, several more remount squadrons were established at home. Thirteen were started in France, increased to twenty-two by the end of November, although this number was not just a matter of adding nine more; several of the original thirteen had been closed, mainly those south of Paris and west of Rouen. As the war progressed, these locations and numbers continued to change. For instance, No. 1 base remount depot for 2,600 animals and two advanced depots for 300 animals went to France with the original British Expeditionary Force (BEF), landing at Le Havre on 21 August 1914. It then quickly relocated at St Nazaire on 3 September, then to the hippodrome north of Nantes. Between 2 October and 10 October it moved by sections to Chateau Madrillet at Rouen, and stayed there for the rest of the war. As the campaign continued, further base remount depots opened at the base ports. At their peak in December 1917 these facilities were training a total of 93,847 horses and 36,613 mules.

The daily work of the depots, as well as receiving and training horses and sending them on, included managing complaints and problems, such as horses going to the wrong units, the perceived unsuitability of horses, and managing injuries in transit, as well as all the normal paperwork. This included such tasks as ordering sawdust for bedding at Calais, drainage pipes to prevent flooding at Boulogne, sand and cinders for bedding at Dieppe, and arranging for bracken to be cut for bedding at Serqueux.

Remount personnel in the Middle East were supplemented by similar units of the Indian Army. Depots were set up in Egypt and Salonika for campaigns there; horses for these regions were initially obtained from Australia and mules from North America, but difficulties with transport meant animals later came from Britain. The depot at El Kantara on the eastern side of the Suez Canal was probably the largest ever such establishment, with 640 acres and facilities for some 8,000 animals at a time. Animals for the Mesopotamia campaign were supplied by the Indian government.

As the numbers of equines used in the war increased, so did the staff of the Remount Service, from 121 officers and 230 men in 1914 to 423 and 20,560 respectively in 1917, reduced again in 1919 to 258 and 6,731. To avoid withdrawing army officers from their normal duties, many of the Remount Service officers were drawn from the landed gentry, Masters of Foxhounds and others with experience of horses, and included the artists Alfred Munnings, Cecil Aldin and Lionel Edwards.

The Remount Service had other responsibilities at home: the Board of Agriculture started a Food Production Department and needed 10,000 draught horses to work on farms; the Remount Service bought 6,800 for this purpose and transferred 3,200 army horses which were no longer suited for military work. They also lent unfit horses to the Department of Draught Horses, which got them fit by ploughing at prisoner of war camps, after which they were returned and exchanged by the Remount Service for another batch of unfit ones.

Buying in North America during the First World War

After the war commenced, it soon became apparent that sufficient numbers of animals could not be obtained in Britain, and a Remount Commission was formed to buy in the United States and Canada. Major General Sir Frederick Benson was sent out to set up the commission's headquarters, arriving in Toronto on 17 August 1914. The first group of officers arrived on 23 August after a ten-day voyage and a conference was held on 25 August to arrange details for the purchasing officers. The headquarters moved to Montreal on 14 November. One of the senior officers was Major Sir Charles Gunning, who was promoted brigadier general and took over when Benson died in August 1916.

The initial personnel establishment consisted of a commission commander (Benson), a paymaster/financial adviser, an embarkation officer and two depot officers, as well as seven purchasing officers, one in Kansas City and the others in Canada. On 1 November another nine officers arrived, one in Toronto and the others in Kansas City, Denver, St Louis, Chicago and Fort Worth. Seven firms of dealers were also used at this time; twenty more firms were added a few months later. Another twelve officers soon joined, situated in both the USA and Canada, and the services of some civilian gentlemen who had been assisting in buying were dispensed with.

By the end of October 1914 seven firms of dealers were being used: two in St Louis, and one each in Kansas City, Chicago, Denver, Fort Worth and Toronto. By the end of the war the Commission had dealt with thirty-two dealers in the USA and seventeen in Canada. One of these firms, Messrs Guyton and Harrington, dropped out of the market in the spring of 1917, having supplied the Commission with over half of all the animals purchased. Ten other specialist mule dealers, one of whom had branches in three cities, were used.

No contracts were made with dealers, but they were notified of require-ments and presented animals at designated collection centres. The principal centres for horses were at St Paul, Sioux City, Des Moines, Chicago, Kansas City and Cedar Rapids, while for mules the principal centres were Fort Worth, Nashville, Atlanta, East St Louis and Kansas City. The states of Illinois and Iowa were the main sources of heavy horses, but these animals were more prone to develop pneumonia than those from other states; this was thought to be because they were stall-fed and thus in higher condition and too fat to tolerate the long journeys.

In common with horse dealers all over the world, those in America and Canada were true to type. They were all out to make the best bargain they could and were ever ready to take advantage of novice buyers. When they realised that only animals that came up to specification would be accepted, they mended their ways and did their best to comply accordingly. The Com-mission found it best to deal with those whom they knew, as taking on new dealers inevitably meant the try-ons started again. Some poor horses were presented for inspection, but these were invariably animals which the dealers were selling for a private person. The dealers were paid weekly on receipt of the proper form signed by the purchasing officer.

In 1918 information was received, and subsequently proved correct, to the effect that Messrs Barrett and Zimmerman of St Paul, with whom the Commission had been dealing, had been giving bribes to a member of the Commission. This person was promptly dropped. Although not immediately adjacent to this item in the report, and certainly not naming him in con-nection with the bribery, at this time 'the services of Lieutenant Colonel McEachran were dispensed with'.

The Commission's officers changed frequently, some departing and more arriving. By 1 January 1916, as well as the four staff officers at headquarters, there were thirty-four officers and veterinarians at the depots, six at the embarkation ports, and three at the feeding station at Covington. On 28 June 1915 a cable was received from the War Office ordering Captain Chaplin to report for duty in England if passed fit for active service, followed by another cable instructing that he should be medically examined, and was only to return to England if passed fit for active service. Conveniently for the Commission (and perhaps also for Captain Chaplin), this examination resulted in the Medical Board finding him quite unfit in consequence of defective eyesight. Captain Chaplin's services were, therefore, retained with the Commission.

During the course of the war some forty-seven purchasing officers were employed. At the beginning, there was a separate Mule Commission, manned by one officer and four veterinary officers. At the beginning of April 1916 the mule purchasing arm was amalgamated into the main part of the Commission. Amongst the documentation produced by the Commission were lists of officers showing their rank and their most recent regiment when in active service (seventy-five of them) and vets (thirty-four of them, most of them either AVS or Members of the Royal College of Veterinary Surgeons).

In the report produced after the Commission had finished its work it was remarked that it would have been easier if there had been standardised books, records and forms which could have been brought into use at once. As there were none, they had to improvise from time to time. Among the many forms used by the Commission were: a Schedule for Boarding Animals with instructions on feeding and care; a Record of Animals Tested and Retested for glanders; a form for animals to be cast, with details of the auction and prices fetched; the Daily State of Mule depots (of the three types and whether fit to embark); the same for horse depots; a request for feed; a Return of Sick and Injured Animals Admitted to Hospital each week with details of the diseases and injuries and of personnel; Equine Death Certificates, and instructions on how to complete them; and several others for the use of Commission personnel and veterinary officers.

Newly purchased animals had to be branded. Each of the purchasing officers had his own personal brand, which was added below the usual broad arrow; these personal brands consisted of one or two letters, with the exception of two, which were a lower-case letter and a square. The brands were applied to the near side quarter of the animal, four inches below and four inches to the right of the point of the hip. Animals from the United States were branded U on the off side quarter, or C for Canada. Mules were marked on the hoof, UD for 'gunners', UC for 'carters' and UP for pack animals. The method of branding for mules had to be changed in 1944. Branding on the hoof, which had been the standard procedure, was ineffective in the long term as the hooves grew and were trimmed for shoeing, and heavy accumulations of mud made the brands impossible to see. Instead they were branded on the right side of the neck (the US Army used the left side), using the broad arrow and the initial of the buyer's surname.

The branding was done at the centres where the animals were brought for pre-purchase inspection. The actual branding process commenced by clipping a clear patch before the branding iron was applied. The instruction was that the iron should ideally be heated in a wood fire until it had just turned red, and any loose cinders attached to it brushed off before use. It should be applied absolutely flat and quickly, and not pressed too hard as this injured the underlying tissue and caused a sore, the result being an unclear mark. Vaseline was to be applied after branding to keep the skin of the newly made scar soft when healing.

There were four types of depot: purchasing, collecting, off-loading and embarkation; where these were adjacent to train stations, they often used the existing stock yards, adding their own corrals, additional buildings and veterinary hospitals. In July 1918 reports were received from all depots concerning repairs being necessary to buildings. Since these were only erected as temporary structures, this was hardly surprising. That September there was a month-long cessation of buying, which allowed a small surplus in the expenses budgets and this was used for repairs, including the replacement of the indoor corrals at the Rosemount depot. Due to the scarcity of labour and a shortage of suitable lumber, which increased prices, this eventually cost twice what had been budgeted, but there was no alternative.

In early 1917 an order from the War Office was received by the Purchasing Commission in North America to the effect that officers of the Commission should wear uniform, and that civilian purchasers could, if they wished, receive honorary military ranks. Many did.

As well as the officers employed by the Commission, there was lower-level labour. Two categories were used: those found by the contractors and those found by the Commission. The first were part of the contract at a stated rate per head, usually two men per 100 animals at depots with enclosed corrals, and were used for entraining and detraining of animals, feeding, and cleaning corrals – basically, all the labour necessary for handling the animals. The second were those employed in the sick lines and for disinfecting, plus other veterinary duties, including dressing wounds and sores. As of 7 January 1917 the number of men employed by the Commission was 211, including foremen, to deal with 46,575 animals. In the early days of the Commission wages were normal, at $2.25 per day for men (except for Newport News, where only coloured labour was available and cost $1.25) and $3 per day for foremen. By 1918 these rates had risen to $3.25 per day for men and $35 per week for foremen. The rate for coloured labour had risen as high as $3.75 per day. This rise in labour rates was probably a result of the war effort when America joined the war.

After the Armistice the American government asked if the British Commission wanted to take over any of the animals they had in stock, but this offer was refused. The last of the animals held in British depots were sold on

4 February 1919; the last of the paperwork was then completed and the Commission closed at the end of that month.

The report on the purchase of horses and mules by the British Remount Commission in Canada and the United States ended with a summary of salient factors which affected the performance of the Commission and which would need to be kept in mind on future such occasions. The first of these was that no one knew how long the war, and thus the life of the Commission, would last. It was obvious that this was unknown, and thus the structures at the various depots were considered to be of only a temporary nature and after nearly four years required extensive repairs. The second was the periodical suspension of purchasing and the orders received on three occasions to dispose of animals and close down the Commission, followed by other orders to recommence buying. This required closing and reopening various depots, with the result that experienced men had to be discharged; since it was not always possible to re-employ those men, new ones had to be trained.

Between the Wars

Between the two world wars it was recommended that depots should be standardised, with a 'kraal' system as used in South Africa (and originally known as the 'Eassie' system). Here the remount depots were built around a railed oval exercise track with paddocks (kraals) with open shelters on one side, yards with water troughs and shoeing facilities. The version of this recommended in 1927 had the working facilities inside the exercise track, and a 'crush' system where animals could be isolated and led elsewhere. The horses/mules were to be let out onto the exercise tracks, one paddock at a time, and encouraged to run round the track for half-an-hour. During this time their feed troughs were filled and hay laid out round the sides. They were then moved from the track to the watering yard and from there to a 'shunt' yard until the second lot were in the watering yard, when they were moved via the track to their original paddock. This was repeated yard by yard until all the animals had been exercised, watered and fed. The whole procedure was to be done twice a day. This system needed far fewer men to operate than any other method.[3]

The mechanisation of the British Army during the 1930s reduced the military requirement for horses, although mules were still used as pack animals in rough terrain, especially in Burma and Italy. But the number of animals required was relatively small and eventually the Remount Department was amalgamated with the Royal Army Veterinary Corps to form the Army Veterinary and Remount Service.

The Remount Department, now based at Melton Mowbray, continues to buy about eighty horses a year as replacements for those who are too old for continued service.

Chapter Four

Transporting Horses by Land and Air

Until the advent of the railways and, later, motorised horseboxes, there was only one way to move horses on land and that was on their own four feet. Either ridden, led from a ridden horse or tied to a carriage or cart of some sort, they would move from their breeders to regular horse fairs, often along the same drove routes used by cattle. When taken overseas, the same applied, walking or riding the horses to the port of embarkation and from the port of arrival to the actual theatre of war.

Road

Before mechanisation, there are a few recorded instances of horses being moved in large carts or vans drawn by other horses, but this was a slow and expensive process, used mostly for valuable racehorses. By the turn of the nineteenth/twentieth century, some horses were moved by road. The first customised horsebox built on a truck chassis was created in 1902; by 1912 the Reading (England) firm of Vincent Horse Boxes began mass production and in 1914 the army requisitioned some of these. These boxes were little used in the field, where road transport of equines was more likely to be in whatever trucks were available. Recommendations for these trucks were that they should either be completely enclosed, or have walls 4ft high with a canopy 5ft 9in high. Trucks with built-in wheelboxes which projected into the interior, or those with any other sort of interior fittings, should not be used. Loose items such as spare wheels should be removed and the floor covered with some non-slip material such as earth or coconut matting. A 4-tonne truck was deemed suitable to carry four loaded pack mules, head to tail across the truck, or two horses with fodder and their saddlery. Since these vehicles were unlikely to have a built-in ramp, to load the animals they either had to be backed up to a slope or bank, or a ramp of hay or straw bales had to be constructed and covered with a tarpaulin or wood to hide any gaps. The same situations could be utilised for unloading, or the animals could be induced to jump out, ideally onto a level and soft surface. In such trucks, the handlers should ride with their animals while in transit.

Mules in Sicily were often transported in open trucks with no more than string to tie them in; not surprisingly many broke the string and jumped out, to be lost or injured.

Trains

Although trains became a useful method of transporting both supplies and animals, their inherent problem is that they can easily be destroyed by enemy action or rendered useless by neglect or accident. And of course in the early days, there were many countries, especially those in the Indian subcontinent and East Africa, where there were no railways at all. The first railway line in Britain ran between Liverpool and Manchester and opened in 1830. Railways quickly spread across mainland Europe, and by 1849 Russian troops were moved from Poland to Hungary by rail, and in 1859 the French moved 115,000 men, 25,000 horses, many carriages and much other material to Italy. In the War of Silesia (western Poland) in 1870 some 456,000 men, 135,000 horses and 14,000 guns and their carriages were carried.

In 1882 the author George Furse was able to report that 'Of all the applications of the scientific discoveries of the present age for war, none have had a greater influence on the movement of troops and their maintenance in the field, than railways.' However, he went on to point out, their usefulness was dependent on the army's ability to bring supplies and materiel to the loading stations and send it on when it had reached its rail destination.

While men could jump onto or down from a train anywhere it chose to stop, supplies and horses required a platform to detrain. Instructions for embarking horses on trains started with a requirement for the carriages to be inspected to ensure that the flooring was strong enough to bear the horses and withstand their pawing. Cross-battens, if not already present, should be provided to give good holding for the horses' feet; straw or a layer of earth would help in this, and also deaden the hollow sound which might frighten the horses. The loading should be done by men with whom the horses were familiar, and they should not have been fed later than two hours before loading started. Where there were not enough dedicated horse-wagons available, those that were should be reserved for officers' horses, while cattle wagons or goods wagons could serve for the other horses, assuming that they had the necessary height and wide enough doors. The wagons should be wide enough for the attendants to be able to move in front of the horses to give them feed and water, and there should be at least one attendant in each wagon.

The horses could be arranged either parallel to the rails, or transversely. The latter arrangement usually meant fewer horses could be carried in each wagon, in order to leave room for the grooms. It did, however, make for a more comfortable ride for the horses, and the noise of trains passing in the other direction was less likely to frighten them. For this reason it was recommended that horses travelling transversely should face away from the other track.[1] As with anything to do with horses, inexperienced animals were more likely to be frightened by travelling by train, and would be calmer if preceded by a calm experienced horse. In India, where many cavalry horses were stallions, it was recommended that they should be separated with a gelding in between.

In 1882 an English railway truck could hold up to eight medium-sized horses, but only six draught horses with all their saddlery and feed for the journey. It was suggested that when these larger horses were carried, some smaller animals such as ponies or donkeys should also be carried to allow them to be packed in tight to reduce kicking. There was a risk that these large horses would rub and damage their tails, so these should be loosely bandaged; they might also damage their poll if they threw their heads up and thus should be provided with a 'bumper' (poll guard). They should not be carried saddled or harnessed unless the journey was less than six hours; they took up less room this way, and there was always a risk that the saddles, if worn, could be damaged. When they were carried wearing their tack, girths and other tight harness should be loosened, and the bits removed from their mouths. However, in cold conditions wearing their saddle did help to keep them warm. On the other hand, in topless trucks in very hot weather the horses should be covered with a light rug to protect their loins from the sun, and some form of ventilation should be provided; at the very least there should be holes in the sides and floor of the truck, which would also give some drainage. Where they were carried transversely to the rails, their saddlery would have to be carried in another truck, which could carry sixty sets of saddlery. Wherever the saddles were carried, they should have a cloth label attached so the troopers could recognise their own. Lanterns would be needed at night, and there was an absolute ban on smoking.

When established units travelled, the animals and their riders, drivers or leaders should always be on the same train, even if not in the same truck. This applied also to wheeled vehicles, which should be carried on the same train as their drivers and teams.

All stations should be provided with ramps to aid loading and unloading horses, and troughs and buckets should be available at all stops, even if the horses were to stay in their trucks. Ideally, larger stations, well equipped with long platforms, sidings and storehouses for feed, should be chosen for loading and unloading horses. Gangs of porters should be available to assist in unloading equipment, and in countries such as India these men would have to be fed as well as paid. Where large trains were involved, and these were numerous, a couple of days should be allowed between trains to allow for restocking feed and other stores.

J. Wortley Axe, one-time president of the Royal College of Veterinary Surgeons, wrote a scathing indictment of existing conditions on railways. Speaking of the common three-compartment railway horsebox, in 1905 he wrote sarcastically that:

> every portion of it appears to have been designed with the special object of making the most alarming noises calculated to frighten the inmates. The same applies with even greater force to the doors, which open onto the platform, or 'dook' as it is called. It is too heavy for a man to let down steadily, and the traditions of the railway would be altogether violated if it were not allowed to fall with great violence upon the siding. Everything about a horsebox comes undone with a jerk and closes with a bang. Some horses absolutely refuse to enter a box of the kind, and much might be done to render them less fearsome to those unaccustomed to travel.

Axe suggested putting some form of sound-deadening material on the access ramps, as the sound of hooves on a hollow ramp was particularly frightening to young horses. He went on to point out the need for improved methods for tethering horses in boxcars, and for allowing them enough room to maintain their balance while in transit. The system at that time, in some companies, was to use two ropes, one short and one longer, tied at one end to the horse's headcollar and at the other to the other rope, leaving a loose loop in which the horse could entangle itself. This, said Axe, was the most common cause of accidents to horses in trains. The method he recommended was a single rope, tied to the front of the headcollar, running up to a pulley and from there down through a closed box to a weight which kept the rope taut. As it was not exposed on its downward route, the horse could not get its feet tangled in it.

Axe further complained about the padding material which was meant to protect the horses. This could not be removed for cleaning or disinfecting, thus passing infection (such as ringworm) from one horse to another. He observed that as long as no scientific study was made of equine safety during rail transit, 'we may expect accidents to continue, and litigants to press the advantages of one system in order to fix blame on another'.[2]

There were instructions for loading troublesome animals onto trains. These included covering its head, two men linking hands behind the animal and rushing him into the truck, or laying down a tarpaulin, getting the animal's hind feet on it, then quickly lifting the tarpaulin and pulling it towards the truck. If all else failed, some animals were more easily persuaded to back into the truck than go in forwards. In general, the animals should be on a loose lead rope held by someone with whom they are familiar, and no attempt should be made to drag them in as this would only make them resist in fright. Nor should the leader turn round and stare into the animal's face.

Many of the horses bought in America had to travel long distances by rail to reach the ports for embarkation. This was not without hazards. On 4 December 1914 a train load of horses, en route from Montreal to Halifax, was derailed at New Brunswick, resulting in the deaths of thirty-one horses, with twenty more seriously injured. The accident was eventually found to be the result of negligence on the part of the railway company, which paid full damages of $7,753.20.

In April 1917 America joined the war. As a result the railways became congested, cars were difficult to obtain and movement of horses delayed. By February the American government had taken over the control of all the railways in an attempt to ease congestion; this was little help, and only two shipments of horses were possible as not all railways would accept horses as freight. In all, fifteen railways were used, including the delightfully named Atchison, Topeka and Santa Fe. The average length of a rail journey was 1,666 miles and eighty-seven hours, with three off-loadings for feed and water. Journeys for horses purchased west of Sheridan (Boise, Spokane or Salt Lake City) were even longer.

At the beginning of the Second World War a division of cavalry was sent out to Palestine and it was decided that, rather than sending all the horses directly from the western ports of Britain, they should go by rail through France and then by sea the rest of the way. A report by the RAVC gives a detailed description of the process and problems encountered before and during the journey. The first step was to select experienced RAVC officers on the grounds that few other officers understood the difficulties involved; the next step was to issue a pamphlet to all officers and NCOs of the regiments involved, along with with lectures and demonstrations on correct procedures. Finally, RAVC officers were distributed proportionately among the trains and ships being used.[3]

Before loading the horses, they were inspected by RAVC vets looking for signs of contagious diseases or fevers which would be rapidly transmitted. They also checked the horses as soon as they had been loaded for injuries caused in the loading process, as well as during the journey. Such animals were taken off the trains and allowed to recuperate before being put on the next available train. Vets had already reconnoitred the proposed routes and found places where these horses could be unloaded. Even without such problems, the whole journey took over a week: a train to Dover, a train ferry for the Channel crossing, and a transfer to French railway trucks for the journey to Marseilles. This took close to two days, and was followed by a week-long sea journey.

It was originally intended that the horses should be taken straight from the trains to their ship, to save on the need for accommodation for horses and humans, but the vets opposed this, pointing out that such a continuous journey would cause heavy losses from additional fatigue and failure to detect health problems before embarking on the ship; instead, a horse camp was established at Marseilles and the horses were given a two-day break before going to their ship. Although sensible, this did mean that due to the difficulty of coordination some of the ships could not be fully loaded at once and had to wait for the next batch of horses to become available. These delays might last between twenty-four and thirty-six hours, and if the ship was to go in a convoy, there might be a further delay while the rest of the convoy was assembled.

All this having been arranged, a Deputy Assistant Director of the RAVC flew to Palestine at the end of November 1939 to reconnoitre, returning nine days later. It was then possible to organise the veterinary arrangements. These started with the allocation of veterinary personnel to accompany each train and ship, and others to deal with any casualties found at Dover and Dunkirk, and organising a mobile veterinary section at the Chateau Reynarde at Marseilles. Veterinary stores including oxygen cylinders were provided for each ship leaving Marseilles for Haifa and a veterinary hospital was set up in Palestine.

The move was carried out in four divisions called 'flights', leaving between late December and the end of February. Their total transit time took around twenty days. A total of 7,906 horses left England; of these, 98 died on the journey, 42 had to be destroyed and 190 were held at Marseilles for veterinary treatment before they could continue the journey. Despite instructions from the RAVC, some essential equipment (hurricane lamps, water buckets and spare lead-ropes) was stored in the baggage cars where it could not be accessed during the journey. And some regiments adopted their own feeding regime despite a recommended scale of feeding and adequate supplies; in several cases this led to the horses getting colic from unsuitable feed such as uncrushed maize.

The weather in Britain and northern France was what might be expected in winter, with icy roads making the march from the collection points to the train stations difficult, and fog in the Channel delaying some departures from Dover. Marseilles was little better, with rain and snow on shore turning the camps into morasses, and gales delaying ship departures. Unfortunately the berths allocated to the horse ships were extremely exposed. There was further heavy weather in the Mediterranean and some horses suffered broken bones. Blackout regulations did not help. Most arrivals at Dover and departures from Dunkirk took place in the dark, making entraining and caring for the horses more difficult. The ventilation was restricted in case light escaped and this led to some horses developing pneumonia.

However, some aspects of the railway side of the operation were successful. There were frequent halts for watering and veterinary inspections, at which unfit horses could be removed. The French railway trucks were clean and in good condition, and the tented stabling (provided by Benjamin Edgington & Co. of London) at Dunkirk and Marseilles proved to be excellent.[4]

The Remount Manual stated that 'as a rough guide, stock should be detrained for five hours after every journey of twenty-eight hours'. At this time they could be fed and watered, walked around and allowed to roll.[5]

De-training required three assembly points, one each for led and ridden horses and another for vehicles, which should be taken there by their team and driver. All arrangements should be in place before the troops could leave their carriages. Ramps should be put in place and material for emergency ramps should be made available. Once unloaded, lead horses should be taken to their assembly point, and draught horses harnessed to their vehicles and taken to theirs.[6]

Sick horses, if unfit to march, could be forwarded by rail when on the line of march but no horse, or officer's sick charger, was to be conveyed by rail at the public expense if it could be left at a military station in charge of a veterinary officer. A full statement of the causes for sending sick horses by rail, with all the attending circumstances, had to be submitted.

Air

Although equines could be carried in aeroplanes, this was not often done, with the exception of valuable racehorses. They had to be carried in breast-high stalls, and their handlers should stay with them in case of panic. Ideally they should be loaded facing aft, but this could be changed if the aircraft's captain required it, perhaps to adjust the trim of the plane. The floor should be covered with stout PVC sheeting, with a deep layer of clean peat to absorb urine and droppings. Pads should be fitted to the polls of the bridles to avoid damage to the animals' heads on loading or unloading, but while in transit bridles were replaced with headcollars. Knee pads might also be needed. Each animal should have a hay-net.

A vet should accompany the animals on planes, and may deem it necessary to use tranquillisers. If it should become necessary to put an animal down during flight, it should be done with a captive bolt humane killer; ordinary ammunition should never be used as it might go right through the animal and then through the plane's fuselage, causing instant decompression and possibly a crash.

This type of transport was rarely used for military animals, although up to twelve animals could be carried in a commercial freight plane. However, for very short distance transportation, mules could be (and were) moved in cargo nets lifted by helicopter.

Over 2,200 mules and ponies were taken in Dakota aircraft to operational areas in Burma, with a few in gliders modified with coconut matting on the floor and bamboo poles lashed together to create stalls. Only four animals had to be destroyed in the air due to what was described as 'disorderly behaviour', but it was remarked that a full nose-bag helped quieten unruly animals. In February 1943 Brigadier Orde Wingate arrived in Burma with his Long Range Penetration Group (the Chindits). Their task was to sabotage the enemy's supply lines and cut the main railway line between Mandalay and Myitkyina. As well as almost a thousand mules, they used several elephants, which carried up to 800lb each, to move their equipment, including rubber boats to cross rivers.

In 1944 a few horses and mules were sent to Yugoslavia, some of which were transported in planes from the Balkan Air Force. Four mules travelled in each plane, and, with no ramps available, deplaned in the dark by the simple method of jumping out.

Experiments were carried out on the possibility of dropping mules by parachute. Each animal was sedated and secured to a padded wooden platform, lashed down with lengths of cotton webbing. The total load was some 1,100lb. Attached to each were two clusters of three 28ft silk parachutes. Loaded into the aircraft by jeep-crane, the load was put on a trolley which ran the length of the fuselage. This was balanced in such a way that it only required two men to lift one side and tip it so that the load slipped down and out of the door. Seven live drops were tried, with the load ejected from the aircraft at 600ft and landing at a speed of about 15ft per second. It took fifty-five minutes to secure each mule to the packing and load it into the aircraft, and five to seven minutes to release it and saddle up on landing. The mules were able to carry a load in less than twenty minutes after landing. Although these experiments proved that it could be done, they were never used in real operations.

Chapter Five

Transporting Horses by Sea

The history of taking horses abroad on ships goes back at least as far as the fifth century BC when the Persians invaded Greece. Vikings took horses to Iceland in the ninth century and the Normans took over 2,000 across the English Channel in 1066. The Bayeux Tapestry shows horses being disembarked from small open ships. This type of ship could be brought right up to a beach and the horses walked up a ramp, but for longer voyages larger ships were needed and the horses were carried on the lower decks or in the hold; once steam ships were the norm and ships were larger, equine accommodation could be added to the top deck. From the early seventeenth century numerous horses were needed abroad during a sequence of wars.

On rare occasions, when ships could be brought alongside a quay or wharf, horses might walk up a gangplank onto the deck of a sailing ship but they could not walk down to the hold and the usual method was to hoist them in slings suspended from a yard-arm, or later by a donkey-engined crane. Many horses did not take kindly to being hoisted in a sling, and would kick and struggle; in one reported case, a horse kicked a member of the ship's crew over the side of the ship and injured him so badly that he was unable to sail with the ship.[1] Many animals were prone to panicking in this situation, but this could be prevented by covering their eyes. It was best if they were loaded last.

The usual method of loading horses used stout slings made of thick sacking or sailcloth, with a wooden strut on each lateral edge to keep it stretched out; they also had a breast-strap and a breeching-strap, to prevent the horse slipping forwards or backwards. The approved method was to lay the sling flat on the ground and lead the horse over it before lifting the sides enough to get it in the right position before doing up the fore and aft straps, and finally lifting it all the way. At least two slings per ship were carried (one large, one small). Larger capacity ships carried more slings and used more than one hatch.

For slinging horses, a four-man crew was required. One man, standing on the off-side (right) of the horse, would bring the sling up under the horse's belly and hold the wooden strut just above the horse's back, then the other side would be raised by a second man and the struts brought together so that the crane hook was above the centre of the horse's back. Then the breast-strap and breeching-strap were fastened to eyes in the sling and the officer in charge gave the order to stand away and hoist. Kicking at this stage should be ignored, as the horse soon calmed down. It was then lowered onto the deck, and once it had gained its footing the sling could be removed and the horse led to its stall. In the case of mules, rather than using slings, they would sometimes be walked over cargo nets and lifted that way, with their legs dangling through the net. There are some photographs of mules in these nets, but instructions on how to get them out do not seem to have survived; it must have been a fraught business.

The standard technique for dealing with troublesome animals was to cover their head with a sack or a coat. Those who did not like the feel of the sling touching their belly should have the sling laid across their back first, then gradually slipped into position, while someone stood at its head talking quietly to distract it. Troublesome animals, said the manual, should be loaded last.

It was not until the First World War that horses could walk down a slope into a lower deck or the hold of some ships; in some cases, the horses were put into a small box on the quay and this was lifted onto the ship. On arrival the process was reversed, but in most cases there was nowhere to put the horses down on dry land so they were put in the sea and either left to swim ashore on their own, or guided ashore with a lead-rope from a boat. In some cases, where the sea was shallow, the beach might be so far from the ship that a flat-bottomed boat was the only way to get them ashore.

Augustus Schaumann, a Peninsular War commissary, described the scene on the beach when the horses of Sir John Moore's force arrived in Portugal at the end of August 1808. These horses had been on board for almost four months, having been initially taken on an expedition to Sweden, where they had been denied permission to land; taken back to England, they were sent on, without being unloaded, to join Wellington in the Peninsula. Brought close to shore in boats, the horses leapt out of them and dashed through the surf to the shore where they galloped about on the beach, kicking and biting each other, and rolling in the sand. When they were finally caught and saddled, it was found that they could not carry the weight of a rider after so long standing in the hold; they had to be led about for a few days to strengthen their back and leg muscles.[2] Sir John Moore wrote to his friend Colonel James Willoughby Gordon, the military secretary to the Duke of York at Horse Guards, commenting 'a great many of the horses of the 3rd German Light Dragoons have proved unserviceable, and many have died in consequence of being worked immediately after being landed from a four months confinement on board ship'.[3] Moore's army also lost twenty-two cavalry horses out of the force which General Baird took to Corunna; these animals died in stormy weather in the Bay of Biscay a couple of months later. Exactly why they died is not recorded but there are three possibilities: in bad weather the hatches to the hold would be sealed to keep it water-tight, and with no fresh air some of the horses could have suffocated; secondly, motion-sickness can be as debilitating for horses as it is for humans; and thirdly, in rough weather the movement of the ship could have meant the horses in narrow stalls were not able to balance themselves and damaged themselves in falling; however, slings were usually available, or could be quickly made from sail-cloth, so the horses were not wholly dependent on their own legs to stay upright.

Although horses could be loaded onto ships quite quickly (as many as forty per hour in the right location and with practice), often the ships did not depart as soon as each was loaded, but instead moved out to holding areas until the whole fleet was ready, with its naval escort assembled and the wind in the right direction. There could be long delays, which were not good for the horses, especially in the matter of ventilation into the hold, until such time as electricity allowed fans to be used. When the ships were moving, carefully angled wind-sails or rotating cowls were placed to direct air down the hatches, but these did not work while at anchor. For this reason, once the need for a naval escort had passed, it was recommended that horses should be the last thing loaded, just before the ship sailed.

Although they sailed in convoys with a naval escort until the end of the Napoleonic War, the horse transports (and all other transport ships) did not belong to the navy but were hired from their owners and crewed by civilian seamen. After 1794 hiring transports for all purposes was the task of the Transport Board. Prior to this, the hiring of transports was done through the Navy Board, the Victualling Board, the Ordnance Board or the Treasury (for army transports). This had caused tremendous problems during the American War of Independence when competition from the various hirers drove up the prices of hire and caused a shortage of shipping.

The Admiralty and other boards which hired ships inspected them for suitability before agreeing on terms for the charter. Obviously the number of horses they could carry was a major factor. Unlike troop-carrying ships, for which the criterion was 2–3 tons per man, for horses the figure was 7 tons, or 10 tons for a cavalry horse and its rider. This did not mean that the 'cargo' weighed that much, but rather that the weight of the ship would be divided by the relevant figure to calculate the number of horses that could be carried. Wooden sailing ships were considered better when going to hot climates as they remained cooler than metal-hulled ships. They also had more space than steamships, and it was suggested that they might be towed behind steamships. Finally the ships had to be checked for vermin and bad smells; if the previous cargo had not been cleared when the ship was inspected, a date had to be fixed for this, and the ships had to be cleaned.

The favoured type of ship for horse transports at this time was the collier, although they had to be cleaned of coal residue and stalls built. After 1803 this was done at the owner's expense, but many owners were reluctant to pay for this, given that in most cases the charter was short and the stalls had to be removed at the end of the charter, also at the owner's expense. Any reusable material was usually sold at auction. There was no thought of retaining such ships as horse transports so they could be ready quickly when next needed.

As well as organising the fitting-out of horse transports, the hiring authority required the owner to provide slings, ship halters, implements for mucking-out and general stall cleaning such as brooms and shovels, pumps and buckets for drawing water and serving it to the horses, and other hardware needed for feeding them. A supply of empty sacks should be carried, to be filled with straw and used as padding for injured or exhausted animals. The masters of these ships were responsible for the feed on board; they had to sign for it when it was loaded, and keep exact records of usage. There was a stocktake at the end of each voyage and deficiencies were charged to the ship.[4]

So many colliers were used that the availability of coal in London, and thus its price, was affected. These ships could only carry up to forty horses, fewer if they were the bulkier and heavier draught horses. If they were intended for a specific purpose, such as troop or horse transports rather than normal cargo carrying, the requirements for internal fittings had to be set out. In the case of horse transports, stalls were built on either side of a central aisle, and there had to be at least 9ft of space from the floor of the stall to the beams of the decks above. Ships with a steep 'tumble-home' (the hull shape where the width at the waterline is wider than at the upper deck) had less head-space behind the stalls but this would have been sufficient room for the grooms to move about to muck out. A beam of 30ft allowed for two rows of stalls with a 10ft aisle in the middle and a good 2ft space behind. The hatchways should be at least 10ft, and no stall should be more than 15ft from a hatchway.

The stalls themselves were small: 7ft long by 2ft wide, with a minimum of 6ft 6in headroom. For mules the stalls had to be 5ft 6in long by 1ft 8in wide. Ponies, donkeys and pack bullocks were housed in small pens, allowing 5ft in length and 1ft 8in in width for each animal. The stalls or pens should have no rough or sharp places where an animal could injure itself. Ships from America had shorter stalls, and the animals had their necks and heads out at the front. Each ship should have 5 per cent of spare stalls for sick animals, if possible on the deck for fresh air.

Later specifications for stalls required that they had an opening gate at the back for mucking out. Otherwise the horses would have to be taken out and put into an empty stall, or, although this does not seem to have been specified, could have been walked up and down the aisles for a little exercise in calm weather. This would require a non-slip surface on the aisles. The dung mucked out was put into baskets and thrown over the side of the ship. However, this should not be done in harbour, nor in the Mediterranean where there is only a slow current and no tide; in the case of steam-driven ships, dung should not be dumped forward of the engine room where it could get sucked in through the intake. Urine was run off the stalls by pipes, either directly to the scuppers, or to a tub which was emptied by hand 'from time to time' or, where the stalls were below the water line, pumped to the scuppers.

In 1813 the first set of official regulations on the transport of horses by sea was issued. These included the idea of sponging the horse's face and nostrils with watered vinegar and adding nitre to the food. These two items remained in the regulations for over seventy years, as did the instruction that horses should be slung in the case of injury or accident. They also stated, sensibly, that horses should be loaded onto ships at night when it was cooler.

Opinions on the matter of shoes varied. Some authorities said the horses should be newly shod before being loaded, others said the rear shoes should be removed and the front shoes replaced with just 'tips'.

Horses should not be fed or watered for two or three hours before loading, especially those who were to be slung on board. Where gangways were used on ships loaded from quays, these should have enclosed sides high enough to prevent the horses seeing water below them, but should not be closed in completely, which the horses would interpret as a 'dark cave' and thus potentially dangerous.

There was a ban on smoking anywhere except the top deck, and often some 'guards' would patrol to enforce this rule, and also to ensure that the stalls were kept clean.

Although there was a major Commission of Enquiry into conditions in the Crimean War, its comments about horses were mainly centred on feeding difficulties; little mention was made about transporting horses by sea from England. It did report, however, that the horses and mules purchased from Varna (near Constantinople) for the Commissariat were poorly cared for on the crossing and 250 of them were considered barely usable on their arrival.

Fanny Dubberly, a cavalry officer's wife, who travelled to the Crimea in a horse transport, reported that the practice of slinging horses in rough weather often rubbed their flesh raw. A later report from W.F. Carter of the US Army Veterinary Corps pointed out that slinging not only compressed the intestines, but could damage the sheath in male horses, leading to various problems. One difficulty with carrying horses in rough weather was that when frightened they tended to panic and struggled to escape; this is why the standard practice was to tie them up tightly. One enterprising person, who clearly had no experience of trying to get panicking horses to calm down, suggested they should be taught to lie down on command!

Mrs Dubberly also remarked on the tightly secured heads of the horses, which made it difficult for them to balance themselves, and on the slippery footing in the stalls. Some vets recommended much looser tethering and sand or shingle ballast in the stalls so the horses could lie down.

Temple Goodman reported events when his regiment left Queenstown near Cork on a P&O steamer in a thunderstorm. Before the horses had time to get used to the motion of the ship a gale blew up:

> We were constantly going round the horses tying them shorter [and getting up those] who had fallen from the rough sea and wet deck. Some even got their fore feet over the boxes, and had to be pushed back before they got any further and someone got hurt from their panicking on the deck. They were on the top deck, terrified by the canvas 'roofs' of the stalls which flapped in the wind. Two horses fell next to each other and could only be got up by cutting open their stalls and dragging them onto the deck.

But all the horses survived and calmed down once the storm had passed. Carrying them on the top deck was experimental, and Goodman was concerned that if the machinery broke down the horses would have to be thrown overboard to allow the men to work the sails.[5]

Further bad storms were experienced by the heavy cavalry when crossing the Black Sea. One particularly bad storm struck the *Wilson Kennedy*, which tossed and rolled so much that few of the horses could stay on their feet. Then, to make matters worse, one deck collapsed and dropped the officers' horses onto the troop horses below. Of the 100 horses on that ship, 99 died, along with another 51 on other ships accompanying them.

Another factor leading to equine debility in the voyage to the Crimea was the decision by the War Department to send the horses by sailing ship, which took a month, rather than by steam ship, which would only have taken two weeks.[6]

In 1854 the 10th Hussars were ordered to move from India to the Crimea complete with 738 horses, which included a mount for every man and a percentage of replacements for casualties. The transports were four steam ships and four sailing ships. The voyage was not trouble free: the right wing of the regiment sailed ahead of the left wing and headquarters staff and encountered a bad storm. The *Jessica*, which was carrying over 100 horses and had a very high deckload of hay, had a particularly bad time. The *Feroze*, which was towing her, also got in difficulties in the heavy seas and the captain signalled that he was going to cast off the tow, as the strain was too great. When the crew of the *Jessica* signalled back that her deckload would hamper them using her sails, and that her crew was in any case too small to handle the sails, *Feroze*'s captain agreed to continue the tow as long as the rope held out;

luckily the storm soon died down. The *Punjab*, on the other hand, although only jury-rigged, sailed so well that she kept getting ahead of her tug, and had to heave-to and wait for it to catch up.

They sailed up the Red Sea to Suez, where the regiment disembarked and marched overland to Cairo, where they lodged in the cavalry barracks at Abbassia. The *Earl Grey* sprang a leak and had to put into Aden for repairs, so arrived at Cairo two weeks after the others. After five days they all marched on to Alexandria: a much more difficult trek than across the desert to Cairo, as the going was bad – trackless and broken country. Arrangements had been made by the Egyptian government for halting places in the desert, with supply departments for provisions and forage, and water troughs which were kept filled each day with Nile water; they also organised transport for supplies and baggage. The transports *Etna* and *Himalaya*, which took the regiment on to Balaclava, had insufficient accommodation and 170 men and 168 horses had to be left behind. The whole journey took 109 days.

During the Second Boer War (1899–1902) a total of 117,595 horses and 80,525 mules were shipped to South Africa from various countries, including North and South America, Australia, Russia, Hungary, Croatia, Spain and Italy; 6,074 of these were lost en route. Many more were sent from England and Ireland. Conditions on several of the transports were bad in several ways. The animals were crammed into poorly ventilated holds, the water was foul and the food inadequate in both quality and quantity. The crossings were often stormy, and panicking animals kicked one another or were hurt on damaged fittings. Even on troop ships there were few men with experience of handling horses and civilians were employed. Few of these knew anything about horses either and many were rogues simply looking for a free passage to the gold fields of Africa; although they were supposedly not allowed to dis-embark on arrival, many managed to do so. These men were liberally armed and had to be searched to relieve them of assorted weaponry, including knives and pistols. Not surprisingly, these men could not be bothered with their equine duties and a post-war court of enquiry revealed many cases of neglect, expecially in the matter of mucking out.

Many animals died on these ships, although the overall death rates were comparatively low. In the worst year (1900) 4.4 per cent of horses and 3.8 per cent of mules died at sea. The overall percentage for the four years of the war was 3.06. These figures look rather different when considered as a product of the country of origin. The overall percentage was just over 4 per cent for remounts (6.2 per cent from Great Britain and Ireland, 5.8 per cent from the USA and Canada, 4.4 per cent from Australia, 3 per cent from the Adriatic side of Italy, and 0.78 per cent from Argentina) and 2.7 per cent for mules. Several factors were involved in these differing figures: ships from Australia and Argentina did not have to cross the tropics, as did the others, although horses going from Australia to Egypt in 1882 via the Red Sea did suffer many losses from the heat in the monsoon season. These horses had not had their coats clipped before leaving the colder weather of Australia. The voyage from Argentina to Cape Town was half that from England, but the voyage from England involved crossing the Bay of Biscay. As it happened, the weather was kinder to those voyages from Australia and Argentina. And ships from Austria, Spain and Italy did not have to cross the Bay of Biscay.[7]

By the end of the nineteenth century almost all ships were steam-driven, and their greater size meant they could carry many more horses: 1,000 was common, and some of the largest ships carried over 2,000. Whenever possible, the horses were carried amidships, as this part of the ship moved less in rough conditions. The stalls were a little larger and other aspects of fitting-out were laid down in government regulations drawn up by the Admiralty.

At the 1902 enquiry into the work of the Remount Department, many of the numerous officers recalled from South Africa to give evidence responded to specific questions with 'I have no recollection' or 'I don't have my notebook with me'. One would have thought that an officer called home from his duty for an official enquiry might have foreseen the necessity to provide fine detail, and that the officers involved with the notorious ships which mistreated their equine cargoes would have remembered not only the names of those ships and their captains but also the dates involved. After reading about all these memory lapses, the inability to bring essential documents to the enquiry, and generally evasive responses, the overall impression is of many incompetents in the Remount Department's employees. One good thing which came about as a result of the enquiry was the production and distribution of a new manual for the Remount Department.

At about this time Captain Hayes, a veterinary surgeon and prolific writer of popular books on horses, published a comprehensive book on the management of horses on board ship. He had, he remarked in his preface, wanted to do this after some voyages to and from India and Russia, but as these had involved only a few horses in small ships he did not feel qualified to do so. Then, in 1900 he was twice given veterinary charge of much larger numbers of horses going to South Africa, which gave him the insight he had wanted. His experience did not extend to mules, of which he only remarked that they were generally hardier than horses, and that he had been told of their predilection for eating haynets and ropes. The answer to this problem turned out to be an application of coal-tar.

Hayes believed that cattle-ships, ideally those with three decks, were best for carrying large numbers of horses. Sitting higher in the water, these ships carried most of the animals above the water line and thus could be more easily ventilated, either by wind-sails above or air-scoops in the sides. He pointed out that white-painted ships were cooler in hot climates.

He believed horses should be prepared before going on board, unless they came straight off grass, or the voyage was expected to be no more than ten days, their corn ration and exercise being gradually reduced. If the voyage was expected to be more than a month, this preparation should take about two weeks. For voyages over two weeks long, horses should either be given some exercise on board, or provided with enough space to lie down. Animals which had been little handled had to be accustomed to this, and to being tied up in a stable; many needed to be taught to eat from mangers and drink from a bucket. This was standard practice in Australia for horses going to India. No food or water should be given for three or four hours before embarking, but they should be watered and fed soon after embarking to help them get used to their new situation.

Hayes' manual also stated that horses should be fed and watered immediately after a sea passage. As well as the obvious benefit that the horses were likely to be hungry and thirsty after the time spent in unloading them, there is some equine psychology involved here: after all the strange events which had been happening to them, the horses would be reassured to find that not only were they on solid land, but that food and water were available, providing something which an anxious horse could use as 'displacement behaviour'.

Admiralty regulations at that time specified the dimensions of horse stalls as a minimum of 6ft 9in long and 2ft 4in wide (Hayes thought they should be wider than this), with a passage of not less than 4ft between two rows of stalls. The stalls themselves were to be divided by boards 3ft 9in high, with a breast board of the same height at the front. That breast board was to be 10in by 3in, with the upper third covered by zinc. In each stall there was to be a food trough of galvanised iron about 1ft 9in by 12in by 9in deep, a staple for a hay net and a firmly secured halter ring.

Scuppers were to be cut in all 'tween decks and under erections, ideally a 4in scupper every 25ft. A permanent water service pipe was to be fitted to all horse decks with hoses attached, carried fore and aft on the upper deck. There should be at least two independent pumps in the engine room in case of breakdown.

There should be side lights (i.e. openings to the outside, not artificial lights) about 12ft apart with wind scoops at each. There should also be wind sails of 2ft 6in diameter with a large mouth (square head preferred), at least two to each 'tween deck compartment. There should also be ventilators with cowls and 'tween decks should have mechanical ventilation by means of fans, or some other approved method, so as to draw out foul air and exhaust it at the top exposed deck.

Electric lights or candle lanterns of sufficient number to give ample light were to be fitted to erections on the open deck. Candle lanterns were to be of an approved pattern and hung in proper hooks.

A pharmacy should also be provided, with a lockable door.

Hayes was keen on 'portable horse-boxes' as an embarkation/disembarkation aid. These were basically little stalls fitted with rings for the headcollar ropes, with sides tall enough to add a canvas cover. Blindfolds were useful for panicky horses. A rope should be attached to one corner of the box; this was to be held by a man to prevent the box twisting round in the air. These boxes were subject to government regulations, which stated that they should be 6ft long, 2ft 6in 'broad in the clear' and 6ft 4½in high, 'made of good wood, well framed, strongly built up and strengthened with iron bands passing right round the outside'. The bottoms were to be battened. There should be a door at each end, hung on strong hinges and fitted with strong bar fastenings top and bottom. Each door should have ring bolts on the outside for tying halters. The inside of the boxes should be lined with leather slightly padded out with straw and there should be wooden runners underneath so they could be slid about on the decks. They were to be fitted for hoisting, and in this case the horse was to remain in them on the journey on the weather deck. These should have a painted cover for protection from rain and sun. Hayes thought the boxes should be a little larger: 6ft 6in long, and 3ft wide to allow a man to get into the box to attend to the horse. He also recommended coir matting to prevent the horse slipping. The box should be openable at both ends, as this made it easier to load nervous horses.

Horses that were to be exercised on board should wear a snaffle bridle; others needed only a stout headcollar with a leading rope on each side to act as reins.

Any horses found to be sick whilst on board should be marked (perhaps with a piece of coloured yarn on their headcollar) to ensure they were properly cared for on arrival.[8]

One situation which the Remount Service warned about in its 1906 manual was that of demurrage, the daily charge levied by ship owners for steam ships which were detained in port beyond the time specified in the hiring contract. To reduce this charge, the embarkation officer, one of the two types of officer employed by the Remount Service, was to order the ship to leave the wharf as soon as possible after the last animal was loaded.

There were two types of official: embarkation officers and conducting officers. The embarkation officers' duties involved seeing that the ship was properly fitted out, that it was clean, that the animals were sheltered from wind and weather (and escapes of steam), and that there was adequate feed and water. They also had various duties concerned with the grooms (known as muleteers): ensuring that there were the correct number of these, with foremen, and that their accommodation was adequate. They were also to ensure that the windsails were properly rigged, trimmed and made fast below, but they did not sail with the ship. Their final task was to see the horses loaded.

Conducting officers accompanied the horses on their voyage. Their duties included ensuring that they had the correct number of animals before signing for their receipt, selecting night watchmen, ensuring that the animals had plenty of water and were given a drink last thing at night, and ensuring that the animals were tied up properly. This latter instruction was contra-indicated by rough weather, as without freedom to move their heads the animals would have difficulty keeping their balance and were liable to fall. They were also to ensure that animals with heavy coats were clipped when their voyage took them through very warm areas.

A standard daily routine was recommended but could be altered by the conducting officer. This was as follows:

6am – water
6.30am – hay and feed
8am – men's breakfast
9–11am – clean out and groom horses
11.30am – water and feed with hay
12 noon – men's dinner
1–3pm – get up forage for the next day and groom horses again
3.30pm – water and hay
4pm – men's tea
5pm – feed and hay
8pm – water and hay

The recommendations on feeding were that for the first two days of the voyage the horses should be fed only hay, then the next five days should include two small feeds of bran and oats, and then for the rest of the voyage grain could be fed in three feeds. Hay should always be available.

The ship was to be thoroughly mucked out at least once a week, and carefully cleaned daily. The scuppers were to be kept clear of dirt and other potential obstructions, with a man going round regularly to ensure this. The conducting officer should perform this task himself at intervals.

The report also commented on the advisability of using a 'mixed' crew: 'Reports are generally favourable to a mixed crew, white and black, as, being quartered separately, it is found that the men of one colour will not join those of another if trouble should arise.' Whether this meant trouble between the men, or some other form of trouble is not specified.

In the First World War, although much larger numbers of animals were shipped from North America and Canada, there were fewer complaints of mistreatment than there had been in the Boer War. Among the 428,608 horses and 275,045 mules the overall loss was 1.96 per cent, and almost half of these were as a result of enemy action, either through shelling or through sinking. The sinkings were mostly the work of submarines.

Submarine attacks were a major concern for one middle-aged lady who crossed the Atlantic as a groom. An enthusiastic traveller, Mrs Bligh saw an advertisement in a Toronto newspaper for men to serve on a government horse transport going to Europe. Passage was free, and a bonus would be paid on arrival. She was able to persuade the employers that she was capable of doing her bit. The ship, which she did not name, held 675 horses, and all but one arrived safely. Some 300 were housed on the main deck and the rest on lower decks, reached via sloping gangways fitted with cross battens to provide foothold. Ventilation for the lower decks was provided by wind-sails. The horses were in large pens, originally tethered, then, on the accompanying vet's advice, set loose, thirty to a pen, although they had to be tied up for mucking out. The implements provided for this were picks, to loosen the trampled droppings, and shovels, with baskets to remove the result, which was thrown over the side. The voyage from Montreal to Avonmouth took three weeks. The horses were fed oats, bran and hay three times a day, but were not groomed until the day before arrival. Mrs Bligh did not report any trouble among the loose horses, so they were obviously happy enough like that.[9]

Fire was also a danger: on 24 August 1915 the *Anglo-Californian*, with 926 horses on board, was just about to depart when smoke was detected coming from the No. 1 hold where part of the forage was stored. Prompt action by a neighbouring ship and the city fire brigade prevented the fire taking hold, and all the horses were rapidly unloaded, except for twelve in the lower No. 1 hold who could not be reached in time and suffocated. Several of the longshoremen and carpenters belonging to the ship suffered smoke inhalation and were taken to hospital. The cause of the fire was unknown. This was not a lucky ship; during the preceding July she had been shelled near Fastnet and her captain and several hands, as well as a few horses, were killed.

A further disaster occurred in Halifax in December 1917 when a neutral supply ship collided with a store ship carrying TNT and oil. The subsequent explosion demolished a considerable part of the city, killing about 1,500 people and badly injuring many thousands more. The Exhibition Buildings where the remount depot was situated were razed to the ground and the stables damaged. Fortunately the loading of two horse transport ships had been delayed, saving some 400 horses; only twelve were killed at the depot, and there was no loss of life among the depot staff. The port was not likely to be usable for some time, so the depot was closed and the remaining horses removed.

At the end of 1916, it was decided to send some horses on the top decks of corn ships. This caused slight delays until the appropriate stalls were fitted, but was effective otherwise.

A total of 194 ships were used during this war, most more than once, and several more than twenty times. Numerous American ports were used, mostly on the east coast, but also New Orleans, which was only used in 1914–1915. Being so far south, it necessitated a long railway journey and was far too hot in the summer. The choice of railway was very much a product of routes and connections between the place of purchase and an embarkation port.

The subject of carrying horses loose in pens rather than in separate stalls was considered and a trial took place on the *Devonian* which sailed on 29 November 1915. This was found very satisfactory, and subsequently most horses were carried loose in pens of five or ten animals. The pens were created by removing the side bars of individual stalls, and there were some occasions when even larger pens were used. It was recommended that vicious animals should continue to be carried in single stalls.

Most of the other instructions for the care of horses on board ships was the same as in the Boer War, but there was greater emphasis on proper watering and constant mucking out, and on the removal of mildly sick animals to separate stalls away from the others for treatment. Terminally sick horses were to be destroyed immediately and thrown overboard. This category included those with septic pneumonia, which was signalled by the odour of gangrene. Exercise should be carried out whenever and wherever possible, although carrying horses in pens rather than stalls made this slightly less important.

The importance of cleaning and disinfecting empty ships was emphasised, and chloride of lime was recommended to purify the air and eliminate 'deleterious matter' (i.e. ammonia) from fouling the atmosphere on board. This should be applied by saturating sacking with water and sprinkling it with the lime before hanging it up, well spread out, in areas where the smell of ammonia was prevalent.

By the end of the nineteenth century, when most ships were steam-driven and no longer needed room to work the sails, four rows of stalls could be fitted on each of the decks, including the top or 'weather' deck; this last should, of course, be covered with an awning. Some stalls, ideally 5 per cent, should be left empty to allow for sick horses to be housed in a double width stall by removing the sides of one stall, but where possible horses should be housed next to their 'friends'.

The regulation height of the division boards between the stalls was, at 3ft 9in, too low, thought Hayes, especially when larger horses were being carried, as they could easily get a hindleg over these boards if they kicked. Mares in season were particularly likely to kick. Getting the horse out of this position was a major exercise; it was almost impossible to just get the leg back down, and the partition would have to be removed and then rebuilt. Hayes thought that an additional 8in would prevent this problem.

One issue with stalls on the weather deck was that if the horses stood directly on the decks, they were prone to slipping and falling. Hayes' recommendation was to fit coir mats (or a good thick layer of straw, soiled hay or sawdust) at the front of the stall. It was the front legs, which carry more of the horse's weight than the rear legs, which were most prone to slipping. As the front end of the stall did not get soiled by dung and urine, some people thought that it did no harm to omit the mucking-out process, although it did mean the horses spent the voyage with their hind legs on an increasingly high and wet surface. Hayes did not agree with this, insisting that mucking out should ideally be done daily, or at worst, every three days.

During the Second World War the transportation of cavalry to Palestine was carried out during what turned out to be the worst weather for forty-eight years in Britain and France, even at Marseilles. Some animals even froze to death in the lines, and then gales delayed the departure of some of the ships for Haifa.

During 1942 numerous mules were sent from the Middle East to India. The first lot of 500 mules left Haifa on 1 May and thus had to pass through the Red Sea during the hottest part of the year. They were put in pens of seven animals each. When they entered the Red Sea they began to sweat heavily, so their watering was increased to five times a day. Some of the pens were in less well ventilated locations and so the animals were moved around, with none remaining in the hotter pens for more than twenty-four hours at a time. They were all taken up on deck for some exercise in the afternoons. Despite losing weight on the voyage, they were all delivered at Karachi in good health.

A further lot of pack mules went from Palestine to Iraq. Denied permission to travel on Turkish trains, they went by train to Aleppo and marched from there to Qamichlye, then entrained again for their final destination of Mosul. This took twenty-five days, averaging 18 miles a day, and pausing for water stops arranged on the route, mainly from wells or the Tigris and Euphrates rivers, using pumps and canvas troughs. They were accompanied by motor lorries fitted-out to carry any sick and lame animals. Of the 189 horses and 2,846 mules, only 4 died and 18 were evacuated as sick or lame.

By the Second World War much bigger ships were available for horse transport, able to carry more animals, more feed and more water. There was also a range of smaller barge-type landing craft which could be used for short sea crossings, to cross wide rivers, or to unload animals from large ships when these could not anchor close in. However, these craft were only suitable for use in calm weather, and were inherently unstable; thus when loading or unloading, an older horse who was used to them should be used as a 'leader' to encourage the others to follow. Once on board, the animals were packed in tightly and linked to each other as well as tied singly to the sides of the boat.

There were several types of craft available: the LCT ('Landing Craft Tank'), the Z Craft, the LCM ('Landing Craft Mechanised'), and the RCL ('Ramped Cargo Lighters'). The LCT was the largest; although it was not fitted to carry animals, it was considered highly suitable for the task because of its size, range, and ability to operate in rivers and get out to sea. With deck space of 62ft by 26ft, it had plenty of room for saddlery and baggage as well as animals, a cargo capacity of 150 tons, plus a drinking water capacity of 38 tons, and a range of up to 700 miles at 7½ knots fully loaded (10 knots unloaded). Its ramp was 12ft 6in wide, and the side walls 4ft 6in high. For voyages of twenty-four hours it could carry various combinations of mules and horses, sometimes with guns and their ammunition. The ramp was at the front (bow) and the engine and bridge were at the back (aft) of the craft; for disembarking, they were driven bow-first onto a suitable beach or other landing place.

LCTs were capable of carrying fourteen to sixteen animals; they had no special fittings but there was a series of rings at deck level, set 4ft apart along each side of the craft. A 2½in thick rope was tied to these rings at 8ft intervals, and the animals were shackled to this, facing forwards. The line nearest the bow, which had a door on each side, would only take four to eight animals, leaving room for these doors to open. Before embarking the animals they should be fed and watered, then all the baggage, men's food, packs and arms should be loaded and stacked aft. The steel floors of the craft should be covered with plenty of hay or other non-slippery material, and a tarpaulin or coconut matting should be spread over the ramp and onto the floor of the craft. The animals should be loaded one at a time and tied to the line furthest aft; once all the animals were aboard, their rations, nose-bags and buckets could be loaded. Where tidal rivers were involved, loading and unloading should be carried out as quickly as possible.

A beach-master should be appointed, and his say would be final. He should choose a beach with a gentle slope and, if possible, firm soil. Where there were sandbanks, or the river narrrowed drastically, it might be necessary to transfer the animals to a smaller craft. This was done by the larger craft stopping in mid-stream, where the current flowed steadily, and lowering its ramp to the horizontal; the smaller craft then approached with its ramp up, before lowering it to the horizontal on top of the larger craft's ramp; the two craft were then securely tied together, the ramps were covered with matting and the animals transferred one by one.

The LST was a larger version of this craft, some 180ft long by 29ft wide. As well as the lower deck, which was well ventilated, it also had room on the upper deck. As many as 400 mules could be carried on trips ferrying them from ship to shore, loaded into pens of eight or ten animals. The quickest way to transfer animals from a ship to the landing craft was over the brow, by lifting the ramp to meet the ship, but this was not possible if the differential was too steep or there was a swell. In this case the recommended method was to move two mules at a time in a cargo net.

With the addition of stalls made of tubular scaffolding poles with their standard couplings, fewer animals could be carried for longer distances (e.g. Tripoli to Cyprus). This arrangement had three advantages: mules could not eat the poles, as they tended to do with wooden stalls; they could be tailored to accommodate different sized animals; and when no longer needed, they could be returned to stores.

The Z Craft was also larger than the LCT, at 72ft by 28ft. Its ramp was 12ft 6in wide, and the range still 700 miles, but with lower side walls, at just 1ft 6in, it was not suitable for carrying animals at sea. It had a lower speed (5–7 knots) but a greater drinking water capacity at 90 tons. It could carry grooms, saddles and four days' rations for 80 medium-sized mules and 4 horses, or 110 small mules and 4 horses, or 75 horses. As before, the animals were tied in rows across the craft, on a non-slip floor and with a non-slip ramp.

There were two versions of the LCM: the Mark I had 25ft by 11ft 6in floor space, a ramp 11ft 6in wide and 10ft long, a carrying capacity of 35 tons and a maximum range of 56 miles at 7½ knots. Its sides were 6ft high. The Mark III was 31ft 6in by 10ft 9in, had a maximum range of 140 miles, a ramp width of 10ft 2in and length of 10ft 2in. With two days' rations, it could carry 18 large mules, 15 medium-sized mules, 15 ponies, or 12 horses. The animals were not tied but instead were held by an attendant, and arranged in a single row lengthwise, facing alternately left and right. This was to prevent the balance of the craft being affected if all the animals pulled back at the same time.

The RCL was intended for inland transport only, such as crossing lakes or rivers, or moving along rivers. It had a wooden ramp and floor and was considered the most suitable craft for carrying sick animals. With room for saddlery and two days' rations, it could carry 30 large mules or 24 smaller mules, in both cases in two rows, both facing outwards.

With all these craft, when it was not possible to get the landing craft close enough to the beach to use the ramp, the animals could be 'launched' into the water and swum to shore, although loaded animals could not do this unless the water was less than 3ft 6in deep. A guide rope should be erected from craft to the selected landing spot. Experienced men were essential for this operation, some being good swimmers (and fitted with Mae Wests). Where there was a distance between craft and shore, or the mules were loaded, they could be given flotation assistance with three Mae Wests, one under the jowl and one each side of the saddle.

In all cases the captain of the craft should be informed in advance that animals were to be carried and thus the drinking water tanks should be filled and their hand-pumps functional.[10]

Chapter Six

Horse Care

Many of the veterinary problems which arose with horses came about through lack of proper care and housing. As one head of veterinary services remarked, 'Freedom from disease is in direct relation to the degree of care bestowed on an animal, and the spread of mange or contagious disease is a certain indication of neglect in management and supervisory care.' For this reason manuals on horse and stable management were printed and issued at regular intervals. All emphasised the necessity for good but draught-free ventilation, cleanliness and a regular stable routine.[1]

There was also the matter of bad horsemanship which led to major losses in the Boer War. Of units of inexperienced men given a mounted role, future Field-Marshal Sir William Robertson had remarked earlier,

> their bad riding galled both their horses and themselves [and] a mounted infantryman who can neither ride nor properly look after his horse is not of much fighting value and he is decidedly expensive in horse flesh. No more unfortunate animal ever lived than the horse of the mounted infantryman during the early period of the march from the Modder to Pretoria.

Many horses died en route to South Africa, but a much higher percentage arrived alive but in very poor condition, needing several weeks' recuperation before they were fit to work; even those which did not arrive in poor condition should have had a couple of weeks to rest and become acclimatised, but few did. The senior generals, especially Lord Kitchener, overrode the instructions and advice of veterinary surgeons, and as soon as he received reports from the major remount depots that shiploads of horses and mules had arrived, he demanded that they should be sent up to the front immediately. It has been suggested that he, and many of his officers, having spent most of their young lives in towns and cities rather than the country, did not know about, nor understand, the requirements of animals. On one occasion Kitchener looked at a herd of starving mules and ordered them to be turned out into a field of maize; the vet protested, saying that if this was done, 90 per cent of them would gorge themselves into a fatal colic. Kitchener was furious and sent for the chief veterinary officer to ask for his opinion. He said the figure of 90 per cent was incorrect, and that 100 per cent of the mules would die. Another typically ignorant order was that all transport should be in a separate 'park' overnight, with the mules sent to the transport lines. The problem with this was that the mules usually spent the night tied to the poles of their vehicle, on which were hung their haynets and mangers full of feed. Away from these handy wagon poles, other complex arrangements involving picket lines and water troughs would have to be made.

Stabling

In a permanent situation, stabling should be built of brick or stone, with flooring of cobbles or 'chocolate-bar' bricks (so-called because they looked like chocolate bars with raised squares on the top) to aid drainage and give a better foothold when the bedding was removed. Wood was an acceptable substitute for the walls but should be of solid timber to withstand kicking. In either case, a good tiled or slate roof should be provided.

The individual accommodation could be either loose-boxes or stalls. Loose-boxes are literally that; the horse is not tied and can move around freely, and thus the box must be big enough to allow this. Each box has its own double door, with the top door left open except in extreme bad weather. Some horses may need a grid over the open half, to prevent their indulging in stable vices such as crib-biting or snapping at passers-by. Stalls are narrow sections of a large building, usually divided by stout timbers, and each horse is tethered on a rope which runs through a ring to a wooden ball too large to fit through the ring. This allows the horse some freedom of movement, and enough space to turn round to be tethered again facing outwards. Each row of stalls should have a paved alleyway inside the building, and again there will be a double door. Individual hayracks and mangers may be fitted, with holders for water buckets. Alternatively, haynets may be used and a ring fitted to tie them to.

The officer in charge of each unit should ensure that he saw every horse every day; this was usually done at midday 'stables'.

On a long-distance march, horses might be billeted at town stops, often in cab or omnibus stables, in mews or inns. These billets should have been listed well ahead of time by a billet master, but they were also checked the day before the unit was expected by a billeting party which moved one day ahead of the unit. The advance party would first check with the local police in each place for information on outbreaks of contagious equine diseases; if these had occurred in the previous six months, the stables would not be used.

Stables would be rejected as unsuitable if they were dirty, too small for the horses to turn round, or had sharp projectiles such as nails on which the horses could hurt themselves. The mangers and hayracks should be securely fitted. Where several horses were to be kept in one stable, they should have solid divisions between them. They were likely to be nervous about a strange place and could react by kicking and biting at their neighbours, even if they were familiar with one another.

The stables should be secure, but if they were lockable, then more than one key had to be available in case the horses had to be evacuated in a hurry. The harness/saddle room should certainly be lockable, as should be the feed store if the unit was carrying its own supplies. As to the type of feed to be supplied by the stable owner, some cab and bus companies offered a mixture of oats, split beans, split peas and maize with chaff. This was an excellent feed for horses that were used to it, but might be refused by those who were not, in which case oats alone were to be insisted on.

The men should be billeted close to their horses; where a large number were in one place, at least one NCO should be billeted with them. On arrival, the unit should form up in some central place, which would serve as the rallying place in case of alarm, and the place for parade in the morning. The men were told when they were expected to get up and get to work with their horses and the time of parade. They could then be dismissed to their billets.

During the Peninsular War both sides used churches to house their horses and men. The question of sacrilege does not seem to have been a matter of concern.

Stable Routine

The stable routine started first thing in the morning, when the stables were opened, the horses watered and given their first feed of the day, then left in peace to eat it while their humans went for their own breakfast. The next activity was known as 'morning stables': the stables were cleaned out, ideally when the horses were outside. The most convenient time for this was when the horses were out at work, with a few men left behind to clean out. Droppings were to be picked up, then the straw separated into dry and wet, the wet being disposed of and the dry shaken out and stood in windrows to air, outside if the weather permitted or at the back or to one side of the stable if not. The straw should be shaken out again at midday stables and any new straw mixed thoroughly with the old to discourage the horse from eating it. The straw bedding was put down at evening stables; it should be at least 12in thick and spread up to the walls. The straw should ideally be wheat straw, but could be barley, oat or rye. Most straw supply contracts specified that at least two-thirds should be wheat. In some places, if there was no straw available, clean peat or sawdust could be used for bedding.

Many soldiers liked to 'pretty up' the beds on Sundays by plaiting some of the fresh straw to lay along the front of the bed in stalls, but this practice was actually forbidden. Droppings should be removed at intervals during the day and before the bed was laid down in the evening.

On returning from work, the horses should be watered, unless they were hot, in which case they should have no more than half a bucketful until they had cooled down a little. (A long drink of cold water can chill their system and may lead to colic.) Their bridles should be exchanged for a headcollar but their harness or saddles left on with loosened girths. They were given some hay while the men went off to change into fatigue dress, after which midday stables was sounded. For this, every man should be with his horse, and all the officers and NCOs of the unit present. The harness or saddle were removed and the horse checked over for rubs and galls, his feet picked out and any injuries or loose shoes reported to the NCO in charge of the stables. After grooming, each horse was taken outside to be inspected by the officer or NCO in charge of the stables, who checked him over thoroughly, and by the farrier, who checked his feet and shoes, looking for risen clenches, loose shoes and evidence of over-reaching or treads. If the horse was perfectly clean, he could be taken to water and then given his midday feed while the men had their own dinner and then cleaned their saddlery.

The normal stable routine at home in permanent barracks was for the horses to be worked in the morning, then, after grooming and midday stables, to be left in peace to relax and rest. At evening stables the horses were watered, wisped, bedded down and given their evening feed and hay.

The stables themselves and their fittings should be kept clean. Stable windows should be cleaned at least once a fortnight, and the interior of the stable whitewashed. Mangers should be scrubbed out once a week, with hot water and soap if they were made of wood, or hot water with soda or salt if metal. Individual water buckets should be kept clean and scrubbed out once a week, and communal water troughs should be emptied out and scrubbed out at least once a week, more often in summer when algae collected.

In all stables, and any other places where straw and hay were kept in bulk, there was a strict 'No Smoking' rule.

Horse Accommodation in the Field

In less permanent situations, such as base camps in the field, tented stabling might be used, but all canvas should be tightly secured to prevent it flapping and frightening the horses. If no overhead cover could be provided, wind screens would help to prevent chills. Wherever possible the horses should be on hard-standing to prevent problems arising from wet and muddy feet. This hard-standing should be raised above the surrounding ground. Drainage should be attended to regularly, without waiting for bad weather. Soil taken from drain trenches should be added to standings and rammed down. Firm approach roads should be made to water troughs, which should also have hard-standing round them.

By the First World War it was decided that anti-bomb traverses should be erected to protect the horse lines; these should be 6ft high, 3ft thick at the top and 7½ft thick at the bottom. They should leave a passage behind the horses 8ft wide. They could be made of plain earth covered with sods, or alternate layers of earth and dung, the final layer being earth. If it was all pressed down well, and covered with sods, flies were unlikely to breed in it.

The picket site should be chosen to keep the horses out of wind, rain and mud. Wind screens could be erected using hurdles made from brushwood, gorse, reeds, etc. Rabbit-wire netting was recommended for making these.

The setting-up of picket lines varied. The picket rope could be at ground level, but it was preferable for it to be breast high, tied to wagon wheels, trees or posts. It should always be firmly secured and kept taut. The horses tied to the line should have at least 5ft between them, or they would not lie down to rest. (Horses can sleep standing up, but they prefer to lie down if possible.) The knot used to tie the horses to the line should be a 'quick release' type. The high line was preferable as it prevented horses getting a foot over either it or the next horse's lead rope, and it allowed horses to be tied to it on both sides.

It was possible to attach a single horse straight to a picketing peg, but in this case the head-rope should be short and a heel rope used. This was the preferred method of picketing kickers. Alternatively one foreleg could be tied to the peg with a rope 12–18in long. Kickers could also be restrained by hindleg hobbles, fitted above the hocks and tied together with a short rope.

For temporary halts, each troop carried a metal ring of about 18in in diameter; the horses would be tethered to this and hay thrown into the middle of the ring; the horses could also feed from their nose-bags.

Picket line guards should be posted at night and when no other attendants were present. They should check head and heel ropes and adjust them if necessary; shorten nose-bags if the horses were tossing them up to get at the feed at the bottom, and remove them when the horse had finished eating; ensure haynets were in a position that allowed the horse to eat comfortably; remove droppings and keep the lines clean; talk to the horses to help them feel secure; and at the slightest sign of a stampede, call for help.

The 1793 Order Book of the Scots Greys issued the following instructions for carrying camp equipment:

> Mallets, tent pins and hatchetts carried in water buckets fixed to the near ring of the saddle behind. The powder bag to be carried by the Orderly Corporal. Kettles to be fixed with strings until straps can be provided. Canteens to be slung on the right side, haversacks on the left side. Picket posts to be strapped to [illegible]. Corn sacks with corn divided between the ends, across the saddle. Hay twisted into ropes and fixed upon the necessary bags. Water-decks neatly folded and placed upon the hay.

Nose-bags fixed to the off-ring of the saddle behind. Forage cords upon the baggage. Scythes wrapped with hay-bands and strapped with the handles to the firelock. Sneads, [sharpening] stones, etc., to be carried by the same men.

Feeding

Although horses are large animals, they do not have a large stomach capacity, and the best rule to observe on feeding is 'little and often'. In military situations this usually means three hard feeds and two or three issues of hay per day, and some grazing whenever possible. The usual corn given to horses was (and still is) oats, which are relatively soft and easy to digest. Barley could also be given, and was the usual choice in India; in America maize (also known as Indian Corn) was often used. All these grains should ideally be crushed for easier digestion. Draught horses might also be fed dried split beans or peas, 'opened up' by mixing them well with chaff (chopped hay or straw mixed in a ratio of three parts hay to one part straw). In the stable this feed is put in a manger, elsewhere nose-bags were used. Whenever possible hay should be given in nets, since if just put on the ground it can be trodden in or blown away. In 1904 the standard army daily ration per horse was 12lb hay, 10lb oats and 8lb straw; previously the hay ration was larger, at up to 18lb a day, with a correspondingly smaller ration of corn. The day's ration should not be given in equal parts. The morning feed should be the smallest, the midday feed a little more, and the evening feed the largest as the horses will have plenty of time to digest it overnight.

The problem with such rigid rations of feed is that all horses are not exactly the same size, and some need more food than others. One trooper reported that his horse, which was quite large, got thinner and more bad-tempered on the standard ration, while other smaller horses got quite fat. There was only one answer: to steal food from the smaller horses, which soon did the trick, giving him a chubby and contented mount.

Hay is dried grass, cut when the grass is tall and flowering. After cutting, it was left in rows to dry and turned several times with rakes or by a machine towed behind a tractor until it was quite dry, and then piled into small heaps which were taken to the stackyard and built into larger stacks, thatched to keep out rain. By the start of the First World War hydraulic presses were in use; these could reduce 1 ton of hay into a 100ft bale. Nowadays it is picked up by a baler and turned into 56lb bales, but even during the Second World War few balers were available. A small amount of red clover or lucerne is good in hay, but hay which contains buttercups should be rejected as buttercups are a blistering agent. The best grasses for hay include perennial rye grass, timothy, fescues and cocksfoot, plus any of the clover family, including red, white and yellow clover, vetch, sain-foin and hop-trefoil.

One manual suggested that hay should be loosened from the bales in a central place, and shaken or rubbed over a sieve (improvised if necessary from rabbit-wire on a wooden frame) with a large cloth underneath to catch the seed and other small bits, which could then be used as chaff. Where mechanical chaff cutters were not available, the manual stated that one man could soon produce a useful amount of chaff using a heavy knife or chopper and a log of wood as a chopping block.

Newly made hay is not as good for horses as older hay, the general rule being that it needs a minimum of four months to mature, but ideally last year's hay is better than this year's. However, hay (or corn) which smells or looks mouldy should never be fed as it will do more harm than good. Good hay smells sweet and grassy.

During the First World War much of the hay used was procured in Canada, as were some of the oats, the rest coming from the United States, Central America and South America. Early in that war the Quaker Oats Company proposed that it should provide a form of oats mixed with molasses and compressed. Exhaustive trials were made but in the end this was not taken up. One of the claims made by the company was that their product was economic to ship, but by that time floating pneumatic suction plants were available to bulk load and unload ships. Canada was the only source which sent grain in sacks. For forces in the Mediterranean, Mesopotamia and East Africa, grain was purchased from India and Egypt, with arrangements made to buy the grain as each crop matured. In 1918 the crop in India failed and it became necessary to import maize from South Africa and barley from Algiers until the Egyptian crop matured.

As shipping became more difficult, it was decided to try to avoid long-distance purchases of hay, and the War Department then took possession of the whole of the British hay crops in 1916, 1917 and 1918. This consisted of some 14 million tons per year. The army did not require all this, and the rest was distributed among farmers and the public, allocated in each county by a committee consisting of farmers, dealers and consumers. A small quantity of hay was imported into southern France from Algiers, while that needed for other theatres mostly went from Egypt and India.

Before hydraulic presses came into use, hay and straw were sold in trusses (bundles or blocks cut from a stack, weighing 56lb of old hay or 60lb of new hay, or 36lb of straw), although compressed hay was available quite early. Castlereagh offered to send a supply to Lieutenant General Sir John Moore in 1808. There was no mention of the compression process, but olive presses were in use at that time, so it was probably done on the same principle, either by screw press or beam press. It was the only practical way to transport large quantities of hay any distance, either by land or sea. Other feed items such as linseed were sold in compressed cakes, as was a form of 'compressed forage' consisting of chopped hay and oats, sometimes with the addition of peas, beans or maize. This was issued on field service, but had to be broken up and damped well before feeding.

If crushed corn was not available and it had to be fed whole, the droppings should be checked for undigested grains of corn; if these were found in large quantities, that horse's back teeth should be checked for sharp edges and rasped smooth if necessary. It is the outside edge of the teeth in the upper jaw and the inside edge of those in the bottom jaw which need attention. The rasp should not be pushed too far back in the mouth, and the edges should be felt with the fingers after every few strokes with the rasp to see if the edges have been levelled. If it is not a tooth problem, more chaff should be mixed with the corn to stop the horse gobbling his food without chewing it properly.

If the straw was used economically, some of the ration could be exchanged for other items of feed: bran, linseed, roots (carrots or turnips but not raw potatoes) or green food. The latter, and the roots, should be chopped or sliced small and mixed with the feed. Carrots are particularly popular and will often encourage a sick horse to eat. In Ireland some horses were given boiled potatoes. A mash of bran or bran and linseed mixed with hot water and left to cool before feeding should be given once a week, usually on Saturday evening when the horses do not work on Sundays. Bran is a mild laxative when given wet; the method is to three-quarters fill a bucket with bran, add as much boiling water as the bran will absorb, cover the bucket with a cloth or sack and leave it to stand until cool enough to eat. Horses which are off work from lameness or an injury should have bran mixed into their other feed. Linseed is also a mild laxative; it is usually supplied in cake form, and should either be boiled for twelve hours, or soaked for twenty-four hours. There is little difference in the result of the two methods, except that the boiling method means someone has to watch it so it does not boil dry. Linseed oil can also be given for horses in need of a laxative; a wineglassful is the usual dose, mixed into the feed. Linseed also helps promote a good coat.

Tired horses which have just finished heavy work can be given gruel. This is made of two handsfull of oatmeal mixed with cold water and then three-quarters of a bucketful of hot water, stirred well and fed while at blood heat. The water in which linseed was boiled is a useful addition to this.

At home, a lump of rock salt should be placed in the manger for the horses to lick at, otherwise they should have a little salt mixed in with their feed. Other than this lump of salt, the manger should be kept clean and any crumbs of grain that are left, especially from a bran mash, should be removed as they will go sour and taint the next feed.

Any horse who does not finish his morning feed should not be worked, but checked at intervals as he might be in the early stages of a fever or some disease.

In 1758, in one officer's notes on horse management, it stated that the horses' feed was always to be measured to the men, in the standard measure of the regiment. The feed was never to be left at the stables, but taken care of in the men's rooms. However, depending on the location, there could be a problem with men who sold their horse's food for drink. The quartermaster was to be answerable, under penalty of severest censure, to ensure that troop-horses never ate more than 20lb of hay or 16lb of corn per day.

Large casks and tubs would be needed for water on board ships, and although not specifically mentioned, the horses might have been taken to the water tubs rather than buckets carried to the horses. In some cases pumps were provided to draw the water up from the tanks in the hold.

On board ships, the bulk of the food was hay, as too much corn or beans can over-excite animals which are not working. Such 'hard' feed was given in nose-bags, mixed with chaff (chopped hay or straw). Some horses had to be trained to eat from a nose-bag, especially when they could not put their heads down and put the bag on the ground. Some nose-bags were fitted with a 'bib' extending behind, its corners attached to a throat strap. This was to catch any feed which got thrown out of the bag when the horse tossed it up to get at the feed in the bottom of the bag.

The hay had to be fed from racks or nets, either being a good way to ensure each animal received its proper ration. If just put on the floor of the stall, much of it would be trodden on and wasted. The daily ration for a cavalry horse was usually 9lb of hay, 11lb of oats, a little bran and 6 gallons of water. Draught horses received the same, but with an additional 2lb of oats. Carrots were recommended as an addition, although these would probably not last throughout a long voyage. Multiply these rations by the number of horses on board and the length of the voyage and it can be seen that a considerable amount of feed and water had to be carried. This required stocks to be assembled close to the departure ports to avoid delays while they were found. At the beginning of 1813 Earl Bathurst ordered the Transport Board to keep magazines containing three months' supply of feed and forage for 500 horses at Cork, 300 at Plymouth, 1,200 at Portsmouth and 500 at Yarmouth; stocks were to be replenished as soon as they were used.

Forage in the Field

In the Peninsula, Lieutenant General Tomkinson of the 16th Light Dragoons commented:

the procuring of forage throughout the winter was attended by the greatest difficulty, both to men and horses. The detachments left their quarters soon after daylight, and were absent from six to eight hours generally, and frequently until dark. The horses got nothing by the way of long forage but the long grass which the men cut themselves ... the horses being so starved they eat the withered grass with much avidity.

Specific areas were allocated to each unit for foraging. Foragers carried a sickle for cutting forage and nets to put it in; when there was a severe shortage of hay, young gorse shoots were found to be acceptable.

At one stage in 1812 there was no straw or hay so the horses ate the withered grass, pulling up the roots and eating these, soil, stones and all. Some died as a consequence. In other places, in late spring, when no ripe grain was available, green barley was fed as a sort of combination hard feed and green forage.[2]

In desert areas of the Middle East, especially Palestine, it was found impossible to prevent sand getting into the forage; some of it was put there deliberately by unscrupulous merchants to make up weight. As well as the usual barley and maize, the horses had chickpeas and a type of lucerne hay called tibben, which they enjoyed. The chickpeas were sometimes fed whole, and when no other grain was issued the horses tended to scour. This was duly noticed and subsequently only barley and maize were issued.

It is well known that British soldiers serving in the Crimean War suffered badly from the conditions in the field and from the poorly managed supply situation. It is less well known that the horses suffered too. There had been large supplies of forage when the army arrived at Sebastopol, but these were soon eaten up. The Commissariat, which was responsible for providing forage for the horses, mules and bullocks which drew or carried land transport, kept no record of lack of forage in the early months of the war, but it was admitted that there had been shortages of hay and chopped straw after a 'great gale' (actually a hurricane) struck on 14 November 1854. Many ships carrying this forage were lost. Some had been carrying trusses of hay as deck cargo, and some 200–300 of these were found floating in the harbour. The few which were recovered were happily eaten by the horses, but no effort was made to bring them all in. Adequate transport from the coast to the army inland was also lacking, and forage had to be carried up to the battalions on bât horses; these were themselves so weak that they could only carry a portion of what was due. The Commissariat felt they had made a full issue, but the regimental quartermasters thought it was a 'short' issue. Although no doubt they complained about this, nothing was done, with the result that the shortage of feed, coupled with exposure to cold wet weather, led to a heavy loss of horses.

The light cavalry brigades were particular victims of this. Apart from the short supply of hay and straw, they had little barley, at some times as little as 1½lb per horse per day, when the proper ration was 12lb. Three weeks later it was suggested that the horses should be moved the 6 miles from their position at Inkerman to Balaclava, where there were some supplies. But the horses were already too weak to be ridden and had to be led to Balaclava; many couldn't manage even this, and had to be left behind, and others died on the road. In all, during that winter nearly 40 per cent of the light cavalry's horses died, leaving them almost totally ineffective as a fighting force. This loss was nothing out of the ordinary: the artillery lost 42 per cent of its horses, and the heavy cavalry 47 per cent. The Commissariat lost 38 per cent. It was later revealed that there was a quantity of buckwheat and millet at Balaclava which might have been fed to the horses but was not.

These shortages also affected mules and bullocks. Pairs of bullocks pulled wagons called arabas which could carry 700lb of feed; mules could only carry one 160lb sack of barley and it required sixty-three mules to carry the day's rations. The assistant deputy commissary in charge of the supply for the light cavalry was never able to get more than thirty-five mules a day, even fewer than that on many days. As well as low stocks, even when boats of supplies did arrive, the assistant deputy commissary reported 'a dozen or more Heavy Dragoons, or as many Artillerymen jump in, carry out the sacks, load their transport, my few wretched Turks or Maltese having a very poor chance in the melee'. At another time the men of the heavy cavalry had to go on board the ships to get their grain sacks filled as there was none onshore. On 21 November, he added, he had been informed that the depot mules were exhausted and incapable of further work. As well as insufficient feed, this was due to the state of the 'roads', with very heavy mud which impeded movement. In normal conditions carts could reach their destination in about seven hours, but when the roads became impassable quagmires, carts had to be replaced by pack animals. It took them between twenty-four and thirty-six hours to get to their destination, and this, combined with their smaller capacity, reduced the carrying power by two-thirds.

One other cause of problems with feeding the horses was that when their nose-bags wore out, they were not replaced as quickly as they should have been. This meant that the grain had to be fed on the ground, leading not only to waste but also to intestinal problems as the horses tended to swallow earth and small stones with the grain.

Commissary General Filder had contracted for 800 tons of hay to be sent from Buyook Tchakmedge, on the Sea of Marmara, and hydraulic presses were sent out to Constantinople from England to prepare it for shipping. This was some 15 miles from where the hay had been collected, but the bad weather made it impossible to move it to the presses. It doesn't seem to have occurred to anyone to take the presses to the hay. Less than 700 tons of hay were actually made, and the situation then descended into farce. The contractors turned out to be men without adequate capital, who had borrowed money at high interest rates under a scheme by which the money due to the contractors had to be paid straight to their lending banker. This gentleman was reluctant to advance money for hay which might be rejected as being of poor quality, or when the full quantity had not been made. The Commissariat did indeed refuse to accept delivery on both these grounds and withheld payment. The contractors, having no money to repay their debt to the banker, made a new contract to sell it to the French Army. The British Commissariat then claimed that the hay was *their* property, and both parties applied to the Porte to compel the contractors to deliver the hay which they believed they had bought. Eventually it was secured for the British, but they were not able to move it in the bad weather and in the end the unfortunate horses never received it.

Many of the problems experienced by the Commissariat were clearly due to the harsh weather in that first winter, but another major cause was that the government, ever eager to save money, had reduced the number of commissaries. A Land Transport Corps was set up at the end of January 1855, at that time officered mainly by officers taken from the regiments serving in the Crimea.

Temple Goodman reported that one of his horses had eaten all the boards and rafters within his reach. In some cases hungry horses ate each other's manes off. When food was available, Goodman reported that the horses had barley and chopped straw, which they ate pretty well, and that green forage was cut every morning.

During the Second Boer War it was noticed that Boer horses were fed by grazing as far as possible, this being supplemented by oat straw. Oats were a universal crop on Boer farms, and for use as fodder they were cut just before ripening and tied into 6lb bundles, each bundle being a day's ration for the small Basuto ponies the Boers rode. It proved almost impossible to obtain any for the British horses.

Where there was grazing available in unenclosed spaces the horses could be hobbled before being turned loose, but there should be guards with them, encouraging them to move forwards as a flock of sheep does, but also making sure they did not stray. In enclosed spaces the horses did not need to be hobbled, and their first action was usually to roll. Where this free grazing was not possible, every opportunity to allow the horses to graze (for instance on road sides and banks) should be taken.

The report on horse buying in North America in the First World War said that the quality of forage provided by the various contractors was, on the whole, excellent. There were, however, periods when the harvest was bad and there was a shortage of hay, and consequently the best quality feed was not always available. Other forage provided included oats and bran.

Watering

Horses need up to 10 gallons of water a day. In stables they usually take 3–4 gallons at a time, except in the early morning when they take about half this amount. They usually take about five minutes to drink. Some horses play with the water in a trough when they have had their fill, shoving their face in deep and sloshing it about and snorting bubbles. In permanent stables water would be available from a tap or hose, and could be given to horses individually in their stable.

Watering should always be done before feeding, never immediately after. On long marches frequent small quantities of water should be given, but never from public water troughs as these may have been used by horses with contagious diseases. The horses should not be allowed to drink their fill on the march, unless they will be able to walk for 30–45 minutes afterwards.

In camp, where the water might be some distance away, units should be marched to it at the walk at stated intervals. Each man could take two horses, riding one and leading the other, but never more than two. The practice of tying several horses together often means that each horse does not get all he needs if he is disturbed by the others in his 'string'. The same rule applied when watering at a trough. Kickers should always be watered separately.

If watering at a shallow stream, it should be dammed or dug out to deepen it, as horses cannot drink freely or quickly in less than 4in of water. The place chosen for watering should be as close as possible to the camp, have a sound bank and bottom, with wide approaches and exits, and should be capable of watering several horses at once.

If using a stream, the place chosen for the horses to drink from should be downstream of where the men obtained their drinking water, but upstream of where they did their washing. Watering should commence at the lowest part of the stream, with later parties working their way up so the water is not fouled. Where the bottom is muddy, gravel, if available, should be thrown in to help prevent the horses stirring up the mud. Steep banks should be ramped in two places, one for access and the other for departing, with the latter being downstream from the former. The manual 'Notes on Horse Management in the Field' did not approve of walking horses into ponds or muddy bottomed sluggish streams to drink.

It was always preferable to water from troughs, if necessary filled by pumping from streams. To prevent dirty water entering the trough, the inlet pipe should be immersed in a bucket held a few inches below the water surface. In camps where there was no natural water source, troughs had to be provided. A makeshift trough could be created with a sheet of canvas stretched between four posts.

When the mounted troops arrived in Gallipoli in 1915 the weather was extremely hot, but this turned to torrential rain that was followed, in late

November, by a three-day blizzard. The horses lacked rugs, shelter and enough men to care for them. Inevitably they lost condition and many were transferred to Alexandria. Surface water was hard to find; a reservoir was built and several wells dug, but this water, although acceptable for horses, was not fit for troops. A steam ship carried water and mule-drawn water carts were employed. This restricted the equine population, although for them food and fodder were plentiful and generally good. Haynets had to be used as otherwise it blew away.

Elsewhere, especially in Palestine, obtaining water whilst on the march was difficult. In this dry terrain water was scarce and the horses were only watered three times a day instead of the recommended four. This was then reduced to twice a day, although it was found that they drank more overall on this regime than with more frequent watering. During the period May to October 1917 it was only possible to water once a day, and later this was reduced to once every thirty-six hours. One officer reported that he kept a biscuit tin of water handy and wiped his horses' mouths and nostrils with a wet cloth; another discovered that exhausted horses who would not eat dry food would accept small balls of moistened grain if fed by hand.

The Desert Mounted Corps commonly made marches of up to 60 miles in a day across waterless desert terrain, often in temperatures of over 100 degrees (Fahrenheit) and with few wells available. Many of the wells were as much as 150ft deep and water could only be obtained by letting down buckets on lengths of telegraph wire. It took up to an hour to water each troop of thirty horses, which meant that instead of watering four times a day, as was usual, they could only manage it once a day.

Grooming

All the manuals on horse care emphasised the importance of daily grooming. It is important for the horse's health that his pores are cleaned of dirt and scurf; this helps prevent skin diseases and galls from saddlery rubbing on dirty patches.

The grooming tools are a dandy brush, a body brush, a curry comb, a wisp and a hoofpick. The dandy brush is like a domestic scrubbing brush but with longer bristles, and is narrow enough to be held in one hand. The body brush is wide and flat with quite short soft bristles, and with a strap across the back for the groomer's hand to slip through. The curry comb is a flat metal plate with rows of teeth to clean the body brush, fitted with a handle so it can be held in one hand while the body brush is scraped across it to remove the accumulated scurf. The wisp is made from a twisted rope of hay.

The dandy brush is used to remove dried mud from the coat, and to brush out the mane and tail. The latter is done by separating small bunches of hair and brushing them downwards until it has all been done. The body brush is used to remove the scurf from the coat, and should be dragged across the curry comb every few strokes. The curry comb should never be used on the horse itself. The wisp is used to stimulate the body, being banged down quite hard and then dragged over the coat. If the wisp was dampened, it gave a nice sheen to the coat.

Part of a unit's pride in the appearance of its horses concerned the tail. In 1777 the Royal Scots Greys were taken to task over the poor state of their horses' tails, and responded that on account of their pale colour, the tails were frequently plucked and the hairs stolen for use as fishing line. In November 1780 it was ordered that the horses' tails were to be firmly tied with a piece of tape, and a month later that a 2in length was to be cut off each tail in order that they might grow full and square. In preparation for a review in 1782 it was ordered that manes and tails were to be washed and the manes plaited.

All brushing should be done in the direction of hair growth, never against it. The groomer should stand well away from the horse and work with a straight arm, putting his weight on the brush so that it penetrates the coat. It should not take more than an hour to perform a good grooming. The job is finished by sponging out the animal's nostrils and mouth, and wiping the eyes and inside the ears if necessary, and finally under the tail, and, if a male horse, inside his sheath.

The hoofpick should be used to clean out the hooves, at least once a day, and certainly when they came back from work, especially if this had been on stony ground, when small stones or other objects which could cause lameness might have been picked up. On the march picking out should be done at the end of the day and during any longish stops, especially if the terrain was stony. Apart from undesirable objects lodged in the hoof, the hooves need to be cleaned of any remnants of dirty bedding, as this can cause thrush (detectable by a foul smell from the frog) and soften the horn, which can then break, making it difficult to fit shoes.

At the same time incipient problems with shoes can be detected. If the feet are always picked out in the same order the horse will become so accustomed to this that he will need no more than a tap on the fetlock to shift his weight off that leg, and may even have the 'next' foot lifted as soon as the previous one is released.

If the horse was hot when being groomed, the saddle was left on or a numnah or sack laid across his loins until he had cooled down, with the legs being groomed first. Ideally the horse should be groomed immediately after work, when his pores are open; it is also easier to remove the effects of perspiration before they dry and become caked on.

It should not be necessary to wash the horse's legs and feet, but if this is done, they should be dried well afterwards, otherwise they may develop greasy heels or mud fever. Greasy heels are most common on heavy horses with feathering on their lower legs and require treatment with bran or oat-meal poultices. Mud fever, which is actually a type of dermatitis, tends to follow frequent work in deep mud, or constant washing of the legs without proper drying after.

Horses shed and regrow their coats twice a year: in the spring they cast their winter coat for a finer summer coat, and in autumn they grow a thick winter coat. With that thick coat they sweat if worked hard and it is difficult to get them dry, which leaves them at risk of a chill. They also take longer to groom and the long coat may harbour lice, mange and other skin diseases. The practical answer to this was to clip the horses and give them a rug when they were not working. Obviously horses which were transported from a cold climate in the winter to a location near the equator needed to have their coats removed, and many of the transport ships carried clippers for this purpose. Clippers were originally powered by hand (winding a handle which trans-mitted the rotation up a cable to the clipper head and making the two cutting blades pass across each other) and later by electricity.

Until the winter of 1917 British horses on the Western Front were normally clipped right out, which may have contributed to the heavy mor-tality rates the following spring. Riding horses continued to be clipped right out (the 'full' clip), but a 'half' or trace clip was used on animals which were only worked at the walk and thus did not sweat so much. Typically the head, neck and belly were clipped clean, but the hair on the legs left long.

Clipping was done once in late autumn and again in late January/early February. After some experimentation, it was concluded that if clipping was done once only, between mid-September and the end of November, although the winter coat continued to grow, it would be short and thick, providing protection from the cold but still easy to keep clean.

Shoeing

In its natural state of carrying no weight and living on grassy plains, the horse does not need shoes, nor to have the growth of his hooves pared away. But in a domestic situation, where the horse is carrying or hauling weight and needs extra traction to do so, or spends much of his working life on metalled roads (or in a military situation, frequently on rough mountain tracks), he does need shoes to protect his feet and gain extra grip. In recent years experiments have been made with shoes which are glued to the horse's feet, but for many hundreds of years horses have been shod with iron shoes nailed onto the horny part of the hoof at the palmar surface.

The area through which the nail is driven is comparatively narrow, and a badly applied nail will soon cause lameness or a serious infection deep in the foot. At the very least the shoe will not stay on, and will be 'cast'. For this reason, and also because not all horses' feet are exactly the same, farriery – the making and fitting of horse shoes – is a very skilled job. Before the profession of veterinary surgeon came into being in the mid-eighteenth century, it was farriers who were the skilled horse 'doctors'.

Many of the problems which lead to lameness stem from faulty conformation, but a skilled farrier can solve these problems with specially shaped shoes. A typical example would be a horse whose front feet are 'pigeon-toed' (i.e., pointing inwards instead of being straight). Using shoes built up more on one side, with this increasing gradually over several months, will cause the horse to use his feet differently and in time his muscles and bone structure will adapt themselves, correcting the fault.

Shoes were usually replaced at monthly intervals. With much roadwork they would be worn down, and the horny exterior of the hoof would have grown enough to prevent the frog touching the ground, so even if the shoe was not worn, it would still have to be removed and the horn trimmed. The frog is a V-shaped spongy tissue on the underside of the foot, and it is important that it touches the ground as it serves as a form of shock absorber. The nails holding the shoes on were oblong in section, and shaped so that they came out of the front of the hoof. The farrier then nipped off the end of the nail and hammered the rest of it over downwards to hold the shoe on. These tips are called clenches (or clinches). Sometimes these loosen and are then referred to as risen clenches; they must be hammered back into position or the shoe will be loosened and may come off.

To remove the old shoe, the clenches were nipped off and the shoe pulled off with pliers. The hoof could then be prepared for the new shoe, which might need to be held in place to check the fit before heating the shoe and using the anvil to make minor modifications to perfect the fit. The shoe should always be made to fit the hoof, not the other way round.

The shoes themselves had a central groove on the underside (for grip) in which nail holes were punched. The shoes would have three to five nail holes on each side, the farrier choosing how many to use. Usually six nails were used on the fore foot and seven on the hind. Fore and hind shoes were different shapes, as were the hooves, the front feet being almost circular, the hind feet narrower but still rounded at the front. Either could have a short section of the shoe turned down at the rear for additional grip on slippery surfaces, and one or two clips (one at the front for fore feet and two at the quarters for hind feet) which gripped the hoof horn.

On Sir John Moore's winter retreat to Corunna in early 1809 through the snowy mountains of north-west Spain, one young ensign was puzzled to see seemingly fit horses destroyed. He reported that he was told

> that from the roughness of the road, hardened by continued frost, they
> cast their shoes, and that they had not a nail to fasten on those picked

Driver of the Royal Wagon Train, 1808.

C.C.P.LAWSON

Cornet Henry John Wilkin of the
11th Hussars, Crimean War.
Note the ornate parade bridle.

Cavalry sword drill.

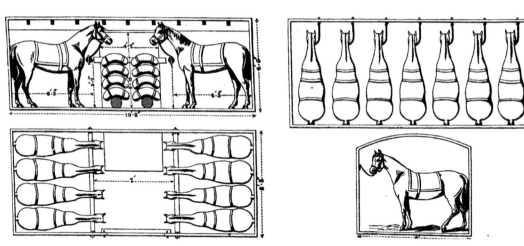

Different ways of carrying horses in a railway carriage.

Simple cart set up to carry wounded,
with springs to hook onto the stretcher.

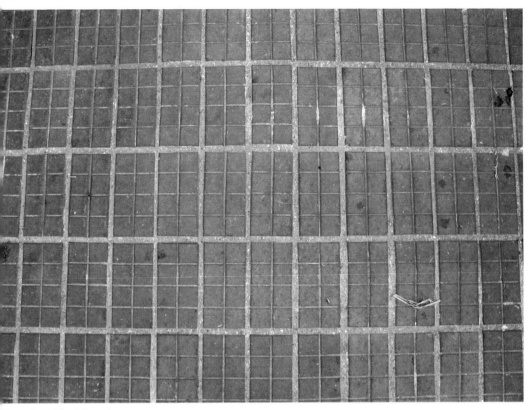

'Chocolate block' paving.

Scrap horse shoes awaiting collection.

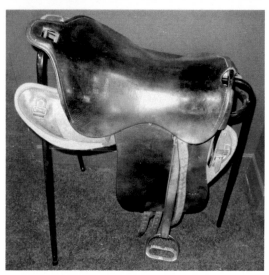

Standard pattern army saddle.

Ammunition boxes on packhorse, First World
War. Model at Royal Logistics Corps Museum.

A Suffolk Punch, one of the best heavy horses. Note the magnificent musculature.

ussex Yeomanry First World War re-enactment team. A useful sort of cob pulling a horse mbulance.

King's Troop Artillery teams – note six horses and three drivers per gun.

A General Service wagon being used for a funeral. Sussex Yeomanry re-enactment team.

Type of horse shelter at No. 5 Veterinary Hospital, Rouen, France. (*Army Medical Services Museum*)

Three mounted soldiers in the rain in France, First World War.

Pack horses can cope with deep mud better than lorries, First World War.

Pair of horses harnessed to a General Service wagon. Note the folded blanket under the saddle.

Pack mules carrying petrol cans, Second World War.

up, nor a shoe to replace those lost; and they added that there was not a spare nail or shoe in any of the forge carts, which retired with the cavalry.

Another man remarked that it was a common sight 'to witness the poor animals ridden with blood gushing from their hoofs'.[3] It was common practice at this time (and later, when the same problems occurred) for any dead horses encountered by the road or on a battlefield to have their shoes removed for reuse.

In 1811 the Board of General Officers recommended that a farrier major should be appointed to each regiment, but this was not done until 1852, when a farrier major was sanctioned for the cavalry.

There were also problems in keeping horses shod in the Crimea, as there was a shortage of proper army farriers and they had to use civilians who, according to a report from the principal veterinary surgeon, 'were of little use, being the refuse of the shoeing forges in large towns'.

Until the late 1850s, when factory-shaped blanks of the new Universal Pattern shoe were produced, each shoe had to be made by hand from bar iron. They were made in several sizes, to fit horses from heavy draught types to smaller riding horses, and were modified as needed for the individual animal. Obviously regiments of ridden horses had mostly one size, and many soldiers carried spare shoes for replacement on the march. There would, in any case, be an accompanying farrier's cart with shoes, nails, a forge and fuel, an anvil and the farrier's hand tools as well. These tools included a large and small hammer (for shaping shoes on the anvil, and for driving nails), tongs (to hold the shoe in the fire to heat it before final shaping), hoof knives and nippers, rasps, and a stand for the hoof to rest on while it was being rasped.

The Army Veterinary Department produced annual statistical returns of sick and lame horses in the late nineteenth century.[4] The report for 1887 also discussed farrier training. Farriers took three years to train, and each cavalry corps had a sergeant farrier, a shoeing smith and a trainee to keep forty horses shod. In the field farriers were in the fighting line and had to perform their shoeing and shoe-making duties as well as fighting duties. The introduction of machine-made shoes and nails in the late 1850s made life much easier; it was not easy to make shoes or nails in the field and the machine-made items were so well shaped and well finished that the work of shoeing each horse was much quicker. Even non-experts could be easily taught to fit these shoes, at a great saving of cost. This report also suggested that the use of heavy forges and the wagons which carried them could be dropped, and small pack-saddle forges used instead. On the subject of winter shoeing, and the problem of horses slipping on icy surfaces, the report remarked that the best solution was to fit small pegs called 'cogs' into the heels of the shoes.

When the Remount Commission was buying horses and mules in America in the First World War they found very little shoeing had to be done, as the animals there had exceptionally good strong feet; only a small percentage needed shoes at all, and then only on the fore feet. They found that animals shown by dealers for purchase were invariably shod with shoes with heavy calkins; these were usually removed before inspection and always after purchase, as no animals were shipped with shoes on unless their feet absolutely demanded it. In depots all the work horses were shod, while those awaiting shipping had their feet trimmed.

Shoeing smiths were not included in the Commission's ordinary labour, instead forming a separate charge; a contract was made for the shoeing at so much per head for a complete set of shoes, or only fore feet, or for taking shoes off and rasping. In 1918 six army shoeing smiths were sent out from England to join the Commission and were attached to various depots where they proved most useful, as good men of this type were exceedingly difficult to obtain in America.

In Sicily in the Second World War there was a desperate shortage of shoes and nails; the situation became so extreme that, as had happened before, shoes had to be salvaged from dead animals. A factory was set up in Naples to make shoes, using local blacksmiths supervised by a farrier quartermaster sergeant and two farrier sergeants. It also became necessary to set up a farriery school in Capua. The staff there comprised four farrier sergeants and a clerk, with catering provided by an Italian cook.

Facilities for training farriers were created in India and Burma, and these produced about fifty farriers each year. In September 1940 175 horses and 30 mules were sent to Aden from India with an assistant veterinary surgeon and a six-months' supply of stores. There was the usual shortage of shoes, and casualties among the farriers meant it was almost impossible to keep all the mules shod, and this inevitably led to sore feet.

There was an Army Veterinary Corps School of Farriery at Woolwich. One of its instructors, Lieutenant Charles Budd, invented and applied for a Patent (No. 17,803, 1915) for what he called 'An Apparatus for use in Instructing Persons in the Art of Farriery'. This consisted of a pivoted arm attached to a stand. The arms of the pivot were shaped like a horse's leg (actually there were two, one for the fore leg and one for the hind) and at the end there was a gripping device which held a hollowed out hoof. The purpose of this apparatus was to show the pupil how to grip the horse's leg between his own legs, remove a shoe, pare the foot and apply and secure a new shoe, thereby obviating the need for live animals to practise on. The application ended with the comment 'The invention is also applicable for use in teaching veterinary work.'

Chapter Seven

Veterinary Matters

Horses, like human beings, suffer from numerous complaints. These fall into three types: those which cannot be cured or are seriously contagious and require the animal to be destroyed; those which can quickly be cured so that the animal can be got back to work; and those which can be cured but take some time for this to take effect and thus the animal cannot be got back to work quickly.

There are many complaints which occur rarely, such as inflammation of the liver; these are shown in the annual lists of sick and lame animals submitted in the 1880s, but the reports show few such cases.[1] Here we will concentrate on the common problems which were likely to be encountered among military animals, together with an indication of their treatment and long-term prognosis.

Animals in barracks or semi-permanent camps could be treated in situ unless their problem was one which required hospitalisation for special treatment. For problems encountered on the march or in temporary camps, it was better to move the animal to an evacuation unit or hospital. This decision was made by the veterinary officer attached to the unit. Whenever possible, cured or recovered animals were returned to service from these establishments, but not necessarily to the unit they came from; animals which fell sick or were injured on the march were usually, when cured, sent to a remount depot for reallocation.

There are only a few anecdotal mentions of equine maladies in the Peninsular War, and these relate almost entirely to lameness.

Contagious or Infectious Diseases

These ailments were usually referred to in that form, although it is difficult to distinguish between the two. They were at the top of the list of equine health problems, as one sufferer could rapidly infect a whole unit.

Glanders and/or Farcy

These two ailments are different forms of the same disease, either of which may morph into the other. Glanders (caused by the bacterium Burkholderia mallei) is manifested by discharge from the nose, ulcerated mucous membranes inside the nostrils and swelling of the lymph glands beneath the lower jaw. Farcy is seated in the tissues beneath the skin, breaking out in open sores in such places as the inside of the hind legs. These exude highly infective purulent matter. The disease can pass to other mammals, and sometimes to humans (usually stable workers) in whom it is fatal.

Suspected cases, and other animals which might have been in contact with the sufferer, were given a 'mallein test', with the mallein either injected under the skin or dripped inside the lower eyelid. The diagnosis can be confirmed in three to five days. There were some anecdotal reports of glanders and farcy in the Crimea, but no mention of what treatment was given. It was carried back to England from the wars in South Africa; by 1892 more than 3,000 cases had been reported, and in 1904 there were more than 2,000. Reported cases fell after that, only nine outbreaks being reported in 1926, and none after 1927.

Early in 1916 a serious outbreak of glanders in England was reported by the War Office. At this time none had been reported in North America, but extra precautions were put in place by the Remount Commission. By September 1918 the depot at Lachine was quarantined with several cases of glanders; it was prevalent all over the Mid-West, with heavy mortality in American remount depots all over that region. All horses were tested on purchase, on arrival at depots and again prior to departure. By the end of October all depots were practically clear. In June 1917 and January 1918 there were reports of glanders in horses arriving in England and Egypt which led to all horses being mallein tested with some positive reactions.

The law in what *Black's Veterinary Dictionary* refers to as 'most civilised countries' designates glanders as a notifiable disease; it requires destruction of the animal. It has recently been reported in the Middle East, India, Pakistan, Mongolia, China, Africa and Brazil. There was one serious outbreak in 1943 in Uttar Pradesh involving fifty animals; all the infected animals were immediately destroyed, but otherwise glanders was not a problem in the Second World War due to rigorous mallein testing before purchase. Given its prevalence in hot countries, it might have been expected in Burma during the Second World War, but it was not a major problem there.

After the 1880s, if a horse was suspected of having glanders, farcy (or mange), the commanding officer of the unit should be informed and a report of the case sent to the War Office, whose opinion should be obtained before the animal was destroyed. All the horses in the same stables, or even the entire troop, should be immediately isolated from other horses. If suitable ground was available, these horses should be picketed out as far away as possible and their stables immediately disinfected. Any which showed symptoms should be segregated, if possible in a loose box, tied up by the head but able to lie down. Particular men should be told off to attend to them, and their bedding, grooming equipment and stable furniture should be kept separate. There should be no interchange of men, saddles, kits or stable utensils between the isolated unit and others. The horses should not be allowed to drink at communal troughs, or to come into contact with the other horses at exercise.

Infected stables should be scraped, washed, disinfected and left open for several days to expose them to the air. The bedding should be burnt. The rest of the stables occupied by the affected unit should be kept thoroughly clean by frequent white-washing and scrubbing the racks and mangers.

Glanders and farcy are usually introduced into a unit from outside, often by remounts or in billets occupied on the march. Horses owned by civilians which are in the habit of entering the barracks or camps, e.g. those removing manure or bringing forage, should be inspected occasionally by the veterinary officer to guard against their introducing disease.

Mange
There are four types of mange, all caused by a parasitic mite which burrows under the skin, making treatment difficult. Those found most often in horses are sarcoptic mange and chorioptic mange. The former can be found all over the body, the latter, also known as 'leg mange', is usually found either on the long feathered leg hair on such breeds as the Shire or Clydesdale or at the root of the tail. Sarcoptic mange can be transmitted to humans, where it is known as scabies. Both types of mange are extremely itchy (often making it difficult to examine the victim without sedation) and the animals can rub themselves raw against any convenient surface, thereby leaving eggs or mites to be picked up by the next animal which comes into contact with it. The hair becomes full of skin scales and dandruff, and self-inflicted wounds are common from the scratching or biting. Localised thick 'nests' of scurf are common on the dorsal hock or palmar knee. As the mites prefer longer hair, clipping affected animals helps. It also affects camels.

Treatment now, as in the First World War, when the Remount Service in Britain complained of numerous animals arriving with mange, consists of dipping twice, at an interval of eight to twelve days. In Britain it is a notifiable disease.

Strangles
Strangles is an acute contagious fever of the upper respiratory tract. Victims stop eating, have a high temperature and a dull aspect. It is mostly found in young horses and is most serious in them. The victim will have visible infection of the mucous membranes in the nose and around the eyes, and the lymph glands behind the jaw swell and become painful; after about ten days they will be found to have a soft spot which is the abscess forming a 'point'. This will then burst, releasing a considerable amount of pus, after which the animal improves, becomes much brighter and starts eating again. These abscesses can be fomented to speed the pointing process and can be lanced by

a vet. Captain Hayes advocated this, followed by inserting a piece of lint to help release the pus. The disease is spread by the nasal discharge and is very contagious. The victim should be isolated for four to six weeks and his stall, rugs and grooming kit disinfected thoroughly. Soft food such as bran mashes should be given, and after the abscesses have opened, Hayes recommended a quart of beer a day with liberal feeding.

There was a strangles epidemic in civilian horses in Britain in 1939, which quickly spread to army horses.

Influenza

Caused by a virus and highly infectious, equine influenza produces a high temperature and a dry cough turning into a wet cough. It is rarely fatal, except in very young foals; sufferers usually recover in a couple of weeks if rested and kept warm. Some horses lose their appetite but can be tempted to eat several small feeds a day.

There was a serious outbreak of influenza in India among Australian remounts in April 1915; before it appeared many horses in the infectious stage had been sent to other depots and units. Eventually nearly 17,000 animals were affected. A year later there was another outbreak in Egypt, also among the remounts from Australia. In all, 86 per cent of the 3,900 horses and mules contracted it and 561 developed severe catarrh or pneumonia. It took over six weeks for recovery. There was another outbreak in horses sent from collecting depots in the Mid West of North America to the east for onward shipping.

Ringworm

There are two types of ringworm; one is caused by parasites of the class Microsporum or Trichophyton, the other is a fungal dermatitis. Both are commonly found around the withers and saddle area, but may spread else-where. It shows as circular bald scaly patches. The parasitic version may be itchy, and can be spread by scratching against hard surfaces. The fungal variety can be picked up from the soil when lying down or rolling, or from infected stalls or grooming kit. It lurks either on the skin or hairs of the animal and causes raised patches of dry crusty hairless skin, usually circular, which grow larger as the fungus works its way outwards.

The incubation period is usually one week. Treatment consists of removing the hair around the lesions (this should be burnt) and applying a dressing twice a week. Two weeks of this should be sufficient, but a cure is not guaranteed until new hair has grown in. Dressings may be tincture of iodine, gentian violet or one of a number of proprietary ointments.

Epizootic Lymphangitis

One of the three main diseases which caused difficulties in Burma, epizootic lymphangitis was (and is) widely found in Asia; it was also known as African glanders. Unlike many of the other contagious diseases, this was found only in horses. It was unknown in Britain until it was brought there at the end of the Second Boer War in 1902. It was made notifiable in 1904, and was soon eradicated. There were a few cases reported after the First World War, but none has not been reported since.

It is caused by the fungus Histoplasma farciminosa and infects the horse by entering through a wound; it spreads through grooming tools, rugs or flies. It takes about a month to incubate. The initial symptoms are thickened and enlarged lymph glands, often at the knees or the point of the shoulder. Tumours on the shoulders can reach the size of a hen's egg, but the smaller ones are usually the first to burst. They then often turn into ulcers, which are slow to heal, if at all. Ulcers may also be found on the mucous membranes inside the nostrils. A few victims may seem to recover naturally, only to relapse later. It is still notifiable, and all cases must be destroyed. Hayes does not mention it, so it must have been extremely rare when he was writing in 1927, and earlier when he was working in India.

Surra
Most often found in horses and camels, surra occurs in Africa north of the tsetse fly belt, and in Asia and Central and South America. Also known as Trypanosoma evansi, it is spread by blood-sucking flies and possibly vampire bats. Symptoms in camels are fever, anaemia, emaciation and paralysis. In horses, oedema (dropsy-like swellings) are common, affecting much of the body. There are some modern drugs available for it, but previously the only way of dealing with it was to destroy the affected animals and spray DDT around the horselines and stable blocks.

Hayes wasn't certain that surra was transmitted by blood-sucking flies, and remarked that there seemed to be no available treatment, the animal dying a couple of months after being infected. The blood lost its red colour, and the visible mucuous membranes became pale yellow; the animal would continue to eat well, but still wasted away until it died.

Other Diseases of Warm Countries
In a belt across Central Africa the tsetse fly (Glossina morsitans) is such a problem that it is almost impossible to keep horses where the flies exist. They look like small honey-bees, and their bite transmits the blood disease trypano-somiasis, causing intermittent fever, anaemia, weight loss and eventual death. It is not unlike surra, which is not found in Central Africa, and is also known as sleeping sickness. Mules seem to be less susceptible to it than horses. In the First World War the German commander-in-chief had tsetse fly surveys done, then made his retreat through the worst areas. This caused the loss of some 12,000 animals among the pursuing British.

African Horse Sickness
This is a highly infectious and deadly disease which affects all equids. It is caused by a virus carried by the biting midge Culicoides imicola, which infests Africa south of the Sahara, Morocco, the Middle East, India and Pakistan. It comes in four forms: pulmonary, cardiac, mild and mixed (pulmonary and cardiac together). When detected, the sufferer had to be destroyed and his fellows watched carefully.

Cattle Diseases
Rinderpest, also known as cattle plague, is an acute feverish disease of cattle. It is caused by a virus, and kills 90 per cent of any herd which it infects. In heavy cattle-raising areas this often results in famine. There was a major outbreak in Britain in the mid-1860s, which killed some 320,000 cattle; it was eradicated in 1877. Rinderpest is still found in vast areas of Africa and Asia. It does not affect horses or humans, but did keep AVC vets busy.

Anthrax is caused by the Bacillus anthracis. Although mainly thought of as a disease of cattle, it can affect horses and also presents a considerable risk to humans; it is a notifiable disease. There are two forms of equine anthrax, one of which shows itself in severe swelling of the throat, neck and chest. The swellings become so enormous that the animal cannot swallow but thin saliva drips from the mouth. It has great difficulty breathing and will eventually die in convulsions. The second form starts with shivering fits which lead to fever; the animal tries to lie down and then gets up again, clearly has abdominal pain and what seems to be severe diarrhoea. As with the first form, the animal dies in convulsions. Like rinderpest, it is generally found in warm or hot countries.[2]

Skin Problems

In the Second World War in Italy there were some cases of equine filiariasis. This is caused by a small worm (Seturia equine), the larvae of which are carried by mosquitoes and other biting flies. It starts with bleeding on the skin of the neck and back, then moves on through fever, anaemia, dropsical swellings and sometimes conjunctivitis. It was prevalent on mules from Sicily, particularly in hot weather. These mules also tended to harbour lice, but this was controllable with clipping and a preparation called Derrimac.

On 29 June 1915 there was an outbreak at the West Alton depot of what later became known as 'gangrenous dermatitis'. Dermatitis is simply an inflammation of the skin but this variety was potentially far more serious. It quickly affected the heels and coronets of horses, resulting in the sloughing of affected parts. It spread so quickly that nearly all the horses in that depot, as well as the majority of others, were affected. If caught early it was easily cured, but if not detected in the early stages it took a long time to heal and in many cases caused permanent disablement. This disease materially interfered with the shipping of horses and it was not until October that any marked cessation in the number of cases took place. Several ships had to be delayed, partly due to this disease (and partly to difficulty in the shipping companies getting sufficient attendants).

Rainscald

This is a fairly common wet weather (usually winter) condition in outdoor horses and ponies, caused by a type of dermatitis (Dermatophilus congolensis) which is transmitted by contact, lice and flies. Wet skin is an important predisposing factor due to both maceration of the skin and release of infective spores. The condition is classically found along the centre of the back, with lesions most common in the saddle area and over the rump. Fresh lesions present as thick crusts and scabs in the hair which become more diffuse scaling, often with a crust. Removal of the fresh crusts brings the hair with them, leaving weeping sores on the underlying patch of eroded skin. This condition will generally resolve itself within a month in dry conditions. Rugging generally seems to do more harm than good, presumably as it creates a moist microclimate, and a more effective treatment is to keep the horse indoors.

Urticaria

Urticaria is relatively common in horses. It is caused by a variety of stimuli, including bites/stings, contact allergies, excitement, stress, heat or cold. Characteristic signs are multiple weals up to a few centimetres in diameter which develop rapidly, usually over the lateral chest, neck and face. Again the animal should be kept indoors.

Mud Fever

Generally thought to be associated with muddy winter conditions, mud fever is seen with almost equal frequency in the summer when horses walk through wet grass. It usually occurs on white or pink skin, generally on white pasterns and occasionally muzzles. In the vast majority of cases the condition is nothing more complicated than a bacterial skin infection consequent to softening of the skin in wet conditions.

The condition typically starts with oozing, suppurating sores associated with varying degrees of pain. Crusts soon form and stick the skin and surrounding hairs together; deep horizontal cracks may appear on the pastern. The legs may swell, seemingly out of proportion to the size of the sores, and lameness and severe pain may occur in some horses which makes them react violently to interference with the sores. Since these crusts need to be removed before treatment with creams, sedation may be needed in particularly painful cases. To soften the crusts before they are removed, warm poultices or antibacterial washes may be needed. After treatment, when the sores are healing, oil-based barrier creams should be applied to waterproof the skin and prevent reinfection.[3]

Lice

Horses suffer from two sorts of lice, those which bite and those which suck. The chewing lice (Bovicola equi or Trichodectes pilosus) feed on dead skin. The sucking louse (Haematopinus asnii) will eventually cause severe anaemia, especially in young animals. Horses which grow thick coats in winter can suffer from them anywhere over the body, but they, and those which do not have this thick hair, usually have them on the tail or under the mane. The lice are very difficult to see without a magnifying glass, but should be suspected if the horse constantly rubs itself against hard objects. Lice can be killed with sprays or powders, but the treatment will have to be repeated several times to ensure newly hatched eggs are killed as well.

Clipping and mane hogging deprive the lice of a cosy place to hide, and in early days was almost the only way to alleviate the problem. Proper grooming will also help, especially by removing dead skin.

Breathing Problems

Many breathing problems can be traced to cold draughty stables or picket lines without wind breaks.

Pneumonia

Pneumonia usually starts with dullness, fever and shivering fits. The pulse is rapid and breathing becomes rapid and shallow. There may be a wet cough, and the eyes may be bloodshot. The mucous membranes of the nostrils become red. Hayes remarks that 'we may [ignore] the suggested treatment of bleeding, blistering and purging'; instead he advocated careful nursing, avoidance of excitement, and perhaps a little opium. Modern treatment uses antibiotics.[4]

Catarrh

Catarrh usually starts with sneezing, followed by a heavy discharge of watery matter which over a few days becomes thick and yellow (known in racing circles as 'the snots'). There is coughing, fever and shivering fits. Hayes remarks that it usually clears up on its own in a couple of weeks.

Roaring and Whistling

Roaring and whistling are caused by obstruction of the air passage, which sometimes suffers a degree of paralysis. Hayes remarks that they can be caused by an overtight bearing rein. Both take place during inspiration, but whistling can also occur during expiration. Roaring may be hereditary. Both are considered serious unsoundnesses, and sufferers would have been cast by the AVC.

Shipping Fever and Transit Tetany

Shipping fever is a form of pleuropneumonia, brought on by the stress of prolonged transport, whether by rail or sea, accompanied by a bacterium. Although it is normally found in cattle, many horses suffered from it while being transported from the Americas during the Second Boer War and the First World War. It was endemic in American stockyards – used by the Remount Commission. It was said at the time to be followed by pneumonia.

In horses it is caused by exhaustion from the stress of travel, and is much like battle fatigue in humans. The horse will usually have a high temperature, may be prostrate, and refuses to eat; the condition may lead to pneumonia. Without this, recovery takes some two to three weeks in a quiet comfortable stable.[5] A Dr Bell produced a serum which was tried but proved to be of little or no help and not worth the expense, so was discontinued. Hayes does not mention shipping fever by name.

Transit tetany is more common in lactating mares, but it does occur in other horses. The main symptoms are sweating, difficulty in breathing, and stumbling and staggering when taken ashore from ships. Modern treatment involves injections of calcium gluconate solution, but before this there was little to be done.

On 26 February 1915 reports came from America that horses were travelling badly on board ship; they seemed healthy when boarded, but were all carrying the seeds of what was called shipping fever. This meant that all horses purchased had to be 'salted' (i.e. exposed to the disease for long enough to be sure they were not going to succumb). At that time there was no reserve of salted horses so they had to cut their losses. Sanction was obtained from the War Office to sell or dispose of such animals as were useless, from whatever reason, so periodical sales were held at each depot. On the whole good prices were obtained. This included mares in foal.

In June 1918 the practice of holding freshly bought animals at the purchasing points until sufficient numbers had been accumulated to make up a full train load was found unsatisfactory, as too many were going sick, so they were moved on quickly to permanent depots before they had time to develop symptoms of shipping fever; this was the right plan as they got proper attention at the most important period of the disease, viz. the early stages.

Lameness

Lameness has numerous causes. It can have a sudden onset, or begin more slowly, often from strains, sprains or more insidious causes, such as spavin, ringbone and arthritis.

Sudden Lameness

The commonest cause of sudden lameness is a sharp object in a foot. When the horse is working or on the march and suddenly goes lame, it is usually due to a stone or sharp object. He should be stopped immediately and his feet examined. Contact with a sharp object might just cause bruising, in which case all that is needed is rest, or it might puncture the sole or frog, in which case the wound should be located and the object removed if still there.

One cause of sudden lameness was referred to in reports as 'picked up nail', where a horse had trodden on a nail and driven it up into his foot; this was most common in places where the army had been for some time, as such nails mostly came from camp fires and camp kitchens where wooden boxes were burnt. It was recommended that containers for found nails should be placed at regular intervals, and troops encouraged to pick them up whenever they saw them. Some units made a sport of this, competing against one another to see who could find the most abandoned nails. The Germans also threw down caltrops, devices made of thick sharpened wire with four points, arranged in such a way that one point was always upwards and thus drove into the foot of any animal who trod on it.

The foot should then be poulticed to draw out/prevent infection. The best poultice is a hot bran mash, but not so hot that it scalds the skin above the hoof; other material for poultices might be grated turnips or carrots or linseed meal. If a poultice boot was available it should be used, otherwise a piece of an old blanket or canvas could be used but should not be tied so tight that the flesh swells. These poultices should be applied twice a day.

Hayes suggested making a poultice boot by cutting a circle of hard wood about 1.5in thick, a little larger than a horse shoe, smoothing the edges then nailing leather to it so that it can be drawn together and fastened around the pastern. Modern stables can buy rubber/plastic boots.

Quittor

Quittor is a suppurating canal in the foot, which usually opens at the coronet and extends down through the foot. It is most often caused by a corn or a prick in shoeing, but it can also be caused by frost-bite. Treatment consists of removing the shoe and checking that the wound is not in the sole, in which case it should be poulticed to draw out the infectious matter. Quittor should not be neglected as it may lead to damage to the bones in the foot or lateral cartilages. Before modern sulpha drugs and antibiotics were available, it could take months for such injuries to heal, and the horse could suffer a degree of lameness indefinitely.

Corns

Corns are bruises of the membrane beneath the horny surface of the sole, usually at the thin point by the heels and next to the inside edge of the hoof.

This is called the 'seat' of the corn. They are most commonly found in the front feet, and are almost always due to faulty shoeing, so the first thing to do is remove the shoe and pare out a little of the horn to see if there is any suppuration, in which case proceed as for other wounds of the foot. If not, the foot should be reshod with a three-quarter shoe. For this, and for quittor, Hayes advocated the use of a red-hot iron to burn out the seat of the trouble, a practice which has long since been abandoned. Mild corns should be better within a week, but with severe corns it can take up to seven weeks before the horse is fit to return to work.

If no obvious wound in the foot or leg can be found, the problem may be a sprain, in which case Hayes advocated the application of a cold water bandage. In modern stables cold water from a hose is run over the affected leg.

When frost nails were not available, or had not been fitted, animals could slip on icy surfaces and sprain their joints in trying to save themselves. Other sprains occur in tendons, usually in the front legs and usually as a result of excessive fast work when the animals has not been brought to such speed over a period of time. They are quite common in badly trained and poorly bred weedy racehorses. In heavy horses sprains are caused by excessive weight-bearing. In either case, hot bandages are applied (and the other leg also bandaged to give extra support when the horse shifts his weight off the injured leg). Sprains should be given up to two months to heal, even though the horse may appear to be sound before this time. Until quite recently, standard treatments for sprains included 'firing' of the lower legs by the application of a hot iron or blistering the affected leg by application of a caustic material. The theory behind these barbaric treatments was that the injuries caused by the treatment would stimulate the flow of blood to the injury.

The location of lameness is usually below the knee or hock. The affected leg can be found by watching the horse's front legs as he trots towards you (his head will nod towards the ground when the uninjured leg is put down), or his hind legs when he trots away from you (the hock of the sound leg will rise higher and drop lower than that on the injured leg). If no obvious cause of lameness can be seen on the leg, punctures of the foot should be suspected.

Over-reaching, Brushing and Speedycutting
These are all injuries caused to the legs of the horse when he strikes himself with his own feet.

Over-reaching is when the toe of the hind hoof strikes the back of the front leg, either on the fetlock or just above the heels. The injured horse should immediately be taken out of work, lightly bandaged and taken home. There is often a lip of skin left, which should be carefully replaced before bandaging, or cut off if it is hanging by a thread. When the injury has healed, the shoes on the hind feet should be shortened at the toe, or the horse shod with toeless shoes. Horses which are prone to over-reaching can be fitted with boots to prevent injury.

Brushing is when the inner side of the hoof strikes the inside of the opposite fetlock at the trot. It may be caused by poor action, or the horse being tired or out of condition. If it occurs on the march, a pad of blanket tied round the fetlocks will prevent further injury. Modern horses can be protected by fitting a boot which reaches from the fetlock upwards, and which is padded on the inside. Remedial shoeing may help.

Speedycutting is when the inside toe of a forefoot strikes the inside of the opposite leg just below the knee, usually at the gallop. It may happen when the horse is tired or moving in deep ground or just has bad action. Remedial shoeing may help.

Broken Knees

The injury known as 'broken knees' does not literally mean the bones of the knee are broken, but that the skin of the knees is damaged when the horse stumbles and falls onto his knees. They usually occur where the horse has bad action, or where his feet are too long at the toe or the shoes too thick, or when the horse is tired or, in young horses and remounts, not accustomed to carrying weight. The horse will be lame for some time and should be walked gently for exercise. In severe cases the bursal capsule may be damaged and the synovial fluid lost. Although it will heal, the knee will always be stiff and the horse unfit for work. The wound should be well cleaned with tepid water to ensure there is no grit or dirt present, then ointment applied. Hayes advocates hanging a wet linen cloth over the injured knee. The cloth should be kept wet to prevent it sticking to the wound.

Other small injuries which have broken the skin, such as kicks, should be cleaned well with tepid water, and later fomented with hot water if they are not showing signs of healing. Sulpha powder can also be applied. Such wounds should not be covered. Depending on where they are, the animal need not necessarily be taken off work.

Splints, Side-bones and Spavins

These are ossifications on or very near leg joints, usually produced as the result of strain. Splints occur on the top of the cannon bone just below the knee. They will produce lameness while they are forming, and in animals under six years old they may recur later. All that is needed is a few weeks' rest.

Side-bones are ossifications of the lateral cartilages in the horse's foot, normally as a product of age. In young horses they are an unsoundness and may, in the army, lead to the horse being cast.

Bone-spavins occur on the inside of the hock joint and, as with splints and side-bones, they produce some lameness when they are forming but not afterwards. The lameness is usually more acute when first starting work in the morning but then wears off as the day progresses. All that is needed is rest. Another type of spavin, called bog-spavin, presents as a puffy or 'boggy' swelling on the inside of the hock. Horses with upright or straight hocks are more prone to these spavins. When the joint is badly inflamed, it should be bathed with cold water followed by rubbing with liniment. They are more likely to occur in elderly animals.

Wounds

Wounds can result from some minor accident such as a kick or from something more serious such as being struck by shrapnel or some other form of battle wound. They were historically caused in cavalry engagements by a strike with a sword, often by the horse's own rider mishandling his sword and hitting his horse on the head. In war situations such injuries may be so serious that the horse has to be destroyed.

If a wound is bleeding heavily, a pad should be placed over the wound and a tight pressure bandage applied until the bleeding stops. This is the only time a tight dressing should be applied. When the bleeding stops, the wound should be cleaned to remove all dirt, then antiseptic should be applied and a clean pad and bandage put on. A veterinary officer may decide to stitch the wound closed.

Eye Problems

Ophthalmia can be specific or periodic. The first symptom is usually found in the morning when the horse has one eye half-closed and weeping copiously. *Black's Veterinary Dictionary* says 'any effort to examine the eye is resented'. The eye will be inflamed, the weeping turning from clear tears to a thicker liquid. The inflammation lasts about ten days and then the horse gradually recovers, but such attacks tend to recur, in which case it becomes known as periodic ophthalmia. The origin is microbial, but it is not contagious. Frequent attacks may lead to blindness.

Harness Galls and Sores

During the Second World War saddle injuries were common everywhere but were particularly prevalent in Burma, mainly due to a combination of the climate and the low standard of animal management. Burma has over 100in of rain in six months, making it impossible to keep saddlery dry. Sores can also be caused by badly fitting saddlery or harness, and in riding horses by a clumsy rider who constantly moves around in the saddle.

The best way to prevent sore backs on long marches is for the men to dismount for at least five minutes whenever possible and ideally to walk with their horse for a while, thus resting their own muscles as well as the horses'. One cavalry officer remarked, 'We have a singular notion in cavalry that it is a dishonour for a man to walk or be seen off his horse; the sooner we get rid of such ideas the better for horses' legs and backs.'

Treatment simply consists of rest, or possibly using a differently positioned harness. Sore backs are often also a little swollen and cold compresses will help reduce this, together with ointments.

Oedema

Horses sometimes develop 'filled' legs when they have been unable to be exercised for several days, perhaps due to frost, etc., and sometimes from overwork. They should be rested and their legs well rubbed by hand to help the circulation.

Dietary Problems

There are various afflictions of the digestive system, the commonest being colic. Like human bellyache, the usual cause is injudicious eating or injudicious feeding (or watering after feeding), or severe infestations of intestinal parasites. Unlike humans, horses have no ability to vomit and get rid of the problem food that way. Symptoms start with sweating, fast breathing, an anxious expression and constipation. The horse may kick or bite at his belly, or want to roll, but should not be allowed to as this can lead to dangerous torsion of the intestines. Instead he should be walked around until he has calmed down or passed some faeces or urine. Warming the belly with hot rugs relieves the pain, as does hand rubbing or wisping the belly.

Hayes recommends giving a drench of opium, turpentine and linseed oil, or, in Asia, a ball made up of opium, asafoetida and camphor. If these do not work, try a further drench of opium dissolved in water, or warm water enemas. Modern drenches consist of two tablespoons of medicinal turpentine, one teaspoonful of ground ginger, one teacupful of whisky and a pint of olive oil. These quantities are the dose for a heavy draught horse; smaller horses should be given smaller doses. Drenches can be repeated at three hourly intervals until four doses have been given, but the amount of turpentine should be halved.

Animals living or working in desert areas, or regions where forage is sparse, may develop sand colic from ingesting quantities of sand or fine soil when trying to graze, or from being given food straight onto the ground. When horses are kept for any length of time close to a sandy beach, they will lick up the sand in an attempt to get salt. Eventually, this seriously damages the intestines and the horse becomes thin and debilitated.

Two other serious ailments are contagious vesicular stomatitis and gastro-enteritis; these were found in many post-mortems. There were many cases of vesicular stomatitis, which resembles foot and mouth disease, in early 1917, one month alone producing 2,596 cases. Thought to be caused by a virus carried by mosquitoes or other biting insects, it is extremely contagious. Gastro-enteritis is an inflammation of the stomach and intestines, often brought on by poisons. This leads to debility as the horse is unable to eat.

Poisoning may come from various substances. There were some early cases of poisoning from linseed cake, which could be prevented by boiling them, and on one occasion castor beans were found in the oats, probably from a bulk-carrying ship that was not cleaned out properly before loading the oats. Other poisonous plants include the leaves of many evergreens such as yew, or the seeds of corn cockle (Agrostemma githago) or ragwort (Senecio jacobaea), which is not normally eaten unless dead or wilted. When poisoning is suspected, an emetic should be given until veterinary assistance arrives. Strong tea or coffee, boiled hard, is useful for this.

Drenches

When a horse has to be given a drench (also known as a draught) for colic, poisoning or other illnesses, two men will be needed to administer it. The drench should be prepared in a bottle or drenching horn and shaken well, then one man holds the horse's head well up and the other puts the neck of the bottle or horn in the horse's mouth behind the teeth and allows a little of the medicine to trickle in and down the throat. As soon as any of the drench begins to escape from the mouth, the bottle should be removed and the mouth held shut until the medicine has been swallowed, this being repeated until the whole dose has been taken. If the horse makes a fuss, more assistants may be needed, and sometimes a twitch must be used. (A twitch is a loop of fine rope attached to a short pole, the loop being passed over the horse's top lip and twisted until it is tight. This is not as cruel as it sounds, and it does keep the horse still.)

Gas

In the First World War the poisonous gases released by the Germans against British troops also affected horses. One version of these was used to create a smoke-screen or 'fog' to hide troop movements, rather than directly affect troops. Released from 'candles', these were made either from lead chloride, chlorates and compounds of nitrogen, or from distilled pitch, saltpetre and sulphur. The damage to horses and other animals from these came from grazing or drinking in fields where the candles were lit. The other types of gas were originally released by the Germans from cylinders in their trenches. This method was soon abandoned as adequate concentrations of the gases were difficult to achieve in this way owing to rapid diffusion into the air, and because climatic conditions were frequently unfavourable and there was a danger of the prevailing wind turning and blowing the gas towards those who were using it. Subsequently explosive shells were used to deliver the gases.

The most infamous was mustard gas. It was a severe irritant, and a very small droplet produces a blister as large as a fifty-pence piece and does serious damage to the lungs and air passages when inhaled. It affects the epithelial cells, blood, capillaries and nerves. Lesions appear on the skin about two hours after exposure and these can take weeks to heal. Horses' skin is thought to be four times more sensitive than humans'. It also affects the eyes, first causing severe watering and then, after about a day, temporary blindness. Symptoms include salivation, nasal discharge, yawning, neighing, a choking cough, apathy and unsteady gait. There may be sudden deaths from heart failure. If the horse survives, recovery and convalescence can take a very long time.

Treatment needed to be administered as soon as possible, first fitting an equine gas-mask and keeping the animal still unless it was essential to move it, in which case it should be done very slowly. The eyes and mucous membranes should be thoroughly irrigated with warm water, ideally containing sodium bicarbonate, soap, hydrogen peroxide or potassium permanganate; the whole body should be washed with the same solution, or liberally sprayed with warm water. Any visible drops of the gas should be dabbed off (not wiped) with cotton wool, which should then be burnt. The water for the eyes should contain a little liquid paraffin, cod-liver oil or castor oil to help prevent the lids from sticking together. Ongoing treatment consisted of treating sores with sulphur ointment or gentian violet, and the usual treatment for asphyxiation.

The other well-known gases were phosgene (a lung irritant) and lewisite. Phosgene acted on the pulmonary alvioli; its effects were more serious in horses which were working at the time of contamination. Symptoms included a profuse nasal discharge, persistent shortage of breath, coughing and a blueish colour to pale skin as a result of lack of oxygen in the blood. Lewisite had much the same effect as mustard gas; it was not visible to the naked eye but could be smelt (like musty hay or green corn). Rapid treatment might alleviate its effects, but it was generally fatal within twenty-four hours. Horses which did recover took a minimum of seven hours in mild cases, but anything up to four weeks otherwise.

In some cases oxygen was given, usually at veterinary hospitals, using a special respirator which fitted over the nostrils and mouth and fastened to the headcollar or bridle. The oxygen was administered from an oxygen cylinder via a valve and tube.

Prevention methods included gas-masks for horses. For foot protection, a metal plate embedded in rubber was fitted between the sole of the foot and the shoe, and satin boots were used to cover the lower legs from the knee and hock down. None of these measures was entirely effective. It was recommended that areas contaminated with liquid gases should be marked, and decontaminated by scattering chlorinated lime. Dry grass pastures should be burnt, otherwise affected pastures could be left to the wind and rain to clear naturally.

In all cases affected by gases, saddlery, harness and horse clothing should also be treated with a bleach preparation, but this tended to damage the stitching. All surfaces of stables and outside hard standing would need, at the very least, to be washed down and may have needed replacement. Personnel performing these tasks needed to wear protective clothing.[6] In fact, there were comparatively few horse casualties from chlorine gas. On the Western Front equine casualties from mustard gas were low, at 211 dead and 2,200 wounded, compared to 58,090 killed and 77,410 wounded by gunshot.

Veterinary Drugs

As time and science progressed, the number of drugs used to treat horses increased rapidly. Before the First World War there were few proprietary drugs, most of the recommended items being made up by the vet. By 1939 there were 795 types of drugs and dressings on the official list; by the end of the Second World War this number had grown to 1,156.

Non-urgent Operations

In the Second World War Major General Wingate in Burma told the deputy director of the veterinary service, Colonel Stewart, that he had a problem with noisy mules and donkeys which betrayed their position to the enemy by braying and neighing. He wondered if there was a way these animals could be silenced. After some experiments, an operation to remove their vocal cords under general anaesthetic was perfected, with over 5,500 animals being successfully operated on. Almost all were completely mute, although a few retained a little voice. The main post-operative difficulty was with maggots in the wounds, but anti-fly spray solved this.

Another operation which was carried out, especially in India where stallions were common (but troublesome), was castration. Ovary removal was found effective on vicious female mules. In both cases the main post-operative difficulty was with maggots in the wounds.

Statistics

In the late nineteenth century the Army Veterinary Department produced annual statistical returns of sick and lame horses. These were divided into ten classes of ailments, plus two other lists, one for admissions into veterinary infirmaries and the other for numbers of horses and mules cast and sold during the year. The classes included general diseases; respiratory afflictions; digestive conditions; circulation problems; contagious and infectious diseases; and problems and injuries to the legs and feet. The statistics for the year 1882 – at a time when the total number of horses in the army was 11,727 –

showed admissions to infirmaries of 9,913, of which 4,711 were from cavalry regiments and 3,940 from artillery regiments.

In the First World War British Army animals on all fronts exceeded 1,000,000 by 1917; the average daily number sick was about 110,000. Total hospital admissions between 1914 and 1918 were over 2,562,000; 78 per cent of these were returned to duty. By the summer of 1918 there had been many casualties from plane-dropped bombs. To give an idea of the magnitude of the work performed at the veterinary hospitals, between August 1914 and 23 January 1919 no fewer than 725,216 animals were admitted to hospitals, 529,064 died, 127,741 were destroyed as incurable, 29,524 were sold to agriculture and just under 20,000 were still under treatment at the end of the war.

All horses had their own medical papers, which went with them when they changed units or went into or out of hospital. From these it could be seen whether the animal was a sickly individual and should be cast or was generally fit enough to be retained in service.[7]

Chapter Eight

Veterinary Administration

Before 1796, veterinary work was done by regimental farriers who held contracts for shoeing and medicines. In that year the Army Veterinary Corps (AVC) was formed. It became the Royal Army Veterinary Corps (RAVC) in 1918. As with many such organisations, it went through a series of name changes, from Department through Service to Corps.

In 1795 William Stockley, a graduate from the London Veterinary College, was attached to the Fencible Cavalry and in 1796 Professor Edward Coleman, head of the Veterinary College, was appointed Principal Veterinary Surgeon to the Cavalry and Veterinary Surgeon to the Board of Ordnance and charged with the creation of the AVC. Coleman remained in this position for forty-three years, despite having little actual experience or knowledge of veterinary work and a tendency to milk all financial systems to his own advantage. He did, however, make vast improvements in veterinary hygiene and arranged for part of the Board of Ordnance's stables at Woolwich to be turned into a veterinary infirmary.[1]

Structure and Chain of Command

The AVC, as a main administrative service, was headed by a Director General (DG), who acted under the Quartermaster General of the Force. There was a Deputy Director (DD) ranked as colonel and an Assistant Director (AD) ranked as lieutenant colonel with each army and cavalry corps. There was a Deputy Assistant Director (DAD) with each division; each of these posts required clerical assistance employing clerks trained in AVC work. Most AVC personnel except those in mobile sections were more than forty-one years old or otherwise unsuitable for front-line service. During the First World War there was no depot in France for reinforcements, these going out direct from Woolwich.[2]

After the Franco-Prussian War of 1870 a number of military reforms were made, and for the Army Veterinary Service (AVS) all vets, with the exception of those attached to the Household Cavalry, were transferred to one list and wore the same uniform. The Army Veterinary Service was renamed the Army Veterinary Department and the Principal Veterinary Surgeon became a member of the War Office staff, moving his office from Woolwich to Pall Mall. In 1891 he was retitled Director General Army Veterinary Department and regulations were published to provide for an establishment of field veterinary hospitals and store depots, although no provision was made for trained staff, only one hospital for 300 animals was provided for a force of some 36,000 horses, and the equipment was largely obsolete.

Under professional care the health of army horses was vastly improved. Glanders was brought under control through better understanding, while more thorough hygiene of stables and better understood equine dietetics all improved matters. However, on the line of march, sick and lame animals were either left by the wayside or, if they could still move, sent to the rear with the baggage. At first there were no sick horse hospitals; during the Peninsular War sick horse depots were set up, but these did not have trained staff and the horses were left to get along as best they could on their own.

At the start of the Second Boer War in 1899 the veterinary service had no real organisation and it was left to the commanders in the operational theatres to organise a system. But they, like the local civilian authorities, had little veterinary knowledge and produced mainly useless archaic systems. The Director General Army Veterinary Department tried to improve the situation by borrowing field veterinary hospitals from India. In the first year of this war these were the only veterinary organisations available. This all caused a major fuss and eventually Edward VII signed a warrant to create an Army Veterinary Corps, with the general director ranked as major general (although remaining a colonel).

The total equine losses in the Second Boer War were 326,000 horses (67 per cent) and 51,400 mules (35 per cent). Glanders and epizootic lymphangitis were widespread and there were thousands of cases of mange. At the end of the war some 140,000 horses and 74,000 mules were declared surplus and promptly sold off, spreading glanders and epizootic lymphangitis through South Africa, and units returning to England without sufficient vets to check their horses before they departed took epizootic lymphangitis with them, which took several years to eradicate.

Courses for Non-veterinary Officers

In 1880 an Army Veterinary School was established at Aldershot. This was not to train veterinary officers from scratch (they all had to be qualified vets before acceptance into the Veterinary Department) but to train non-veterinary officers from mounted regiments in what was referred to at the time as Veterinary Sanitary Science.

It had long been obvious to the veterinary profession that good animal management was effectively good preventative 'medicine'. Unfortunately at this time (probably because many of them had been brought up in towns and not exposed to animals) the fighting forces of the army knew little about horses, a failing which went all the way up to general officers. This ignorance caused so much wastage in France in the First World War that it was decided to provide classes at veterinary hospitals on the lines of communication, as well as those given at the Army Veterinary School at Aldershot. Each course took ten days and taught ten officers and fifty NCOs, with lectures and demonstrations on the basics of recognising the signs of disease, using good stable routines (cleanliness, watering and feeding), grooming and clipping (and learning the early signs of disease or loss of condition), proper fitting of saddles and harness to avoid sore backs and galls, the correct use of picket lines, and farriery. Although such short courses could not be a complete education in horsemastership, if nothing else they did serve to engender a respect for the veterinary profession and a willingness to follow its instructions.

At Aldershot the aim was to enable these officers to understand the proper management of horses and other animals used in the army on ship or shore and how to prevent casualties. The school also gave lectures and demonstrations during the courses on conformation and age, the principles of shoeing, and the points of minor surgery or medicine which would enable them to save the life of an animal when no veterinary officer was present. When these courses started, attendance was voluntary but the Principal Veterinary Surgeon of the Forces believed it should be compulsory. Originally the courses were held three times a year and lasted five weeks, ending with an examination. Between 1880 and 1885 some 345 officers attended the course, of whom 285 passed the exam and 60 failed.

In 1889 attendance was made compulsory, and the courses extended to a full month, with a written exam at the end of each week. In that year 112 officers attended courses, 61 from cavalry regiments, 12 from the Royal Artillery, 3 from the Royal Engineers, 12 from the Army Service Corps and 24 from infantry regiments and the Indian Army. There were also special classes for veterinary officers who had been abroad and wanted to catch up on the latest developments and treatments.

By 1900 topics on these courses included construction of stables, management of horses in the stable, on the line of march and on board ship (and principles of embarkation), the foot and the principles of shoeing, sore backs and minor diseases, dietetics, conformation, teeth and age, detection of lameness, recognition of various kinds of grass in hay, and description of grains.

The 1932 Regulations for the AVC had little to say about these courses, other than how the school establishment received the questions for the exams, but did require details of the courses to be published annually.

Another important part of the work of the Veterinary School was training farriers to work as veterinary assistants. Unfortunately no details of this course have survived, but generals in the field had for some time been asking for such trained men to reduce the number of horses lost on the march or in the field hospitals. The first trained men went with the expeditions to

Bechuanaland and Suakin and were found to be most valuable. It was then proposed that all sergeant farriers who had a third class education certificate should attend the courses, as well as men of the same educational standard who had been passed as competent to shoe horses. They also suggested training two men per battalion of infantry to shoe horses and then passing the more intelligent of the two to attend the Veterinary Assistant course. In his report, Fleming went on to discuss reorganisation of the existing system of farriery. At that time it took at least three years to train a farrier, with most of this time spent in learning to make shoes and nails. This was tolerable during the time of long service, but not when short service became the norm. Shortages of shoes and nails were increasingly common until the introduction of machine-made shoes and nails. This meant that it was no longer necessary to take heavy forge wagons on campaign, along with the coals to fire them and the iron to make the shoes; smaller forges could be carried on pack saddles and men quickly trained to put on shoes. The farrier sergeants would do the necessary training and could then be released to work as veterinary assistants in the hospitals. It was proposed that a minimum of 10 per cent of men in mounted regiments should be taught to put on shoes.

Fleming also mentioned winter shoeing and described his solution to the problem of slippery roads. This was a simple invention: pegs which screwed into the back of shoes, which could be fitted when the horse left the stable and removed when he returned.

As with all military functions, the AVC submitted various returns and statistical reports, often in an annual summary of its activities. Few of these have survived, but there are some, which, added to the frequent printings of the regulations, do give a partial picture of what they were doing.

There are several returns from the 1880s, starting with an 'Annual Return of Sick and Lame Horses' for the year 1882. This consists of a set of tables, listing afflictions by class, divided into specific ailments/diseases/accidents, and showing against each the numbers held over from the previous year and those admitted since, then whether they were cured, relieved, incurable, died or destroyed, or still under treatment. To give some examples, Class 1 consisted of seventeen 'general diseases', including five fevers, anaemia, asthenia, rheumatism and exhaustion. Of the 972 horses in this class, 177 died or were destroyed, 602 were cured, 100 relieved or incurable, and 93 still under treatment. Class 2 covered ailments of the respiratory apparatus; of the 2,155 total admissions, 1,694 were cured, 174 died or were destroyed and 180 were still under treatment. Class 10 was 'locomotory apparatus', divided into forty-one afflictions. Thirteen of this type were fractures of various bones and most of the sufferers were destroyed;[3] 192 cases were splints, ringbone and spavins, 605 were sprains and 1,065 were various problems located in the foot. All the ailments in the other classes were on a very small scale.

There were also listings of the numbers of horses cast or sold, divided by regiment and reason; by far the greatest number were for 'old age' (807 out of 1,223). There was also a table showing hospital admissions by the 'different branches of the service' by number and percentage. For cavalry regiments this was 5,317 of an average strength of 11,351 (47 per cent) and for artillery 3,940 of 4,259 (92 per cent). The other units were non-combatants: the Royal Engineers, Commissariat and Transport Corps, Military Police and Regimental Transport. Overall, 9,913 horses were admitted, from an average strength of 11,727, with 82 per cent listed as sick and lame and just under 5 per cent as died or destroyed.

These figures look very large, but it should be remembered that some of the sick and lame horses may have been the same animal admitted two or more times and that many others may have been purchased or cast from the average strengths.

The 1884 return reported on the previous year's bad outbreak of glanders, 'that much-dreaded malady', in the 3rd Hussars while they were stationed at Aldershot; this was thought to have come from billet stables in East London (where the disease was always more or less present) used on the regiment's march from Colchester to Aldershot. The report commented that this disproved the notion that the disease arose spontaneously. There was also a serious outbreak of strangles, an infectious disease mostly found in young horses, and the stables at Hyde Park Barracks and Woolwich, both of which were long known as being insalubrious, had many cases of equine influenza.

The report for 1886 included sections on Egypt and South Africa. Interestingly, among the mortalities in that year, there was one horse of the 1st Life Guards which contracted rabies after being bitten by a prowling dog when the regiment was drilling at Wormwood Scrubs. Mortality in Egypt was just over 4 per cent of horses, just under 2 per cent of mules and 34 per cent of camels. This high mortality among the camels included three which suffered fractured vertebrae through being run over by a train. The report omits to mention how this came about, but one might surmise that the camels had sat down on, or too close to, the tracks.

In South Africa the highest mortality was from horse sickness in Natal, an affliction which made annual appearances, so Mr Nunn – 'one of the most intelligent and enthusiastic officers of the Veterinary Department' – was sent to investigate. He had had training at the Brown Institute in London and at Mr Pasteur's laboratory in Paris. While on station, he was also to report on other contagious diseases in South Africa, 'a task for which he is particularly fitted by his long experience as Inspector under the Contagious Diseases (Animals) Act in the Punjab'. He had also been, for some time, the Assistant Superintendant of the Horse Breeding operation in Bengal, and 'is [thus] well qualified to give an opinion' on the type of horses in South Africa for sending to India.

Uniforms

Veterinary officers were included for the first time in the 1882 Dress Regulations. As part of the regimental staff, they dressed much the same as the other staff officers – very plainly, with no facings on their collars or cuffs, although from 1817 these had been embroidered to regimental pattern. By 1883 all regimental uniform was abolished, and the usual uniform for veterinary officers included a tunic, with their rank indicated by the number of knots in the braid on the sleeves and the length of the feathers on the cocked hat. This was gradually replaced by a forage cap. The colour of the service dress was fixed as khaki in the Dress Regulations of 1904.

Reorganisation

Between March 1902 and September 1910 there was an ongoing reorganisation of the Veterinary Department, which occasioned much correspondence. It started with what one letter referred to as 'the discontent of the Army Veterinary Department', which wanted earlier promotion, increased pensions, free passages to postings abroad for wives and families, and combatant rank. The first three were granted quite quickly, the last was not. By the middle of 1904 increased rates of pay for warrant officers and other ranks had been added to the list.

The correspondence became quite sharp at times. One of the grievances concerned the length of service required – fifteen years – before veterinary majors were eligible for promotion to lieutenant colonel. The Director General of the AVD wrote to the Director of the Quartermaster General's department, noting that this provision had been omitted from an Army order, and wondering if the omission had been deliberate or accidental, and stating that he thought it was desirable and should be re-inserted. The Director of the Quartermaster General's department pointed out that 'presumably [it was] you [who] worded the Royal Warrant in question' and would he therefore say whether the omission was deliberate or not. This drew a response that it had been omitted after a 'verbal reference', to which the Director of the AVD replied that there was no record of such an instruction having been given. This argument went back and forth a few more times before the Quartermaster General's department gave in.

By September 1902 a more detailed list of issues had been produced. The main grievances concerned rank, followed by the lack of trained subordinate staff, the lack of control over men employed in veterinary hospitals (at that time such men were lent by combatant units and could be withdrawn at short notice by their commanding officer), a general dissatisfaction with pay and pensions, and several other matters relating to service abroad and the rates of pay attached to it. All of this became the subject of a committee of enquiry into the conditions affecting officers of the Army Veterinary Department, headed by a Parliamentary Under-Secretary of State, the Earl of Hardwicke. The committee reported in April 1903; among its recommendations, duly sanctioned by royal warrant, was the creation of an Army Veterinary Corps for NCOs, while officers remained in the AVD. Two veterinary hospitals were sanctioned, one at Woolwich and the other at Aldershot, although one cavalry commander objected to having such a hospital which was not under his control in his barracks. Two more hospitals followed, one in Wiltshire, the other in Ireland. Mobilisation stores were also set up at these locations. The AVD and AVC were amalgamated into a single organisation in February 1906. In 1909 a Special Reserve of Veterinary Officers was created.[4]

Recruitment to the AVC

The AVC was very selective about who would be considered for commissioned rank in the Corps. Candidates had to be between twenty-one and twenty-eight years old and unmarried. They must be British subjects and sons of British subjects, and of 'pure European descent'. They must be a member of the Royal College of Veterinary Surgeons. The head of the veterinary school from which they had graduated would be asked for a report on the candidate's professional ability.

In addition, all candidates had to sit a double entrance examination, written and oral, covering cattle as well as horses. If these were passed, and the candidate was found physically fit in a medical examination, he was appointed as a lieutenant on probation, then had to undergo 'such courses of instruction as the Army Council may direct'. These are not described, but were probably basic military instruction. On passing the examinations for these, the lieutenant's commission was confirmed. Some vets were sent to individual mounted units, while others worked in veterinary hospitals at home and abroad, and in evacuation centres abroad.

After three and a half years the lieutenant became eligible for promotion to captain, and after eight and a half years (three years of which had to be in service abroad) a captain became eligible for promotion to major. Promotion to lieutenant colonel was made by selection from majors with not less than fifteen years' service, with at least two years in India.[5]

Hospitals/Evacuation Centres

Evacuation of sick and wounded animals from their unit was considered essential, as keeping them with their unit impeded that unit's mobility and used personnel who should be combative. Evacuation stations were allotted at one per corps, and situated close to the corps' railhead. They had one officer, thirty-eight other ranks and one horse ambulance, which was indispensable. Mobile sections took horses to them and they passed them on to hospitals. Special sick-horse trains were organised when there were sufficient animals to fill them. Horses able to walk were evacuated by road; twenty animals could be attached to a rope in pairs and needed only three men to accompany them, one each at the front, middle and end. This method was also used by the Remount Service.

On arrival at hospital reception, each animal had a mallein test and if necessary went to the mange unit to be dipped; debility cases went to the convalescent unit for rest and feeding up, the others to the general hospital, except for those that were obviously incurable or permanently lame, which were quickly disposed of. Few stayed in a hospital for more than six days. Some draught horses, not fit enough for the front, were branded VB ('Veterinary Base') on the foot and kept for work on the lines of communication. Many of these were blind as a result of eye diseases, but this did not stop them working. Cured animals were released to the remount unit. It was a point of honour that these should be immaculately turned out.

The convalescent depots were not just for horses out of hospital, but also for those needing an extended rest; work at these did not include any medical or post-surgical care, just grooming and feeding up, using good quality food-stuffs, including linseed cake and locust beans. In addition to chaff-cutting and grain-crushing, these depots had facilities for boiling food, stabling for bad weather and paddocks. These convalescent depots developed out of the situation at the beginning of the war when hostilities on the Marne and Aisne produced numerous debilitated horses. Some 3,000 of these were turned out to grass; in two weeks they were transformed and the idea of convalescent depots was born, with the first at Gournay-en-Bray, about 20 miles north-west of Paris. There were three hospitals nearby. Where small paddocks or sand corrals were used, they had to be periodically rested, cleaned out and fresh sand added. The animals loved to lie in this soft surface, and rolling was the order of the day when they were turned out in the morning.

The ideal location for veterinary hospitals was close to the main remount depots, as these were a major source of cases, especially of animals newly arrived from overseas. Outside western Europe, there were veterinary hospitals in India, Egypt, Salonika and Gallipoli, with mobile veterinary sections elsewhere. India also had camel hospitals.

Originally intended for 250 animals, there were five hospitals each with 2 officers, 5 sergeants, 6 corporals, 10 dressers, 4 artificers, 83 horse keepers (mainly cavalry reservists) and 4 batmen. These hospitals had accommodation for 1,250 animals, barely 2.5 per cent of the total force of 53,000 and totally inadequate. Reorganisation allowed 1,000 animals per hospital, then 1,250 and then 2,000, with a total of 544 personnel, including farriers and saddlers.

These larger hospitals were divided into five subdivisions. Each block had its own dressing sheds, forges and water troughs, etc. The stalls could easily be converted to loose-boxes. Mangers were made of iron sheeting which was easily disinfected, while hayracks and other fittings were improvised from hay-bale wire. Each hospital and convalescent depot had its own chaff-cutting and corn-crushing machinery. The personnel had well-equipped barracks with messes, dining halls, a YMCA, force canteens and church huts. There were also gardens and most veterinary hospitals were self-sufficient in vegetables.

The British Expeditionary Force in 1914 had six veterinary hospitals (each for 250 animals), eleven mobile veterinary sections and two base store depots. As the 53,000 animals with the force on initial mobilisation rose to 456,000 animals, the infrastructure also increased to 18 hospitals (each for 2,000 animals), 4 convalescent depots (for 1,200 animals), 50 mobile veterinary sections and 16 veterinary evacuation stations. They also used horse-drawn and motorised horse ambulances. Twenty-six motorised two-horse ambulances were presented by the RSPCA, which had raised the money for them by subscription. They were sometimes used to take milking cows to human hospitals or troops to the front line. In Flanders, the AVS had five canal barges pulled by steam tugs. Each barge carried up to thirty-two horses on a smooth and comfortable journey. All evacuated animals had their own papers, detailing not just their problem but what unit they came from, and all were mallein tested on arrival; if any had a positive reaction, the information was sent to their unit vet, who could then test all the others. The evacuated horses had colour-coded labels on their headcollars: white for medical cases, green for surgical and red for communicable diseases.

Over the course of the four years of war the percentage of cures fell, which inevitably reduced the efficiency of the animals. In the first year it was 84 per cent, falling annually to 82, then 80, then 78 and gradually lower. In the first winter there were only a few brick sheds and no other covered accommodation for sick animals or new remounts. Heavy draught horses suffered badly from catarrhal and other respiratory infections.

During the First World War all veterinary officers had to keep a war diary, in duplicate, from the first day of mobilisation. These were to be updated daily and had to contain 'a concise and accurate record of all matters connected with the campaign in so far as they relate to the duties and experiences of a RAVC unit, a veterinary officer in charge of a unit, or an administrative veterinary officer'. The entries should relate mainly to technical matters, or others which might be useful on future occasions either at war or during peace. Only one side of the paper should be used and the handwriting should be legible. The original copy should be sent in monthly, and the duplicate copy, clearly marked as such, to the RAVC records department at home.[6]

The official Regulations for the Veterinary Department were produced periodically, but apart from changes to the contents of the medicine chest and some of the instruments, they remained much the same throughout the war. Their main content related to administrative work: use of the correct forms and other procedures such as those applying to marching, and the correct method of obtaining medicines, instruments and surgical equipment. There were lists of veterinary stores, with items including sponges, tape and flannel for bandages. Other items, shown on a requisition form for farrier sergeants' supply of medicines, included scales and weights, and a mortar and pestle. The medicine chests were packed to a standard pattern, and the manuals showed what items were where, from the bottom layer to the lift-out tray; some included an 'ointment slab' which would have been used for mixing ointments in quantities larger than a mortar would hold.

There were sections devoted to veterinary schools and farriery, and there were several pages on glanders and other infectious diseases, including the correct way to dispose of carcasses (ideally cremation, but otherwise to be buried at least 6ft deep, with the skin slashed and the carcass covered with quick-lime).

Interestingly, the earliest of these sets of regulations dealt separately with treatment and medicines for officers' chargers; this must presumably have meant the officers' privately owned horses rather than those issued by the army.

The RSPCA provided invaluable help throughout the First World War, not least by offering its inspectors and helping to locate grooms for recruitment to the AVC. A special fund was set up, and the proceeds initially devoted to providing stabling for veterinary hospitals, remount depots and convalescent depots in France. It provided stabling for 12,500 horses. They sent many other donations, including the twenty-six motorised horse ambulances mentioned above, along with eighty horse-drawn horse ambulances, clipping machines, chaff cutters and corn crushers, ovens and boilers for the preparation of hot feeds, equipment for a 'carcase economiser' detachment, bandages and poultice boots, and a ton of white paint for operating theatres. They also sent gifts for AVC personnel, including gramophones, games, books, cricket and football outfits and boxing gloves.

At the beginning of the war there were five veterinary hospitals for 250 animals each, plus eleven mobile sections and two base store depots, manned by 122 officers and 797 other ranks; by the end of 1917 there were eight hospitals, four convalescent depots, seventeen veterinary evacuation centres, sixty-six mobile units, five base store depots, a bacteriological laboratory and seven 'carcase economisers', staffed by 651 officers with 15,200 other ranks.

After the First World War

Shortly after the First World War ended, on 27 November 1918 King George V conferred the title 'Royal' to the Army Veterinary Corps (now RAVC). It took some time for the number of officers to reduce as they were busy ensuring that contagious diseases did not come back to England with the equine army, but by the end of March 1920 there were only 334 officers and 1,280 other ranks left. Postwar mechanisation and economic necessity saw a drastic reduction in numbers of animals but by 1931 another war in Europe was seen as inevitable and, despite mechanisation, it was evident that equines would still be needed. Given the likelihood of chemical warfare, the RAVC started research on protective measures for animals.

After the Armistice the best animals in the Vichy French remount depots in Syria and Lebanon were taken over by the RAVC. In all, some 10,500 animals were recovered alive, but many had been neglected and left without feed or water. Using local labour, the better animals were collected in depots and individually inspected, mallein tested and divided into categories, using distinctive brands. Some 7,300 were deemed fit for service. The light draught horses, all originally imported from France, were good, docile working horses; the French riding horses were not as good, some well-bred but most common and badly shaped, old and in poor condition. Heavy draught mules, mostly from France or Spain, were of a good type, while the mountain artillery mules were of a fine type, very quiet and mostly in good condition. There were also some Syrian and Barb horses from Spahi regiments, but most of these were small and in poor condition.

The vast number of human deaths from the Spanish 'Flu in 1918, much of it spread by troops returning home from the war, is well known. Where animals are concerned, the spread of such plagues is often the result of war, from the disruption of normal veterinary services and the upset of the normal patterns of animal care and livestock movement. At the end of the First World War western Russia developed rinderpest which spread rapidly to neighbouring countries; by 1921 this disease had killed 5.6 million animals. In 1919 foot and mouth disease in western and central Europe caused heavy losses of stock.

In 1944 it took strong controls to prevent African Horse Sickness from affecting the Middle East and spreading to other countries around the Mediterranean. The RAVC worked to control such situations and help local livestock industries until civilian organisations could take over.

The Second World War

In September 1939 bases at home and in northwest Europe increased the RAVC establishment from 18 officers and 68 other ranks to 42 officers and 441 other ranks. A veterinary air-raid precautionary organisation was needed for all large towns and cities in the threatened areas: Greater London, for example, had some 50,000 horses and cattle, 24,000 sheep and pigs and 2 million cats and dogs, and heavy casualties were expected. It was decided to grant emergency commissions to young veterinary surgeons rather than call up reserves. Some 247 volunteered immediately and plenty of others continued to do so until 1943. In all, 519 officers served during the war. Other ranks were also easy to recruit: veterinary students, hunt servants, grooms, stable lads and farm workers eagerly volunteered, but throughout the war there was a shortage of farriers and saddlers.

Many of the horses and mules used in this war served in Greece and the Balkans. All the veterinary and remount units were near Athens. Some 830 mules arrived from India and 250 were sent up to the front soon after landing. A second contingent of 338 mules and 60 horses was sent from Alexandria, but their ship was sunk near the Greek coast; a few of the horses were rescued but the mules were trapped below and could not be saved. The British troops were unable to maintain their positions in Greece and had to evacuate. One RAVC officer and 112 other ranks were captured; the rest managed to get to Cyprus.

As a result of the rapid increase in numbers of animals in 1941–1942, the Indian Army Veterinary Corps in the East found itself in need of many more veterinary units and it was decided to open a large training centre at Ambala. However, GHQ blundered by sending a brigadier to Ambala to draw up a plan for the establishment, despite the fact that a plan had already been worked out by the senior veterinary officers. Lacking veterinary experience, the brigadier ignored this plan completely and proceeded to draw up his own version. Described politely as 'very remarkable' and less politely as 'absurd', his thoughts on personnel allocated only one lieutenant and a few instructional staff for a squad of 400 trainees, with no idea of what should happen if this lieutenant fell sick. Many other 'inadequacies' occurred in his establishment plan, but the commandant's protests were ignored.

Recuits for the teaching posts streamed in, many sent from other units; it soon became obvious that their units were glad to get rid of them. After six months or so a revised establishment was introduced, the failures of the first plan having been observed, but the new version was still inadequate; one of its major failings was the lack of sufficient clerks. Few experienced clerks were available and the standard of those who were available was very low. Other Indian staff recruits also caused difficulties; when they joined they were given ten weeks' basic military training and six weeks' technical training. The military training was slowed down by the fact that many of these recruits were malnourished. Few knew anything about animals and most regarded them with deep suspicion, but it was found that a short course of riding instruction usually overcame their fears and also improved their self-confidence.

After four months' training and one month's leave, many failed to return. Desertions became commonplace and it seemed that many of the men listed as deserters had never even joined their unit; they enrolled, drew the enrolment money and disappeared. Some made a habit of enrolling at different centres. All this took up a great deal of administration for the courts of enquiry which had to be held.

Further revisions of the establishment followed. After the fourth, the Centre finally had the establishment it should have had from the beginning. All it lacked was a technical training officer, a post which was finally sanctioned in December 1944. By the end of 1945 the Centre had been tasked with agricultural and resettlement training. It had to build, stock and equip a model farm and provide instructors for this and cottage industry courses. However, all went well, and when the commandant retired, his successor sent him a copy of the Inspection report of the Lahore district which praised the professionality of the Centre. It had been a long struggle, but they got there in the end.[7]

During the Second World War it became obvious that the small number of equines needed did not warrant two separate departments, and in 1941 the Remount Department was taken over by the Royal Army Veterinary Corps, which then became known as the Army Veterinary and Remount Service. This allowed a tremendous economy in staff, manpower and units. The activities of the old Remount Department were nothing new to the veterinary service since veterinary officers had always been attached to buying commissions.

One change was that mobile veterinary units kept a 'stock' of fit remounts which they issued to units that had evacuated sick and wounded animals. They had powerful lorries with trailers which could transport up to twenty animals. These were particularly useful in the Italian campaign for evacuating casualties to veterinary hospitals and delivering remount replacements to the forward areas where there was no rail transport. The amalgamation of the two arms working with animals in 1941 was beneficial to other corps such as the Royal Artillery and the RASC.

By 1941 the increased importance of operations involving animals in Egypt and the Sudan led to the transfer of the Deputy Director of the Army Veterinary and Remount Service to Cairo to take responsibility for all operations in the Middle East. Although the number of ridden animals was falling, due to increased mechanisation, the saving of petrol by the use of equines for draught and pack purposes meant many of the surplus animals could be retrained to work in pole or shaft wagons and to carry packs. By 1942 some 2,300 had been transferred to the companies set up to use them.

In India and Burma the amalgamation of the veterinary and remount services did not take place until after the war. Despite mechanisation, and the expectation that few animals would be needed, in 1941 there was still an establishment of 42,000 equines, 3,800 camels and 17,500 cattle, plus five months' supply of veterinary stores. Many of these animals were sent to the Mediterranean countries and Iraq. Veterinary personnel reduced dramatically until the fall of Singapore and Malaya made it obvious that pack animals would be needed for the eastern front in hill and jungle country. Additional veterinary surgeons and their assistants were recruited and trained, bringing their number up from 40 to 329 by the end of the war.

In Burma the Japanese advanced rapidly, forcing the withdrawal of British and Indian troops, including veterinary personnel. There was also much sickness amongst the animals and by June 1942 there was only one veterinary surgeon, one assistant surgeon and six Indian other ranks to care for 225 sick animals in the hospital, as well as those out working with troops. Many animals were killed by bombing and others suffered girth galls, but the records for this period were lost so no accurate figures are available.

One difficulty that emerged early in the Burma campaign was the inadequacy of field veterinary equipment. The veterinary chests were not resistant to rain or the ever-present damp in jungle areas. Many types of drugs and dressings were spoiled, as were the metal containers in which they were kept. Some of the drugs, such as chloralhydrate, were hygroscopic and not only attracted damp but conveyed it to the metal containers and other contents of the chests. These hygroscopic drugs had to be replaced by substitutes.

The first veterinary hospital was set up in Assam, where the jungle had to be cleared before the tents could be set up. Since the men doing this work were stripped to the waist, their numbers were soon depleted by malaria; this was followed, once the monsoon rains started, by trypanosome diseases of the blood, known locally as surra, in the animals. A further base was created at Dimapur by the same methods and with the same consequences, except that jaundice and dysentery joined the malaria, affecting about half the men.

The usual wartime shortages of drugs occurred, including a product known as naganol which was used for treating surra. This disease was caused in both horses and humans by a protozoa transmitted by insects. The main supply of naganol came from the German company Bayer, but in 1928 a French substitute was produced, followed by another from the British company ICI. It became so important that instead of the usual delivery systems, RAVC officers collected it in person from the ships and took it to the forward areas themselves.

The system which supplied drugs and equipment essential to the continuing welfare of animals in the field (but not those needed for specialized treatment) were supplied in standard chests built to withstand transportation and climatic changes. Over 207 tons of these were supplied.

In southern Europe, by the end of 1943, the DDVS was anxiously awaiting a remount depot, a hospital, a laboratory, a base veterinary store and three conducting units to deliver remounts to field units and evacuate casualties. One large field remount depot did arrive in January 1944 and another in February. This one, the pre-war Italian remount depot, was better situated in a rural area. With stabling for 2,000 horses and 10,000 acres of paddocks, it was divided into three separate centres, suitable for convalescents and newly purchased mules which needed to be brought up to fitness for duty.

In December 1943 the staff headquarters of the veterinary service moved to Naples. After consultation with American units, the RAVS was designated the responsible adviser on veterinary and remount matters for the British 8th and the American 5th Armies. Remounts were to be held in a common user pool to be allocated to whichever of the allied forces needed them for operational requirements. The two armies estimated they needed thirty-three pack companies, but only thirty were available, coming from Cyprus, France, India, Italy and North Africa, totalling some 10,000 animals.

In Italy in 1944 veterinary stores were found to be in short supply, including bandages and cotton wool, ready prepared ampoules of various drugs, and anti-tetanus serum for gunshot wounds. However, there were only thirty-six fatal tetanus cases in May 1944.

Other duties performed by the RAVSC at the end of the Second World War included overseeing slaughterhouses and butcheries. India particularly faced numerous problems: many of the buildings were poorly constructed with inadequate lighting and poor drainage, and had insufficient equipment for dealing with large quantities of meat and offal; meat was commonly transported in unhygienic conditions; slaughtermen were mostly ignorant of the basics of hygienic handling of meat and were not instructed in simple public health rules; diseased meat rejected from military butcheries often found its way into the bazaars and from there into officers' messes and restaurants; religious prejudice meant a proportion of the meat ration was issued to units on the hoof, thus evading veterinary inspection and often being slaughtered by untrained men in unit lines.

The RAVC also carried out slaughterhouse inspections throughout the Middle East and ended up supervising the rebuilding of slaughterhouses and giving the workers hygiene training. Where local conditions made it difficult to obtain good quality animals, the RAVC set up their own depots for fattening cattle, sheep and goats, breeding and rearing pigs and also rabbits, whose flesh was in demand in military hospitals. In Sicily vets were needed for meat inspection at the abbatoirs in Syracuse, where much of the beef and mutton was affected by trichinosis, brucellosis and anthrax, and hygiene standards were very low. Experience had shown that giving troops fresh meat, rather than tinned, was good for morale.

A Civil Affairs veterinary service and the veterinary panel of the Allied Post-War Requirements Panel were set up at the end of the Second World

War. As well as conserving and replenishing flocks and herds, the RAVC worked on replacement of draught animals which had been seized, especially by Germany, which, contrary to the popular impression that it was highly mechanised, was dependent on an establishment of over a million horses. Many of these were available for distribution to civilians and within three months over 44,000 of them were branded, tested for disease and distributed. Healthy but otherwise unserviceable animals were slaughtered to feed sur-rendered troops and displaced civilians. As well as captured animals, those surplus to military requirements were also distributed. This situation per-tained in South-East Asia as well as the Middle East and Europe; there were few private vets in Burma or Malaya even before the Japanese invasion. The Civil Affairs Service sent vets to Burma to serve until the Civil Veterinary Department was reinstated. There were serious outbreaks of rinderpest in both countries. Already suffering from a rice famine, the loss of over 50,000 buffaloes used to work the rice paddies exacerbated this until the RAVC brought the situation under control.

In Europe, as soon as hostilities ended, vets were released from their duties with pack units to collect enemy animals; these were sorted and branded on the right shoulder with the broad arrow and 'C' for captured. They then went to temporary collecting centres, from where the sick were transferred to veterinary hospitals. The best of the mules and riding horses went to remount depots, and the rest were handed over to local farmers. Some 3,500 of the good ones went to India and Burma, and 12,000 went to relief work in Greece and Yugoslavia. There were 8,000 captured animals in northern Italy, a large proportion of them draught horses. Another 60,000 animals were sur-rendered to the 5th Corps in Austria. Many of these were good quality horses, including some Hanoverians and Trakheners, and several which proved successful on the racecourse.

The RAVC continues its work with army animals. Most of the horses are used for ceremonial purposes, but the greatest number of animals now kept healthy by the RAVC are dogs.[8]

Chapter Nine

Training Horses and Riders

Training Horses

In the eighteenth century British riding was heavily influenced by an Italian named Domenick Angelo, of whom George II remarked, 'Mr Angelo is the most elegant rider in Europe.'[1] In 1754 Lord Pembroke started a private riding school at his house in Whitehall and another at his Salisbury seat of Wilton. Angelo was installed as his manager and riding master. When in due course Pembroke was appointed to the command of the 15th Light Dragoons, he sent a number of the regiment's riding instructors to Wilton to be trained by Angelo. His influence soon became so widespread that his methods of breaking, training and riding horses were adopted by all the mounted units of the army. In 1761 Pembroke wrote *Military Equitation: A Method of Breaking Horses and Teaching Soldiers to Ride*, based on Angelo's teaching.[2]

Pembroke stated that all horses bought for the cavalry should be of an age when they would already have been backed (i.e. saddled and ridden). The instructions for the Remount Department when they were buying horses overseas were that all the horses should have been broken to saddle. In the Americas this was generally done by the rough method seen in cowboy films: tie up the unbroken horse firmly in a small corral and strap on the saddle, stick a rough rider on top, let the horse go and wait for him to stop trying to get rid of the nasty thing on his back. Repeat this process for several days until the bucking reduces or does not start at all. This was mostly done with the local 'stock' or cowboy-type saddle in North America; when the horses reached the British Army, they would have to be accustomed to the smaller European-style saddle.

Pembroke advised that even if described as 'backed', the horse's education should be started again. His method was very much the same as that used today: first the young horse wears a headcollar and is led about with it, then a bridle. The trainer or groom will take every opportunity to lean across the horse's back, first just laying on an arm, then applying more pressure. When this is accepted calmly, the saddle can be put on, girthed loosely to begin with, then more tightly, and finally a lightweight rider can sit on it. Before the saddle is used, the horse will be lunged. This involves a very long rein, fitted either to the far side of the bit and passed through the closer side, or to the centre of the noseband of a type of breaking bridle called a cavesson. The horse is then encouraged to walk further and further away from the trainer (being led by an assistant on the far side, if necessary), going round in a circle. The trainer holds a long whip with a very long thong, with which he follows the horse round. It is for guidance, not punishment. Once the horse understands he is to move in a circle, he can then progress to a trot and finally a canter, doing all this in both directions, and using voice commands.

When the horse is used to doing all this, first without and then with the saddle, a rider can be added, being led at first and then, once the horse is happy with the weight, on his own. The rider gives the aids for the various gaits and halt with his legs and hands as the trainer gives the vocal commands. Then the lunge rein is removed and the rider is on his own, although the trainer is still close by. Finally, the horse is taught to obey the rein aid to turn to left or right, and all the basics are done. Unlike the American system (the 'indirect rein'), where the rein is laid on the horse's neck to direct him to move away from it, the European rein aid is direct, using pressure on one rein to give a signal through the horse's mouth that he should turn in that direction.

Later stages involve the rider adding his back to the hand and leg aids, stiffening his back to 'block' down as a slowing or stop aid, or using one leg to make the horse move his quarters away from the pressure. This latter aid will also have been given when the horse is being led, by the trainer holding the reins/lead rope in one hand and reaching back with the other to push against the horse's side. At some point during this process the horse must be taught to stand still while the rider mounts and wait until he gives the aid to move off. This is a comparatively simple process, consisting of the vocal command 'No' every time he tries to move and praising him when he stops.

Another stage in horse breaking which some trainers of riding horses like to use is long-reining. As the name implies, these are very long reins fastened to a headcollar or bit which the trainer holds while standing behind the horse, closely at first and then further and further back, using voice commands as well as light pressure on the reins. It is an essential part of the techniques used to train a horse to harness. Once the horse is accustomed to the trainer behind him, some lightweight harness can be fitted and a very light object such as a log (or these days, a small tyre) added to drag behind. This stage will require an assistant at the horse's head to reassure him that it is not a dragon behind him. Next, a lightweight two-wheeled cart is substituted for the log, and heavier carts are gradually introduced. Once the horse will go quietly in single harness, he can be introduced to double harness, using a very experienced calm horse alongside him. After this, it is just a matter of increasing the weight and the noisiness of the load.

All this training, for both riding and driving, must be done in small increments, as the object is not only to accustom the horse to the idea of carrying or pulling loads, but also to develop his muscles in the process. He may happily accept the mental parts of his job, but if he is rushed into full work before his muscles are built up, he will soon 'break down' and be useless for a long time or, indeed, for ever.

Lewis Nolan advocated keeping young horses with more experienced animals rather than as a group on their own. A young horse who regularly sees other horses leaving the stables in saddles/harness, and being worked under saddle or pulling a vehicle, will soon come to accept that is what horses do, and will not make a major fuss when he is asked to do it. Nolan also remarked on the inadvisability of using stallions, although there were some regiments in India which did. He said, 'the entire horses when brought into contact, if once they got their noses together, reared, fought, and broke from the ranks'. He did not mention the additional difficulties of handling stallions in the summer when there were 'in heat' mares around.

For the horse whose work will be no more than carrying a rider from point A to point B on roads, there is little more to be done, other than to teach him to cross flimsy bridges. These may move under his feet, and his hooves will make a noise: both clear indications to the equine mind that a troll lurks beneath. As so often, when teaching the young horse to deal with scary new things, the solution is for an experienced older horse to 'give him a lead'. These flimsy bridges may be encountered on back roads or when going across country; in the First World War the cavalry carried their own little fold-up bridges for crossing trench lines. The artillery used a larger stouter version of these.

For the horse whose role is to be in the cavalry, or to carry an officer who needs to move around a battlefield, more is needed. This would include crossing low objects, such as field walls or hedges. A single horse might jump a higher hedge, but en masse such obstacles were more likely to be broken or cut down to an easier height. The obstacle most likely to be encountered going across open country was a ditch, stream or dry river bed. The 23rd Light Dragoons suffered badly at one of these at Talavera in 1809.

It was not the practice for heavy cavalry regiments to teach their horses to jump but light cavalry did, as they were expected to be able to cross any normal country. As a book written by an anonymous author remarked: 'War is never carried on, on a lawn, and seldom on a plain.' In 1758 it was reported that a troop of light dragoons, quartered at Maidenhead, spent some days digging large trenches and jumping their horses over them, and leaping high hedges with broad ditches on the other side. Their captain swam his horse over the Thames and back again and then the whole troop followed. Of course, horses requisitioned from hunting stables in the First World War would have been experienced at dealing with all obstacles.

Pembroke believed, as did several more recent writers, that both horses and riders should be taught to swim in case they needed to cross a river where there was neither bridge nor ford. The horse, once aimed in the right direction, should be given his head, and the rider should take his feet out of the stirrups in case he and the horse parted company.

Once the horse has learned all the basics, his balance needs correction. The newly broken horse tends to go 'on the forehand', with his weight thrown onto the front legs. This is hardly surprising when one considers that the weight of the rider and all his gear is also at the front end of the horse's body. This makes it more difficult for the horse to lift his forelegs and he is thus prone to stumble or even fall on his nose over rough ground at speed. It makes him less manoeuvrable and difficult to stop if he takes it into his head to run away with his rider, as was all too often the result of charging. Over a long period this wears out his forelegs before their time.

The horse needs therefore to adjust his balance, learning to put more weight on his quarters and raising his forehand. This is achieved by working in small circles, with frequent changes of direction, and gradually bringing his head up and his nose in. This should be done initially by teaching the rein-back, at first from the ground; the teacher stands in front of the horse, takes one rein in each hand just behind the bit, and with the vocal command 'Back', gently pushes him until he steps back. The horse's face should be perpendicular during this exercise. This rein contact is next taken up by the rider. Rather than from a complete stand-still, this is best done immediately after stopping, when the horse is effectively still in movement, and the rein-back is almost like a bounce.

The other essential for shifting the horse's balance backwards is that he should be ridden to the halt rather than allowed just to shamble to a stop. The reins are applied first, then the legs to push him forward and 'up to the bit', then the rider tightens his loin and back muscles to 'block down' onto the saddle. It should never be forgotten that the horse's back is sensitive enough to feel the rider's body weight and balance, even through a saddle, and to respond to shifts in these. His free movement is dependent on the rider's ability to move with him and if the rider becomes rigid, the horse's movement is restricted.

Another useful way to increase a horse's suppleness is to ride him in and out of a sequence of upright poles, gradually decreasing the distance between the poles and increasing the pace at which the exercise is performed. This is known as bending and is a popular contest today among young riders at gymkhanas.

Pembroke had more to say on getting horses accustomed to all the things they might encounter in the field of war: 'In order to make horses stand fire, the sound of drums, and all sorts of different noises, you must use them to it [sic] by degrees in the stable at feeding-time; and instead of being frightened of it, they will soon come to like it, as a signal for eating.' The training of horses afraid of burning objects (common in war) should begin by making them stand while some straw is set alight at a distance, making a fuss of them, then increasing the amount of burning straw and decreasing the distance until they are familiar with it and no longer scared. The same applied to the frightening sight of a mass of shining arms, regimental colours and standards, and the sound of swords being drawn and returned to the scabbard. Pembroke also mentioned the scary potential of dead horses, which are naturally frightening to a horse and a common sight (and smell) on the battlefield. In addition, horses must be taught to stand quietly when the rider uses a firearm (having first been accustomed to the sound of firing in the stable at meal-times). They should not move after the weapon is fired until told to. Ideally they should be turned away from the direction of fire, so the bang is not directly over their ears.

Modern army horses still undergo what is now called 'nuisance training', as do police horses. Balloons, waving flags, football rattles, umbrellas and fire-crackers, as well as such modern horse frighteners as skateboards, are all utilised in this training.

Training Riders

The first requirement for teaching someone to ride is a very quiet horse, usually referred to as a schoolmaster. The riding master was supposed to give instructions in '. . . a cool and temperate manner and to refrain from swearing or using improper language, and from harshness to either man or horse'.

The next step is to instruct the rider on what to wear and how to wear it. Obviously in modern military terms their underwear will have been issued and be suitable for the purpose, but in earlier times they might not have been and it was important that the new rider should understand that his genitals needed to be kept up out of the way. Bumping about in the saddle and landing on the testicles is not conducive to happy riding!

The new rider starts by learning how to mount. Facing the rear on the nearside of the horse, take the reins in the left hand, place the left foot in the stirrup and spring up from the right foot whilst pressing down on the stirrup, leaning a little over the horse's back and swinging the right leg up and over the saddle. Once sitting upright, the stirrups can be adjusted to a length which is both comfortable and allows the toes to point upwards. The flat of the stirrup iron should be under the front of the ball of the foot, not with the foot pushed right through which could lead to the rider being caught and dragged if he is thrown (a hazard when the rider wears shoes which do not have a definite heel). Then the thigh muscles need to be adjusted so that a flat surface is against the saddle; this may need to be done manually, by placing a hand under the thigh from the back and gently moving the thigh muscle backwards, but can also be done by putting the leg back, pressing it against the saddle and then dragging it forward. This is comparatively easy for male riders (unless they have fat legs) as their thighs are naturally flattish inside, but can be more of a problem with women whose thighs tend to be fuller. It is necessary to organise the thigh muscles like this as otherwise it will be very difficult for the rider to keep his feet pointing forward rather than at an angle sideways, which may cause the teacher to make rude remarks about penguin feet.

At this stage, the riding master's assistant will be holding the horse; it will then be put on a lunge-rein and the rider taught to relax and feel the way the horse moves underneath him. There was much talk in those days of gripping with the knees to retain the seat, but while this might be useful in a sword fight it is not at this stage. The first lesson will conclude with the rider learning to stop the horse (a most reassuring lesson) and start him. Future lessons will deal with the trot and canter. The canter is easy to sit on, the trot less so until the rider learns to soften his back and absorb the motion, or to 'post' (also known as 'rise') to the trot, although the latter is less used in military riding. Once the pupil is confident at all gaits on the lunge, he can be released to ride on his own and finally in a class. All of this is usually done in an enclosed area, ideally an indoor riding school or manege. Some cavalry regiments had their own riding school; others were trained at Maidstone or Woodbridge, either first or second hand. This training was given by experienced riding masters, rough riders and officers such as Paget and Le Marchant; the pupils, once proficient, went back to their own regiments to pass on their new knowledge to others.

At the start of the First World War it was by no means certain that new officers would be able to ride; this was an increasing problem as more and more young gentlemen grew up in towns rather than in the countryside. As a result, most regiments insisted that officers new to the regiment should attend the riding school for as long as the commanding officer thought necessary.

Fashions in the way the riders sit ('the seat') have changed. In the eighteenth century the normal seat of legs bent at the knee, with a stirrup short enough for the rider to clear the saddle when standing, gave way to a straight leg and the feet thrust forward. This became known as the 'hunting seat', where the rider leaned back over fences. There is a certain merit in this position, as it avoids the commonest fall, which is forward over the horse's shoulder when he trips, pecks on landing or refuses a fence. However, this seat does not help the horse when the rider's weight is thrown backwards, and even on the flat it puts the rider's abdominal muscles in tension which impedes the free movement of his upper body.

This type of seat was gradually overtaken by what is now called the 'forward seat', where the rider sits upright with his lower legs and feet below him. This is referred to by instructors as the 'head, hips, heels' line. This seat gives the rider not only free use of his upper body and arms, but also of his legs, which he will need when putting his legs or feet back to give an aid. To achieve this, his weight should be on his fork, not on his buttocks or tipped forward (testicle hazard!). The advantage of this seat, as well as giving flexibility to the rider, is that it allows him to achieve good balance and what is known as 'an independent seat' without the necessity to grip with the knees. The problem with gripping is that the leg muscles soon fail to function that well, and the rider tends to 'clothespeg' himself up out of the saddle. The advantage of the independent seat is that the rider absorbs not only the normal motion of the horse, but also much of the types of movement that will otherwise unseat him, such as sudden stops, stumbles or shying.

The next stage for the cavalryman was to learn the use of weapons when mounted. This started the same way as for foot soldiers, with the use of the sword, including parrying, especially against blows aimed at his right forearm, wrist and hand. These constituted some 70 per cent of cavalry wounds, with another 20 per cent being to the head.

Prior to 1796, the general standard of swordsmanship was poor. Men were as likely to injure themselves as an enemy, and frequently missed their opponent and gashed not only themselves but also their horse's head and neck. Major General John Gaspard Le Marchant noticed this while serving as a major in Flanders in 1793–1794, and in particular observed the shortcomings of the cavalry sword. After much research and experiment, he designed a new cavalry sword, and produced a manual of exercises.[3] The Duke of York approved both and ordered all light cavalry regiments to be equipped with the new sword and to use Le Marchant's exercises.

The basic sword exercise was the use of the 'six cuts', practised on foot against a circle painted on a wall. This had the addition of crude features to simulate an enemy face, and was divided by three lines: ear to ear, and diagonally left to right and right to left. The pupil stood about 4ft away and practised the cuts. Interestingly, one of the most effective cuts was not one of the six, but rather straight down onto the centre of the skull.

Once proficient in the six cuts on foot, the trooper was then taught some twenty or so sword positions for use on horseback, including nine 'guards', three thrusts, the parry and seven more cuts. There were two basic uses of the sword: the thrust and the cut. The thrust could only be used one way, but extra care was required when using it against cavalry; if the point was parried, the adversary's blade could get within the attacker's guard, and the heavy cavalry sabre could not be recovered in time to fend off further strokes. For this reason, it was recommended that the point should seldom or never be given in the attack, but principally confined to the pursuit, when it can be applied with effect and without risk. Against infantry, since the enemy was well below the attacker's level, the weight of the sword was felt less and could be used more easily than with an extended arm carried above the level of the shoulder, as was needed for a mounted enemy. Therefore in many instances, the point could be used against infantry with as much effect as the edge and with the same degree of security. Cutting at the enemy's bridle was encouraged, to make the horse uncontrollable when the bit fell out of his mouth, or the cut maddened him through pain.

When cutting, the Regulations stated that against cavalry the action should come from the wrist and shoulder without bending the elbow and thus exposing the forearm; against infantry, because the enemy was below the horseman, it was necessary to bend the elbow to obtain sufficient sweep for the cut to take place.

One of Le Marchant's mounted sword exercises taught not only accuracy of attack with a direct stab (known as 'giving point') but also control of the horse. A 4in diameter ring was suspended from a pulley and the rider rode straight at it at speed from various distances and thrust his point through it. If he did not stop his horse in time, the pulley dragged him back and off the horse. This exercise was known as 'running the ring'. Other exercises included attacking a straw-stuffed 'man' and a pumpkin on a pole to represent a head.

The 1796 Regulations remarked on this, saying:

To become a perfect cavalry swordsman, horsemanship is indispensably necessary, and without it, very little benefit can be derived from the science. Good riding does not consist in urging a horse forward with precipitation and checking him with violence, but a dragoon and his horse should be so formed to each other to act as one body; for which purpose the rider should make himself acquainted with the temper and powers of his animal, so that by judicious management, the horse may be rendered docile, and execute readily whatever may be expected of him . . . it is alone by temper and perseverance, not by severity, that vice is to be conquered, and those tricks surmounted which in horses generally originate in timidity.

It also suggested that at an early stage in the rider's education, not only should he learn how to manage both reins in his left hand, but that in his right hand he should carry a switch in the position in which the sword would be carried, and keep that hand under control instead of using it to grab for the mane or saddle in a perceived emergency, saying 'the horseman is to depend on his seat, and not offer to hold himself on by any disgraceful means'. In other words, he should have an independent seat.

The next stage was to teach the horse and rider together to perform the various evolutions. These were opening up and closing up the ranks and turning them in a wheel. To form the line, the order was 'Half Wheel/ Quarter Wheel/One-eighth Wheel'.

When moving in a column, it was to be in ranks of four, with a gap of 3ft 6in between them; these could then wheel about to form the desired type of line. The commanding officer organised his troopers into column of fours by 'telling off' each group of four, starting at the rear, with each group reining back to its new position on the command 'Rear rank take order'. These ranks could be in close, loose or open order; in close order each man's boot-top was touching the next man's, in loose order there was a 6in gap between the boot-tops, while open order had the full breadth of a horse between them. The same thing applied to the line when about to charge. The order for this was 'Take Close/Loose/Open Order – March'. Confusingly, the term 'order' was also used to refer to the distance between the ranks, with 'Order' being 24ft, 'Close Order' 8ft and 'Marching in Fours' 4ft.

After each evolution, and on the march, the horses should be straight and the riders facing forward. They might take a quick glance sideways to check their dressing but should not turn their head.

A good charge was so effective at disintegrating a massed enemy that it came to be regarded by many British cavalrymen as the principal objective of the cavalry and thus its training. This led to the conviction, much ridiculed when later commanders such as Haig expressed it, that a good charge was the answer to all opposition.

There were several ways to charge. The preferred method was to form a main front rank (also known as 'rank entire') to make the charge, riding knee to knee, with a second rank holding well back as a reserve in case of need. Part of the training was in this formation, with the first rank attacking and then moving out of the way, either to regroup for a second charge or to let the reserve move in and pursue the fleeing enemy. Each part of the line was headed by its squadron commander, accompanied by his trumpeter to give the commands. The second method was the charge in echelon; sections charged one at a time with a gap of 100–200yd between them, to hit the enemy line in successive places, one at a time. The third method was in 'echiquer', which was a mixture of the two, retaining the 100–200yd gap. The two ranks (called here A and B) were split into groups (1, 2, 3, etc.) and they charged alternately: A1 and A3, B2 and B4, A2 and B3.

When the enemy was formed into a square, the attack was to be made on one face and at least one corner simultaneously. If necessary, further attacks should be made at 150yd intervals.

The trouble with cavalry charges was that they tended to get out of control; sometimes after the first attack on the enemy they just kept going and could not easily be recalled for a subsequent manoeuvre. This happened at Maguilla in June 1812 when, after initial success, the cavalry just continued on, only then to be routed by the enemy. Wellington was less than impressed. He wrote:

> It is occasioned entirely by the trick our officers of cavalry have acquired of galloping at everything and their galloping back as fast as they gallop on the enemy. They never consider their situation, and never think of manoeuvring before an enemy, so little that one would think they cannot manoeuvre, except on Wimbledon Common; and when they use their arm as it ought to be used, viz. offensively, they never keep nor provide for a reserve.

Wellington produced detailed instructions on charging after Waterloo, emphasising the need for a reserve, but there was no opportunity to put these into action for several decades.

Learning to charge was important because the opportunity to do so was normally short-lived and thus the cavalry needed to form up quickly and precisely. Each regiment tended to have its own training routine until General David Dundas' *Rules and Regulations for Cavalry* was approved by George III for use by all regiments. (Interestingly, Dundas had a reputation for falling off, twice in front of the King, and rotating as he did so, which earned him the nickname 'Pivot Dundas'.) Most training sessions for the cavalry ended with a charge. In a charging situation, the only paces used (and the commands for them) were walk, trot and gallop, with the last two divided into slow and quick. The charge was to start with a walk with the sword drawn and the blade resting on the right arm. Then the pace changed to a brisk trot, the sword hand resting on the right thigh, blade pointing forward. This continued until the enemy were no further away than 250yd, then sped up to a gallop; about 80yd from the enemy the order 'Charge' was given and the gallop increased to the fastest possible with the sword arm lifted until the line crashed into the enemy.

Delivered well, the charge was a devastating attack; one only has to look at Lady Elizabeth Butler's painting of the Royal Scots Greys at Waterloo to imagine what it must have been like for an infantryman facing such a thundering mass of horsemen. The other side of this picture is that many horses refused to 'charge home' against a line of bristling bayonets. Infantry or skirmishers had to go first to break up the line or square, then the cavalry could crash over those who stood still and run down those who fled. These skirmishers rode in two lines about 200yd from the enemy. They might be armed with carbines or pistols, but if the latter they should have their sword suspended from their wrist by its knot. They should always fire to their left, with the butt of their carbine against their right shoulder, partly because it was the most convenient, but also so there were no 'friendly fire' accidents.

The old type of cavalry sabre had an ornate grip and guard; the version for the heavy cavalry had an 8in-long basket guard and a straight blade 39in long, giving a total length of 47in. It weighed 3lb. The version for the light cavalry had a single bar 'stirrup' hilt, was 41in long and curved, with a wide tip. It weighed 3oz less than the heavy version. Before the introduction of Le Marchant's new sabre, there was considerable diversity of swords in use. Heavy cavalry continued to use the old-type sword. Officers' swords tended to be more ornate than those for troopers, and they also had a dress sword which was even more ornate. Further changes were made to the cavalry sword in 1820, 1830 and 1853, when a better 'universal' pattern was adopted.

Lancers, as might be expected, carried a lance: a formidable weapon with a sharp tip mounted on a long pole. It could only be used once (unless the thrust missed) and then at speed, but it was a serious enemy-frightener when used en masse. The favourite practice in its use was tent-pegging, when a tent peg was snatched up off the ground. In India this sport evolved into pig-sticking (against wild boar), a notoriously dangerous activity as an enraged boar, even with a lance through its body, could still kill a dismounted soldier.

Lancers needed to develop a strong hand and were expected to learn fifty-five exercises: twenty-two for use against cavalry, eighteen against infantry and another fifteen for general use, including some for use against enemy cavalry armed with a sword. This was where the lance had a distinct advantage over the sword, but there was one drawback: a sword allows its user to operate in a full circle around himself but a lance can only be used in a half-circle to the front and sides.

The lance was little used by the British Army until it met Napoleon's Polish lancers at Albuera in 1811. The King's German Legion sent a cornet to the 15th Dragoons to teach the use of the lance, but it was not until after Waterloo that its use was taught on a grand scale in the British Army. And even then it was not until 1825 that it was used in anger, at the siege of Bhurtpore by the 16th Lancers. The new Lancer regiments formed in 1816 used a very long lance, some 15 or 16ft, but this proved unwieldy and was soon reduced to 9ft. It carried a small pennant just below the head, and it had a small loop for the arm.

The cavalry also used carbines, originally a very heavy version with a 42in barrel. In 1796 the Board of Officers approved a new, lighter and shorter version for the heavy cavalry, and an even lighter one for the light cavalry. This was 41in long overall, and included a swivel ramrod and a bolted lock.

In 1803 a newer version was introduced, even shorter at 35in, with a rear sight and small compartment for keeping cleaning tools. The difficulty with the use of carbines was that, while it was easy enough for a single man to stop his horse and take careful aim, this was less easy in a group when the horses would be less likely to stand still for long enough for an accurate volley to be delivered.

Dragoons also carried a pistol.[4]

Chapter Ten

Saddlery, Accoutrements and Horse Clothing

Riding Saddles

The back of a horse is a convenient shape for riders, with a dip behind the withers to sit in. However, although a skilled rider can do everything bareback that the less-skilled rider can only do with a saddle (the author prided herself on rising to the trot and jumping bareback), in general a saddle with stirrups is needed, especially for military purposes. The mounted swordsman or lancer needs the security of seat which a properly shaped saddle gives, while being able to push down onto the stirrups allows extra security and a solid base from which to wield the weapon. Stirrups also allow a rider to stand up, giving him a better reach in battle.

However, for the benefit of the horse, the rider's weight should not press down directly onto the animal's spine, so saddles are designed to avoid that. The base of every saddle is a wood and metal frame known as the tree. This consists of two arches, one at the front over the withers and the other at the back behind the seat. The front arch is steeper and longer than the back arch to accommodate the higher spinal processes at the withers. These arches are connected by two side boards, shaped to fit the back of the horse below the spine; these join the front and back arches.

Underneath are two pads, one fastened to each side board, which hold the top of the saddle off the horse's back, leaving a gap in the middle (front to back) to allow air to pass beneath the saddle and also to prevent it rubbing. In a civilian situation, each saddle can be fitted to an individual horse by adjusting the padding, but in the field a saddle needs to be usable on any horse, so a more universal type of pad was used.

On top of the tree are the straps to which the girth is attached, and on top of those there is a flap, at the top of which can be seen the bars to which the stirrups are attached. The flap extends downwards to a point which corresponds with about half the length of the rider's calf. The top of the saddle is called the seat, and on each side is a small flap called the skirt which covers the stirrup bars. In various places around the edges of the saddle are fitted rings, usually D-shaped, for attaching various items. At the front there may be a breastplate to prevent the saddle slipping back, and at the rear a crupper which fits over the horse's tail to prevent the saddle slipping forward.

Ideally all the leather used for saddles is pigskin, but sometimes the flaps are made of ox-hide. In India and the Middle East saddlery made of such hides might be religiously offensive, so alternatives such as horse-skin were used. A well-made saddle of these leathers can last for up to thirty years or more, but is less likely to do so in military use, especially in damp conditions which will cause the stitching to rot. Battle damage, such as sword slashes or bullet holes, may require parts of the saddle to be replaced. A regimental saddler may not have been able to carry out major repairs in the field, such as replacing the seat, but could make simple repairs.

As with other equipment, the purchase of saddlery was dealt with by the colonels of regiments until 1855 when the Army Ordnance Department took over the task. One of the favourite suppliers of Peninsular War officers was Giddens, which commenced business in 1806 and took over many of the other long-established firms in a sequence of amalgamations, including Whippy & Stegall and Champion & Wilton; they still have a shop in London as well as one in Newmarket for the racing fraternity.

Until the mid-eighteenth century military saddles had high built-up pommels and cantles and sometimes padding on the front and back of the flaps, all intended to keep the rider in place; this was a necessity when the rider wore armour, which tended to unbalance him.

Changes in the type of saddle used by the army came after Frederick, Duke of York, spent some time in Germany to study soldiering, using the example of the Prussian Army. He found the Prussian cavalry and its equipment impressive, and took home examples of the saddles used by the Life Guards (heavy cavalry) and the Hussars (light cavalry). A few years later, in 1796, the Board of Ordnance recommended a new type of saddle for the heavy cavalry, based on the Prussian model. The new design was of brown leather with black straps, with the panel (sometimes spelled pannel) and pad in one piece and removable. The breastplate was a single strap fitted well below the pommel and the crupper was divided in two. The girth was 4in wide and divided into three for the buckles. The stirrup irons were square sided. Saddles like this remained in use until after the Crimean War.[1] The new type for the light cavalry came into use in 1805 and those for other light units in 1812. Based on the Prussian hussar saddle, these had a fairly high pommel and cantle, the seat being covered by a fitted sheepskin and shabraque, held on by a surcingle or second girth. Some, rather than having thick padding underneath, were fitted on top of a felt pad called a numnah or on a folded blanket. The advantage of the blanket was that it could be folded more thickly as horses lost weight on long campaigns.

The problem with the hussar-style saddle was that it was designed to be taken apart and put on the horse piece by piece, which was time-consuming if horses had to be saddled in a hurry, especially at night. The solution to this was for front-line units to keep their horses saddled at night, with each rider sleeping on the ground at his horse's head, holding the reins.

Some army saddles after this period were made with 'fans' – extensions of the side boards out behind the cantle. Padded like the rest of the saddle, and sometimes with a spoon-like cantle which extended out behind the rider and upwards at a shallow angle, these provided a convenient space for a rolled blanket or cloak. Some officers carried their cloak rolled and attached to the pommel. It was suggested at one point that other ranks should carry their blanket rolled and slung diagonally across their chest as a form of light armour.

Drivers (known in civilian terms as postillions) of artillery and other teams, who rode on the near-side horse of each pair, had saddles with low cantles and very short fans, if any. These saddles did not have the usual attachments to carry the driver's accoutrements, as his baggage was carried on a small saddle or blanket pad on the off-side horse.

In 1855 the Board of Ordnance was abolished. It had historically been a separate organisation, belonging neither to the Army nor to the Navy, but issuing guns and other weaponry to both. It was replaced by the Army Ordnance Department, which took over the duties of the old Board of Ordnance, including the testing and selection of saddles and harness and the subsequent contracts for manufacturing and then the issue of approved types. From then on, the rule was uniformity in everything, including saddlery.

This did not mean, however, that attempts to improve things ceased. In 1855 a Board of Cavalry Officers was formed to report on the best type of saddle. After much deliberation they recommended a saddle with a wooden tree with long points at the front, to prevent the saddle rolling sideways. These trees should be made in three sizes, small (number 1), medium (number 2) and large (number 3), number 1 being ½in smaller in every direction than number 2, and number 3 being ½in larger. Of every batch of saddles supplied, at least half should be number 2, with a quarter each of numbers 1 and 3. They opted for panels, although folded blankets could still be used with emaciated horses. An alternative to the panel was the numnah, placed on the horse with a saddle cloth on top. Instruction in tree-making was organised at the cavalry depot at Maidstone, the first instructor to be appointed being master saddle-tree-maker Sergeant Bird of the 12th Lancers, whom they described as 'a most ingenious mechanic'.

Anxious to reduce the weight of the saddle, the Board wanted to abolish the sheepskin seat cover and the shabraque, as together these weighed between 6 and 7lb. The Universal Pattern saddle which they recommended would weigh about 15lb with panels, which themselves could weigh up to 6lb, being heavily stuffed with horsehair. The 'Universal Pattern Wood Arch Saddle' was used by all regiments except the Household Cavalry.

Further modifications followed until another Universal Pattern saddle – the Steel Arch Universal Pattern Mark I – was approved in 1884. This version had steel arches, but there was a serious flaw in that the front arch tended to flatten if the saddle was dropped, a fairly common occurrence when attempting to put on a heavily loaded saddle at night. Another flaw was that the leather seat had a slit cut along the middle, from front to back, but this was found to 'pinch the men', as it was delicately described, and this slit was omitted from the Mark II.

In 1891 Frederick Smith, who later became the Director General of the Royal Army Veterinary Corps, produced a manual based on a series of lectures he had given at the Army Veterinary School at Aldershot.[2] In this manual he pointed out that sore backs are never accidental, but are caused by poorly fitting saddles or bad riding. Bad riding is simply the result of an (often insecure) rider who moves around in the saddle or leans to the side, thus putting his weight and pressure in the wrong place. Poor fitting of the saddle also puts weight in the wrong place and can usually be remedied by adjusting the padding. This is not easy to do in the field, however, except by using a folded blanket, but should be done by the regiment's saddler at home.

The basic principle is that the saddle should not, at any point, touch the horse's spine, but sit on the muscles either side of the spine. As the horse 'falls away' in condition on a long campaign, it is important that the fit of his saddle is checked every day. Smith also discussed injuries to draught horses, such as sore shoulders caused by the shape and incorrect fitting of the collar or breast harness.

The other injury associated with saddles is the girth-gall, often caused by lack of condition in the horse when his skin is soft and thus vulnerable to rubbing by a hard girth. Often the galls occur when the saddle is not tight enough, which sometimes results when the horse blows itself out on saddling. Although some riders swear by a sharply applied knee behind the girth, it is best to wait a minute and tighten the girth before mounting, and again after riding for an hour or so. Smith believed that a new type of girth was better; instead of a single set of straps attached directly to the tree, this had two straps, one from the front and the other towards the back of the tree, which came together in a V-shape and were attached there to a thick leather plate known as the sweat flap, with the girth straps attached to that. This arrangement gave enough stability that it was possible to dispense with the extended points at the front of the tree. He also believed that a folded blanket was better than the padded panel, and in due course that practice was adopted, along with the V-girth.

Smith wrote a whole chapter on how to fold saddle blankets. They were 5ft 6in long by 4ft 8in wide and the regulation method was to fold them with six folds under the front arch of the saddle and four under the rear arch. He also mentioned six and three folds, nine and three folds and even twelve and three folds. He described how to achieve these numbers of folds, then remarked that he had found these instructions difficult to describe on paper and suggested practising them with a blanket or a piece of paper scaled down to 5½in by 4¾in. However many folds were used, the blanket should never touch the spine as any movement from the saddle would drag it about and cause sores. The standard method of ensuring a proper fit was to put two hands under the centre of the blanket, and adjusting it if this space was insufficient.

Other galls which are likely to occur in a horse in soft condition are from accoutrements such as buckets and other equipment containers attached to the saddle, especially if they are left with a long strap which lets them bang up and down.

The stirrup consists of two parts: the stirrup iron, a D-shaped piece with a flat base on which the foot rests, and the leather, a plain strap with a buckle at one end and holes near the other so the length can be adjusted. This leather slides over the bar, the end of which can be turned up to keep the leather in place; this is usually not done as it is safer for a rider who falls off backwards as the stirrup will then come off the saddle so he is not dragged.

By 1912 the Universal Pattern saddle had changed again. The front and rear steel arches were now jointed, and the long points at the front had been dispensed with, as the new V-shaped girth attachment was found to give adequate stability.

There was a serious shortage of horse equipment in the early part of the First World War, exacerbated by the need to supply the initial mobilisation of the British Expeditionary Force. This shortage became so severe that the War Office appealed for the civilian owners of spare hunter-sized saddlery to donate it, complete with girths and stirrups; bridles were also required. Although such items could not be used by the BEF itself, they could be used for training.

Part of the problem was the small number of British saddleries who could make military saddles and harness. The other part was a shortage of the right sort of leather to make these items. However, the right sort of leather and the necessary expertise were available in America and Canada, and by February 1915 they were providing large quantities of saddlery.

There was also a shortage of saddles in the Boer War. No one in high authority believed that this war would be prolonged or that large numbers of mounted troops would be needed. In 1899 some 16,000 sets of saddlery were already on issue but the reserve was a mere 500 sets; in the event, some

30,000 sets were needed in Natal alone. During the course of this war over 76,000 sets were purchased, including some US Cavalry saddles, which were not a great success due to the different method of girthing, which was not generally understood. Many of the saddles sent to South Africa were lost when horses foundered on the march and had to be abandoned, complete with their saddles: a welcome prize for the enemy.

The average weight carried by a saddle horse in the Boer War was just over 20 stone (281lb). This included the rider at 166lb, his greatcoat, forage nets, saddle blanket and numnah at 27lb, the saddle with wallets and other attachments such as the carbine bucket at 31lb, and various other items including forage for the horse, food for the rider, and small arms with their ammunition.

To put on the saddle, the saddle blanket, if used, should be put on first, with the centre pulled up to keep the spine clear, then the saddle should be placed gently on top, either in the correct place or a little forward, from where it can be slid back. It should never be placed too far back and slid forward, as this pushes the hair the wrong way and will irritate the horse. A hand slipped under the pommel and then the cantle will ensure neither is resting on the spine. The strap of the breastplate is then slipped between the front legs and the girth put through it and loosely done up (to be tightened before mounting). The crupper is slipped over the horse's tail and slid into position. Where a shabraque is used, it is placed over the saddle and held in place with a flat surcingle.

Side-saddles, as well as being used by royal ladies when inspecting troops, were also used by the First Aid Nursing Yeomanry (FANY). This volunteer unit was raised in 1909 as a mounted unit, before women riding astride became common. Earlier versions of the side-saddle were fitted with a single upright pommel around which the rider hooked her right knee, with a second pommel on the offside of the saddle so she wedged her knee between the two, but by the time the FANY was formed the standard side-saddle had a single pommel for the right knee and another curved pommel mounted on the near side of the saddle. This was known as the 'leaping head' and fitted loosely over the left thigh. For jumping, or when the horse was playing up, the rider could bring her left knee up and lock herself on by gripping the two pommels. All versions of the side-saddle had a stirrup for the left leg, with a breakaway fitting at the top of the stirrup leather.[3]

Side-saddles require special girthing to prevent the back of the saddle slipping sideways to the near side. There are two ways in which this can be done: the first is a separate strap, known as the balance strap, which goes from the front girth strap on the near side to a separate girth strap attached to the rear off-side of the saddle; the second is a shorter strap sewn to the girth on the offside which goes to that rear strap.

Bridles

The bridle is the main method of controlling a horse, whether ridden or driven, by the use of reins which go from the horse's mouth to the rider's (or driver's) hand. Just as the horse's back is conveniently shaped for a saddle, so the horse's mouth is conveniently shaped to take a bit, having a gap between the incisors at the front and the molars at the back, across which the bit fits over the tongue, with the ends of the bit in the corners of the mouth. Control is achieved either by pulling the bit straight back against the corners of the mouth, using reins attached to a bridoon bit (now commonly known as a snaffle), or by applying pressure to the bars of the bottom jaw with a curb bit. Pressure is simultaneously applied on the chin groove through the 'curb chain', which is attached to the bit on either side and fits snugly into the groove behind the chin. This pressure is greater or lesser depending on the length of the side bars of the bit and the point at which the reins are attached. Either or both of these bits may have a central joint, and the curb, if un-jointed, may have a 'port', which is a raised section in the middle of the bit to fit over the tongue.

Until late in the eighteenth century military bridles used an unjointed curb bit only, but during the nineteenth century the bridoon was added, creating what is known to civilian riders as the 'double bridle'; with this, the bridoon is used to raise the horse's head and the curb to lower it. From 1902 the pre-ferred military bit was the Universal Pattern Reversable or 'elbow' bit, which is a single bit incorporating the action of both. This bit has two sets of reins and in the civilian world is known as a Pelham. There are two places where the curb rein can be attached to the bit, allowing the severity of the bit to be modified.

The bridle is held together by the browband, a leather strap long enough to fit across the horse's face just below his ears. It has a loop at each end, through which the other leather parts of the bridle pass, continuing up behind the ears. These consist of the strap of the noseband, and the cheekpieces which hold the bit in place. Where two bits were used, the bridle had one cheekpiece for each. The cheekpiece is a single strap which passes from one side of the bit up through the loop of the browband, over the horse's head behind the ears, and down through the loop on the other side of the browband and then buckles to a shorter piece from the other side of the bit. The Pelham or Universal Pattern bit needs only one cheekpiece. The main cheekpiece incorporates the throat-lash (or throat-latch), which goes, as its name suggests, from below the browband around the horse's cheek by his throat, preventing the bridle slipping forward. For added security, the cheekpieces may be sewn on to the bit rather than buckled.

One variation of the bridle incorporated a leather headcollar, and the Board of Cavalry Officers recommended this sort. As described above, the bits were attached by a separate strap through the browband, but the Board felt that the reins should be sewn on to the rings of the bit rather than buckled. Some cavalry regiments also had a metal rein, made of chain, to prevent the rider losing control when the enemy cavalry slashed at his reins with a sword.

There was also a collar-rein, used for leading the horse or tying him up, which the Board felt should be made of twisted white horse-hide and rope; a length of chain could be used to attach the collar-rein to the headcollar, but the chain was prone to breaking and could not be easily repaired in the field, whereas the rope version could be spliced.

The Board recommended that all metal parts should be galvanised to prevent rust, and submitted samples of the types of bits they approved. These were not, however, approved by Major General Cardigan, then Inspector General to the Cavalry, who thought the bits too large and clumsy, fit only for a dray-horse, and the whole bridle ugly: 'hideous and disfiguring'.

There are many variations on bits and bitting in the civilian world, including the unpleasantly harsh 'twisted' snaffle (either a straight twisted bar or a jointed one), but none of these is used in a military situation. Civilian bridles also usually have a separate noseband, to the back of which can be attached a standing martingale, a strap which runs through a neckstrap between the horse's front legs to the girth. A variation on this is called the running martingale, which divides and ends in a pair of rings through which the reins (complete with 'stops' to prevent the rings sliding too far forward) are passed. Martingales are used to prevent the horse throwing his head up, an action which can be painful to the rider if it coincides with the rider's head being thrown forward.

Nosebands and browbands were often used for ornamentation. Decorative bosses were added to the browband, often with a matching boss on the bit. By 1812 cross-pieces went from the browband to the noseband, complete with a boss in the centre, and some also had an ornamental throat-piece with a suspended medallion or plume of feathers. By 1825 Hussars' bridles were covered with cowrie shells. All these decorations were confined to officers' horses, and were only worn in ceremonial situations.

The officer's bridle of the Royal Horse Guards from 1870 was made 'of black patent leather, mounted with brass D-wire buckles, and ornamented with brass bosses, rosettes and scales on the headpiece, studded with steel; the scales are in the form of half Maltese crosses, studded with steel, the centre one being double'. The scales were intended to prevent an opponent cutting through the headpiece of the bridle, thus letting the bit fall out of the horse's mouth and rendering him uncontrollable. The description continues:

> ... the head-piece should be cut two inches wide, thirty inches long and split up eight inches at each end, by a piece being cut out of the centre, so

as to leave two straps, three-quarters of an inch wide, at each side, one to take the cheek of the bridle and the other for the throat band. ... The bit is ... mounted with handsome brass bosses, bearing the Royal crest in the centre – viz. a lion on a crown, surrounded by a motto – to correspond with the rosettes. ... For dress purposes there is a head and rein for bridoon, covered with oak pattern lace.[4]

To put on the bridle, first the headcollar, if worn, is undone, slipped off the head and done up again round the neck; alternatively a lead rope is looped around the neck, both to prevent the horse escaping. The reins of the bridle are put over the head and laid on the neck, then the headpiece of the bridle is presented to the top of the face, with the bit/s in front of the teeth. Many horses will open their mouth to receive the bit, and some will even reach down to take it. For those which do not, the thumb of the left hand is slipped into the mouth between the two sets of teeth and pressed down to open it. In very cold weather a kind person warms the bit/s in his hand first.

Accoutrements

The Board of Cavalry Officers suggested that a cloth should be attached at the front of the saddle to cover the cloak and wallets, and a waterproof one at the back to protect the cylindrical valise. This valise was made of tough cloth or leather, about 2ft 3in long and about 7in wide. It bore regimental devices, or the number of the regiment, stamped on each end, and was used to carry small personal items, such as a spare shirt and shaving kit. Where a shabraque was used, it would cover the valise. The covering cloth could be of a different colour for different regiments, thus making identification easier at a distance. Covering cloths were phased out in the 1870s for officers and in 1894 for other ranks.

The wallet currently in use was, the Board said, too heavy and too small, being made of thick tough leather; they recommended it should be replaced with one made of stout canvas and made large enough to carry a pair of horse shoes as well as the grooming equipment currently carried. All regiments should also have a shoe case, like the one currently in use by the 4th Light Dragoons, which had a strap to fasten the shoes by the toes, which should be stored toe up.

Cardigan did not approve of the proposed canvas wallets either; he thought they were 'most unseemly in appearance' and would not be waterproof. It appears he was more concerned with looks than practicality. Another item approved by the Board but disliked by Cardigan was the mud boots or galoshes known as antigropelos. He thought they were so large they would be an inconvenience in the men's tents and were likely to be left behind in an alert, and once again referred to the look of these boots, saying there was 'something so unmilitary in hussars and dragoons being dressed in mud boots, that it is to me quite painful to reflect upon such plans'.

A new type of corn sack had been approved, with the opening in the middle rather than at one end, and made narrow at the centre so the sack would fit better behind the saddle. However, the manufacturer made the first batch of these too narrow at the centre, so it was difficult to fill them without spillage. A new 'feed bag' (nose-bag) was proposed, made of stout canvas (double at the base) with a canvas head-strap with metal eyeholes and buckle. This was lighter than the conventional nose-bag, made of a coarser material, which was difficult to carry on horseback. As these nose-bags were perishable in the field, the quartermaster general's stores should include an 'ample supply' of them. Likewise, the stores were also to include a supply of spare numnahs for extra padding when expeditionary horses' condition 'fell away' on long campaigns.

The Board disapproved of the current cavalry cloak. These were said to be quite useless in the service, and the men posted as vedettes were not allowed to wear them even in bad weather as they enveloped the arms to such an extent that they could not use their weapons. The Board recommended that the cloak should be superceded by a loose greatcoat with sleeves and a back-band to gather in its width behind when worn on foot. There should also be a waterproof cape, to be attached to the neck of the coat, or worn on its own, with the greatcoat remaining rolled up on the saddle except at night or in cold weather. The coat itself should have a collar with the regiment's facings.

The Board also discussed other items of clothing, including the mud-boots which Cardigan so disliked. These were actually leather leggings designed to cover the leg between the knee and the short-ankled shoes called highlows which preceded the Wellington boot.

Each man carried a wooden picket pin and rope for the hind legs of his horse, and the Transport Corps carried longer pins to support a breast-high rope to which the horses were tied by their collar-rein. This breast-high rope was an improvement on earlier versions where the rope was close to the ground, making it too easy for horses to get a foot over their collar-rein, at which they might panic and pull back, inflicting rope burns on their heels. Each man also carried the grooming kit for his horse, consisting of a brush and curry comb, a mane comb and sponge, and a 'horse picker' (now known as a hoof-pick) to remove dirt and small stones from the sole of the hoof.

A 'bucket' was attached to the front of the saddle to carry a carbine, pistol-carbine or lance, as appropriate to the regiment. The lance bucket fitted the base of the lance-pole, which was held upright by the rider until needed. There was a new type of lance, which the Board approved, and in its final report it included a comprehensive list of exercises with the new lance.[5] Some men also carried a spade, a felling axe and a woodsman's 'bill' in a 'churn', and all carried their picket pin in a narrow pipe.

Pack Saddles

Much of the equipment needed in the field was (and still is in some remote or mountainous areas) more conveniently carried by pack animals, especially where there were no roads at all, such as in thick forest, or where existing roads were unsuitable for wheeled transport. A heavily laden wagon will soon cut up the surface and become bogged down in wet conditions, where an individual animal can pick its way through the mud or large stones. Equally, in hot dry countries wagons cannot cope with thick sand, but camels can. Each type of pack animal needs its own type of saddle, and these also vary according to the load.

Mules can carry about 200lb, and know exactly what that weight feels like, often refusing to budge if the load is heavier. In the Peninsular War Commissary General Kennedy wrote to the Victualling Board asking for the salt meat to be supplied in smaller barrels. The normal '100lb barrel' actually weighed a lot more, as the stated weight referred to the dry contents, not including the weight of the metal-bound barrels and the brine which preserved the meat. The mules would tolerate a 112lb sack of biscuit on each side, but no more. Camels can carry up to 400lb each, and elephants up to three times more than that.

Due to the shape of an elephant's back – sloping from the shoulder to the tail, and with a high spine – pack saddles for them needed to be well padded on either side with a gap in the middle for the spine. They also needed a breast strap and a crupper to prevent the load slipping forward on steep slopes. With a flat platform or cradle fitted across the top of the pads, mortars or heavy parts of guns could be carried. Elephants do not wear bridles, but are controlled by a mahout sitting on their neck.

Bactrian (two-humped) camels have been used for pack-work in central Asia but were rarely used by the British Army, unlike the dromedary (single-humped), which was and still is used throughout the Middle East, North Africa and northern India. Camels of either type need a saddle which does not touch any part of the hump. This means carefully fitting the saddle to each beast. The weight is carried either in front of the hump, or on a platform mounted on pads fore and aft of the hump. As well as carrying small items packed into boxes or sacks, camels were used to carry artillery pieces in teams of seven: one to carry the gun itself, three for the gun carriage and wheels, and three more for the ammunition.

There were several types of General Service patterns of pack saddles for camels. The Egyptian Pattern Mark I was approved in 1900. This had V-shaped wooden arches connected at the top by a metal rod and at the lower edges by wooden sidebars. The front arch was 16½in high and 28in wide across the base, while the back arch was 9in high and 16in wide. Across the sides of the two arches were two pairs of stretcher bars to keep the saddle arch apart, and underneath were padded panels. Rings and thongs were attached for the girth and breast straps. This saddle could be used to carry either two wounded men in cacolets (a sort of chair for those who could sit up) or one flat stretcher across the top. A shade was included for the man's head. The most recent form of approved camel pack saddle, known as the Baladi Pattern, was similar to the Mark I, and came into use just before the Second World War.

As with equines, camels suffered sore backs from ill-fitting pack saddles, especially when they were not removed for several days. This happened on the Nile expedition of 1884–1885, when many camels developed open sores, with attendant maggots.

Nets and ropes were used to attach other loads to the saddle. Camels wore a simple headcollar, steered by a rope attached under the chin; this was an improvement on the earlier local system of a rope through their nose.

The simplest form of pack saddle for equines consists of a blanket or thick pad with pairs of sacks over the top, these sacks either containing the load, or being stuffed and suspended on either side to form a pad for the load. The first British Universal Pattern pack saddle was called the Otago, after the location in New Zealand where miners invented it, using it for riding as well as carrying their equipment. It consists of a simple saddle shape, held in place with girth, breast plate and crupper, and has additional straps fitted on the side to secure the load. The Commissariat 'discovered' the Otago saddle during the war against the Maoris in New Zealand in 1864. Although there were specialised saddles for carrying such things as ammunition boxes or parts of guns as top loads, the Otago was considered the best all-purpose pack saddle.

Another type, known as the Sawbuck, consists of two crossed pieces of wood, much like a carpenter's sawhorse, with side bars to hold the crossed pieces together. Platforms could be added to the tops of these if required, or panniers on the sides.

The pack saddles used by the British Army in the Peninsular War were of a type known as the Devonshire crook after its origin on the farms of southwest England. Two strong willow saplings were cut while green and bent and tied into the required shapes for the front and back arches. Once these had dried out and their shape was fixed, they were connected by side boards. The length of these was dependent on the intended load: short for heavy loads such as sacks of potatoes and longer for lighter loads such as sheaves of corn. These soon evolved into beechwood trees for army use. Infantry battalions had thirteen mules with these saddles, cavalry regiments fourteen and some more to carry their portable forges, armourers' tools and saddler's equipment, plus one each for the surgeon's equipment and the paymaster's books.

The Commissariat hired thousands of mules (with their muleteers) in Spain and Portugal, not because they needed that many but because the muleteers were reluctant to travel far from their home villages and took their mules (and their saddles) with them. Mule pack saddles were quite heavy but very satisfactory, being mainly used to carry a pair of panniers attached at the top and tied together under the mule's belly.[6]

In the Crimea Temple Goodman remarked that he wished he could get an English pack saddle, as the local ones did not fit his cob, whose back was rubbed by carrying baggage hung on a plain saddle.

A new General Service pack saddle with an adjustable tree was introduced in 1904 and has been in use ever since. The steel arches are quite small, and the way the side boards are attached makes it adjustable. They can be turned as far as the horizontal, thus making it possible for the saddle to fit any animal, from a broad-backed horse to a narrow-backed donkey. They could be fitted with a wooden frame to carry machine guns as top loads, with additional lower boards for ammunition boxes. Used on a strong horse, they could also carry a cacolet on each side.

In Sicily, in the Second World War, there were plenty of mules available but the local pack saddles were not up to military loads and galled the animals' backs. The troops improvised with pick handles, ropes and blankets, but these were rarely available in sufficient quantities.

Where possible, personnel who were going to be working with pack animals should practise fitting and loading them. At home, a vaulting horse of the type found in gymnasia was useful for this. It was important to be able to load and unload the animal quickly, as standing around under a load unnecessarily is tiring; animals should be loaded as close as possible to departure time, and unloaded during long stops.

Other Horse Clothing

The first winter of the First World War was particularly harsh. Fortunately, the Director of Remounts had asked the Ordnance Department for more rugs and blankets at the end of 1914. Although saddle blankets could be used to keep equines warm at night in the winter, it was better to use shaped horse rugs which would stay in place. These covered the back and were cut to meet across the breast where they were buckled. These fitted rugs allowed the animal to lie down and move about without dislodging the rug. A padded surcingle passed over the back just behind the withers to buckle on one side. When a fitted rug was not available, an improvised version could be made from an ordinary blanket and some stones and string. One stone on each corner of the rug, and one in the middle were fixed in place by pushing them upwards under the blanket and tying them in place with the string, the long ends of which then tied the two 'lumps' together under the horse's belly at front, middle and back.

For use where the animal was under cover, or in dry climates, these rugs were usually made of jute, bound with leather, but where it was wet they needed to be waterproof and were made of canvas; as lighter waterproof materials were invented, they were adopted for rugs. Whatever material was used for the rugs, the wise horseman followed the old dictum: 'Always see the rug is well forward. Keep your horse's heart warm and you keep all of him warm.'

Furniture

Rugs and blankets were strictly functional, but there were other items of 'furniture' or 'trappings' which were purely for display purposes at reviews and other formal occasions. Large saddle cloths might be embroidered on the back corners; the shabraque might also extend backwards or be augmented behind by separate housings. Both could be rectangular or reach back and down to a point, and were ornamented with ribbon as well as the regimental crest and the names of famous successful campaigns. The same applied to holster covers. Some hussar regiments used a cheetah or leopard skin as a shabraque, either cut straight at the sides and enhanced with lace, or complete with the paws (and claws) on each side. The front legs hung down, while the hind legs were attached to the breastplate straps. The head, stuffed soft, and with artificial eyes and tongue, sat behind the cantle, tied to the crupper. The tail hung on the nearside of the horse's neck.

British cavalry units abandoned the shabraque at the beginning of Edward VII's reign. All these showy accoutrements were mainly for officers; the higher the rank of the officer, the more ornate these were.

Care of Saddlery and Other Tack

The instructions were that all tack should be handled with care, not dropped or thrown, which could damage the tree, or laid down where a horse might step on it. When not in use, bridles should be hung up as though on a horse's head, and saddles placed on a rack or saddle horse with the cantle outwards. In the field, where these items were not available, tack should be kept under cover, with the saddle placed upright, resting on its pommel with the cantle upwards. The stirrups and girth could be hung over the cantle and the bridle draped over it (but not forced down as this might stretch it). The saddle blanket should be placed over the whole, unless the pad was wet, in which case it should be left clear for the air to reach it. Wet blankets should be spread out to dry. Wet leather should not be left near a fire as this will dry it out too much and render it vulnerable to splitting. Black leather should, according to an instruction given to Horse Guards and dragoons preparing for a review, after cleaning, be 'blacked', perhaps with boot polish?

Stitching and buckles on saddles, bridles and harness should be checked at least once a week and repaired immediately if worn or stretching. Girths should be buckled on different holes each side and stirrup leathers replaced if worn around the buckles or holes. Surfaces which come into direct contact with the horse are prone to building up accretions of sweat; this should be brushed off pads and washed off leather. This should be done gently with a sponge, warm (never hot) water and soap. The instructions do not define the soap, but it would have been a form of soft soap. Nowadays there is a yellowish-coloured commercial saddle soap which comes in a tin or as a bar of glycerine soap. Once washed, the leather should be dried with a soft cloth. A knife should not be used to scrape built-up sweat from leather or other materials. The Army Service Corps instructions for 1917 say that leather girths should be treated with grease to keep them supple, but do not specify the type of grease.[7] Bits and other metal items, if made of iron or steel, should be wiped over with water, then with an oily rag, to prevent rust forming.

Chapter Eleven

Harness, Wagons and Order of March

Harness

There is a simple rule for carrying loads on wheeled vehicles: the heavier the load, the more horsepower is required, whether from an engine or from one or more horses. And where horses are concerned, this requires different connections from vehicle to horse, and different types of vehicle.

The smallest and lightest load carrier is called a cart, drawn by a single horse harnessed between two long (usually wooden) shafts. With a light load and good roads, the cart can achieve good speeds; the driver sits at the front of the cart and uses long reins. For a heavier load, the driver walks, leading the horse, with the reins hooked up out of the way. Such loads must be carefully balanced, with as much weight as possible at the front of the vehicle, as otherwise it may lift the shafts, and sometimes even the horse.

For heavy loads a four-wheeled wagon is used, drawn by at least one pair of horses harnessed to a single shaft called a pole, which extends from the centre of the wagon.

Vehicle harness has three functions: to attach the horse and its motive power to the pole or shafts via heavy straps called traces; to provide some stopping power with breeching (in harness use, this is a strong broad strap which fits about 12in below the horse's tail) on which the horse can 'sit'; and to connect the horse's best pulling point (the neck and shoulders) to the rest. There are two methods of doing the latter, the first being the 'horse collar' which is used where weighty loads are involved. The collar needs to be fitted to the individual horse by adjusting the padding, so collars are not used in battlefield situations where the loss of a draught horse with this collar cannot simply be rectified by finding a spare horse. The second type is the breast harness, which is easily adaptable to any horse. As the name implies, it is a substantial item which fits round the horse's breast, with straps to hold it in place over the neck just in front of the withers and to connect it to the traces. In some cases, where the 'driver' rides, further straps may connect the traces to a crupper. These are kept in place by a girth.

With multiple pairs of horses, linkages are needed between each pair and the vehicle. The first of these is the swingletree,[1] a large triangular metal piece which attaches to the vehicle by a swivel at the apex of the triangle and is wide enough across the base to attach the traces in a straight line. The other is called the whippletree or sometimes a double tree (or confusingly, the swiveltree). This is a horizontal bar, connected from its centrepoint to the vehicle by a chain between the two horses, and from its ends to the team in front. They can be hooked up in sequence when using more than four horses. Apart from their use to provide multiple horse power for a wagon, they are essential for use with artillery pieces which often have to change direction at speed.

Artillery

Horse artillery consists of two main pieces, the limber (closest to the team) and the gun, and sometimes also the caisson. The gun, when in use, sits on its two wheels and a rear extension called a trail. In action, this trail rests on the ground to give the gun stability, while the other wheels are removed to the rear with the horses. In motion, the trail is attached to the limber, which also has two wheels. The caisson is a two-wheeled cart which could carry the gun and ammunition but could also carry spare wheels and limber poles.

The rough rule for the number of horses required for each gun says that the size of the ball dictates the number of horses: thus, 4-pounder guns needed four horses and 6-pounders needed six (although twelve were required for 9-pounders). An artillery battery of six heavy guns could involve as many as 200 horses, in addition to those needed for ammunition and supply wagons, plus up to ten for the officers and support staff such as surgeons and farriers.

The field artillery was there to support the infantry battalions to which they belonged; thus they did not have to be fast and the gunners usually walked alongside their gun. The drivers were often hired civilians and the horses belonged to them. The gunners were supposedly trained infantrymen but this training was often perfunctory.

Siege guns were much bigger, and usually moved on four-wheeled wagons. The purpose of these heavy guns was to create a breach in the besieged walls, in the hope that the fallen masonry would create a slope up which the attackers could scramble. Defences outside the walls would include scarps and glacis, cleared areas which the attackers would have to cross in the face of the defenders' weaponry. To avoid this, the Royal Engineers were called in to dig trenches and saps.

In 1793 the Horse Artillery was created to support the cavalry troops to which they belonged. Their guns were usually 4- or 6-pounders, built and mounted to the same pattern as the field guns, but a little lighter so they were able to move faster.

For this reason the drivers and gunners were all mounted so they could keep up with the cavalry. The Horse Artillery was originally staffed by the civilian Royal Corps of Artillery Drivers, but this was not successful; its officers were uninterested in their duty and the corps was described as an Augean stable, being especially notorious in the Peninsula. After Waterloo it was subsumed into the rest of the Royal Horse Artillery (RHA).

The King's Troop was created in 1803 at Woolwich, where it was responsible for improving the standard of riding in the RHA. It remained there until the outbreak of the Second World War but was reformed after that war when King George VII asked that the firing of royal salutes should be performed by an RHA battery. Although bodies known as 'the King's' are usually renamed 'the Queen's' when there is a change of gender of monarch, Her Majesty Queen Elizabeth II asked for the name to be retained as a tribute to her father.

The horses used by artillery units were (and are) of the type known as light draught and most were (and still are) from Ireland. Their colour ranges from light chestnut to black, but never grey or part-coloured.

Having selected the firing site for the battery, the routine was for the teams to gallop to it and turn so the guns were pointing in the right direction, unload ammunition boxes and unlimber the guns, then remove the horses, limbers and caissons to a safe distance (at least 6yd behind the guns and ideally behind a ridge). The ammunition could be roundshot (ball), grapeshot or shells, or a selection of these.

Wheeled Vehicles

As well as artillery pieces, numerous different types of wheeled vehicle were used by the British Army. Many of these were used at home, carrying supplies to barracks and encampments, while others were needed on campaign.

The first instance of an official wagon train came during the Duke of York's campaign in Flanders, when Brook Watson was appointed commissary general to the army. His duties involved the supply of food for the troops, hay and grain for the horses and oxen, straw for the soldiers' palliasses, and candles. He had to hire wagons and their drivers from contractors, but this was not satisfactory as the drivers tended to help themselves to the loads or desert if the contractor failed to pay them. The Austrian Army had a very efficient wagon train and it was finally decided to organise a similar corps for the British Army. A corps of Royal Waggoners [sic], complete with farriers and wheelwrights, was raised in March 1794 and horses and wagons bought. But this too was not a success and the corps was disbanded a year later and the wagons sold off, mainly in bulk to buyers who were then given contracts for their use.

In August 1799, to aid Sir Ralph Abercromby's expedition to Holland, a new transport corps was established, initially known as the Royal Waggon Corps [sic] but later named the Royal Wagon Train. This new corps of five squadrons was overseen by Wagon Master General Digby Hamilton (then a lieutenant colonel), and was so successful that it was increased to twelve squadrons and Hamilton was promoted to major general.

The best type of vehicle to use in the field depends on the country involved. Although it was tempting to assume that a General Service Pattern wagon could be used everywhere, it was usually better to employ whatever vehicles were in common use in each location, as they had evolved over the years to be best adapted to the terrain. They also had the advantage of being available, rather than having to be transported from home to the theatre of war. However, this rule did not apply to the Peninsular War. When British troops arrived in Portugal, it had been assumed that there would be vehicles available, but all they found were bullock carts which were extremely slow and could only be used for short distances. These were very crudely made, often with solid wooden wheels bound with iron attached to a single axle which turned through wooden blocks. These were never greased and thus the whole creaked and squeaked constantly. The 'body' consisted of no more than rough planks nailed to a central shaft and such sides as the wagons had were made of wicker. The carts and bullocks belonged to the drivers, who would not go further than the next village to their own, and absolutely refused to cross the border into Spain; nor would they stay with the British troops if they thought the French were close.

It was not until Viscount Wellington was appointed commander-in-chief in the Peninsula that better wagons were organised for the army. In 1811 he ordered 800 better, and larger, carts with springs. These were built either in Portugal or in England and were driven by men of the Royal Waggon Train and were so successful that a further 700 were ordered the following year. At that time the establishment of the Royal Waggon Train was listed as eleven marching troops of eighty rank and file each, eight in Portugal and three in Ireland. There were 46 officers, a surgeon and a veterinary surgeon, 64 non-coms, a trumpeter, 20 farriers, 20 wheelwrights, 20 collar makers, 10 black-smiths, 200 waggons and 1,000 horses. The cost of all this – not including maintenance of the horses, replacement horses and wear and tear to waggons and harness – was included in the estimates for army services for 1812 at just over £42,000.

At this time it was customary for supply vehicles to carry away the wounded when their load had been discharged, but during Sir John Moore's retreat to Corunna in 1808–1809, orders to leave women and children at the Portuguese ports on arrival had not been enforced and the empty wagons soon overflowed with women and children, as well as wounded and exhausted soldiers, and plunder.

Two-wheeled carts, although obviously not capable of carrying such heavy loads as the four-wheeled wagons, did have some advantages. They could travel on secondary roads which were not suitable for the heavier wagons, and if they did get into difficulties in mud, they could be relatively easily extracted with the help of a few men. Whatever the road, they can move more speedily than a fully loaded wagon, and can carry urgently needed stores from the larger wagons at the back of the column to the front. They are best used on level ground, as an improperly balanced load makes it difficult for the horse to get traction on steep uphill slopes, and it is more difficult to slow the cart going downhill.

Although heavy wagons are useful for carrying heavy bulk loads from ports or railheads to centralised stores, lighter and more speedy wagons or pack animals are better for supplies which have to keep up with the troops. In the Peninsula Wellington organised a relay system to achieve this.

At about the same time the Duke of York decided to buy the Hanoverian Army's field bakery which could make bread for 30,000 men. It consisted of sets of metal oven frames, which were finished with straw and clay, but could easily be dismantled and moved to another site, using ten wagons for twelve sets of frames, plus others for the flour, mixing troughs, etc.

During the Crimean War the Victorian 'celebrity chef' Alexis Soyer designed a brilliantly simple cooking stove consisting of a large drum (rather like the 100-litre oil drum of today) with a small furnace at the bottom and a removable cooking pot at the top. These stoves were not heavy – a mule could carry two – but the total number in use was significant as a smaller version was issued for use inside soldiers' tents.

Since they rarely move at more than walking pace, wagons can be driven by one man seated on the wagon, or walking at the front with the horses, rather than by 'drivers' sitting on the nearside animal of each pair.

General supply wagons were open-topped and their loads kept dry (and secure) with a tarpaulin. They carried all the necessities for living and fighting: food and drink, tents, firewood, clothing and ammunition for both artillery and small arms.

By the time of the First World War decent roads were generally available and the PDGS (Pole Draught General Service) wagon was in general use. In Palestine the GS wagon was considered good in camp or on good roads, but the lighter version (LGS wagon) was better in hilly or roadless country, as it had a lower centre of gravity, four large wheels and a greater angle of lock on the front wheels. It required only two men and four horses, compared to the GS wagon with three men and six horses.

Wagon Convoys

Carlyle remarked of Frederick II's convoy of 1758 carrying the stores needed to maintain the siege of Olmutz:

> The driving of 3,000 four-horse wagons, under escort [over] ninety miles of road ... there are twelve thousand horses, for one thing, to be shod,

geared, kept roadworthy and regular; say six thousand country wagoners, thick-soled peasants; then hanging on to the skirts of these, in miscellaneous crazy vehicles and weak teams, equine and asinine, are one or two thousand sutler people, male and female, not of select quality, though on them too we keep a sharp eye. The series covers ... as many as twenty English miles, unless in favourable points you compress them into five, going four wagons abreast for defence's sake. Defence, or escort, goes in three bulks or brigades: vanguard, middle, rear-guard, with spare pickets intervening.

As far as pack animals were concerned, these were mostly mules, but might include horses and donkeys, as well as other non-equine animals.

In the civilian world columns of mules might be left loose to follow the leader mule, which wore a bell. This was not considered good practice on active military service, when they might come under fire or have to halt to allow other traffic through, so in most situations mules were led. This was done by the handler holding the reins about 6in below the jaw, but on narrow tracks he should walk ahead on a longer rein. Where the terrain was difficult, the leader should use an even longer rein and go ahead confidently; once the mule had seen it was possible, he would follow. A loose head was always preferable, although young mules might need some more positive guidance if they got excited. In situations where the mule might want to escape, such as during shelling, one rein should be passed over its nose and back through the other ring of the bit; this done, a firm pull would tighten the rein over the nostrils and stop the mule by restricting its breathing. Otherwise it was preferable to attach a lead-rope to the ring on the noseband.

When there was a shortage of leaders, mules might be linked together by attaching a rope from the neck-chain to the lead-ring of the follower, and from there to the saddle of the lead mule. Where the footing was particularly bad, these links should be undone to allow each mule to cross on its own. Steepness or rough footing do not bother mules unduly, but slippery slopes such as loose gravel or dry grass do. In this case the leader should attach a rope to the saddle and an extra man should keep upslope of the mule ready to pull if necessary. Otherwise, it is best to give the mule his head, but allow brief pauses to let him get his breath back. On steep down-slopes, the saddle-rope should be used, with the extra man behind to act as a brake. For narrow tracks on the face of a steep slope, or alongside a steep drop-off, it is essential to keep moving unless there is an obstruction that narrows the track to less than the width of the load. In such a case it may be necessary to unload to get past the obstruction. This is essential if the obstruction is on the up-side of the track, as if the load strikes the obstruction it may tip the mule over the edge. Steep turns also require care; they should be taken slowly, and the mule should have his head turned so he can see the edge.

With mules, the men should work in pairs with their mules standing by; thus each will have a thorough knowledge of the other's mule and saddle. This will also mean they can perform loading together, and on the road the mules, being familiar with each other, will follow without necessarily having to be linked. Columns of more than forty animals should be divided into smaller units.

Collecting a fresh load from stores should be done under the supervision of one experienced man, leaving the other to sort and make up the individual loads. The animals should be fully loaded, thus reducing the number of animals in use, although some spare animals without saddles should always be taken along. About one spare to thirty animals is the right number. In general, a broken saddle means the load is also damaged so spare saddles are not needed, but if an animal has developed a girth gall, fallen or been wounded or killed, then its saddle and load can be transferred to the spare. When a column of pack animals is returning unladen, their girths should be loosened by one hole before starting off.

March Discipline

There are numerous reports of chaotic marches, mainly caused by senior officers taking vast amounts of baggage with them on campaign. Some thought their seniority and/or social position allowed them to position their wagons at the front of the column of march and there was also much argument about which regiments were most important and therefore should be at the front.

The Duke of York, having seen this for himself when he was on campaign, decided it was time to put a stop to it, and in 1796 Horse Guards issued a booklet of instructions on baggage and marches.[2] This remarked that when attempting to stop the advance of an enemy:

> instead of keeping all our force collected to oppose him in front, to allot a Part only for that Purpose; and by throwing the rest in different Bodies on his Flanks and even in his Rear as he advances ... and by unremitting Attacks to make his Progress slow and uneasy ... this will depend on [the troops] being free of every Incumbrance of Baggage, Carriages, or even a numerous Artillery.

After some comments on the advantages of this tactic, it went on: 'The Propriety of the following Regulations must therefore be apparent to every one, will be chearfully [sic] entered into ... and will be rigidly enforced, as the Welfare of the Soldier and the Army depend on them.'

Each regiment of infantry was to be allowed two bread wagons, each carrying three days' bread for 400 men, one ammunition wagon, two battalion guns with one wagon, one cart with entrenching tools, two sutler's carts, and one wagon for the sick. For the cavalry regiments, the bread wagons, sutler's carts, ammunition cart and wagon for the sick were the same, but the guns and entrenching tools were replaced with two forage carts. Entrenching tools for an infantry regiment consisted of 20 pick-axes, 20 spades, 20 shovels, 40 bill-hooks and 10 axes, and for a cavalry regiment 8 each of pick-axes, spades and shovels, 16 bill-hooks and 8 axes.

Lieutenant generals were allowed one chaise and two carts, major generals one of each. The carriages of headquarters staff were to be 'exceedingly limited' by the commander-in-chief. Any other private carriages were to be considered as part of the heavy baggage, and had to move well to the rear; if found close to the army, they would be ordered to be destroyed by the baggage master. All other baggage, such as tents, blankets or officers' necessaries, was to be carried on bât horses. Officers' personal baggage was to be carried in a small portmanteau. The officers of each company or troop could have one small tent, and to carry this, plus blankets, provisions, three or four days' corn and 'other useful necessary articles', two bât horses would be allowed.

For each battalion of ten companies of infantry, twenty bât horses would carry the regiment's tents and poles, with two more for the company's officers, four for the field officers and staff and one for the surgeon's chest. For cavalry regiments there were twenty-four horses for tents and poles, sixteen for the troop officers, four for the field officers and staff, and one each for entrenching tools and the surgeon's chest. The picket ropes for the troop's horses were also to go on bât horses. Heavy baggage should be left at a place of safety under escort and guard. The baggage accompanying the regiments would also have an escort/guard, these to number no more than fifty-eight men and non-coms for an infantry regiment and fifty-four for a cavalry regiment.

When the corps advanced in one column, the order of march was laid down, starting with an advance guard of piquets, followed by pioneers, dragoons, infantry and cavalry, wagons and carts, bât horses, general officers' carriages, bread wagons, other carts and wagons and a rearguard as specified by the senior officer. When retreating, this order was reversed, with a rearguard of infantry and cavalry. At least two cannon were always to march with the advance guard when advancing, and with the rearguard when retreating. When the march was made in two or more columns, their precise order was to be specified by the commanding officer. On the march, no horses or carriages were to interrupt the column. If a carriage broke, it was to be pulled aside to clear the road and left with an escort; if it could be repaired in a reasonable time it should be, otherwise its contents should be divided among other carriages.

Unfortunately the regulations relating to officers' baggage were not always observed, especially during the Peninsular War. Many officers, especially generals who were expected to 'keep a table' and entertain their colleagues, staff and visiting dignitaries, were accompanied by a small train of carriages, wagons and carts carrying their personal supplies, ranging from dress uniforms, beds and other furniture to food and kitchen equipment and vast quantities of wine.

Another booklet on march discipline was issued in the First World War for 'officers who have not as yet had any practical experience, so that when they are called upon to perform any of the duties mentioned, they will have some knowledge of what points require special attention'.[3] This suggests that the topic was not part of the general training for officers. Proper march discipline had two purposes: to ensure the well-being of the animals, and to avoid interference with other traffic.

The first point was the desired location of officers in a column or convoy: the senior officer should be at the front, and warrant officers, company sergeant majors and company quartermasters (of the Army Service Corps) should be at the rear. Mounted transport officers should be at the head of their units, and mounted NCOs should be within the column and not on the flank. These officers and NCOs should drop back at intervals to check the driving and the state of the wagons, doing so by pulling into the side of the road to let their vehicles pass. Crossroads were the best place to do this.

The drivers were to keep their wagons well to the left on roads (except in France where they drove on the right). This was easy enough on good main roads but could prove difficult in France where the camber tended to be steeper, in which case the wagons might have to pull into the ditch. Mechanical transport always took precedence over horse-drawn.

Unless a man was needed on the box to work the brake, it was forbidden for civilians or unmounted men to ride on the wagons, unless written (and signed) permission had been given by an officer. Nor should weapons or equipment belonging to unmounted men be hung on the wagons. One man should walk behind each wagon to operate the brake or a 'drag shoe', while the others should march close up to the rearmost wagon of their unit, leaving no gaps. The wagon with the slowest pair of horses was to be situated at the front, the others taking their pace from this. However, the pace was never to be more than 3mph or the marching men would not be able to keep up. If a wagon had to stop for any reason it should pull out of the column, regaining its place at the next halt. If damaged beyond repair, its load should be distributed between the other wagons. The proper distance between wagons was 4yd, and this should be maintained.

On arriving at a steep hill, the column halted and the wagons were sent on one at a time at intervals which varied according to the slope of the hill. Going uphill should not be hurried or the horses would be blown before the top was reached. If they had to stop before reaching the top, a drag shoe or chock should be put under the wheels to prevent the wagon slipping back down. For really steep hills, the horse teams in the rear half of the column were un-hitched and taken to the front where they were hitched in to double up the teams; once at the top all the horses were unhitched and taken back to the bottom to bring the rest of the wagons up. Going down required a slightly different routine, with a special drag-shoe applied to the leading wagon. Once safely down, it continued far enough to allow the rest of the column to join it on the flat, and the drag-shoe was taken back up for the next wagon.

Before a column moved off, three spare responsible men were needed; ideally they should be NCOs, but experienced privates could also be used. One went ahead as a scout to find the best way (and remove obstacles if pos-sible), while the second remained at the front of the column to set the pace, taking signals from the scout and passing them back as necessary. The third stayed at the rear to watch for loose loads and ensured they were put right. Even the smallest columns should not move off until these duties had been allocated. On arrival at crossroads or level crossings, the column should halt and NCOs on foot should check that nothing is coming.

About 2 miles after setting off there should be a 5–10 minute halt during which the men should check saddlery and harness, tighten girths and check feet and shoes; the horses should be allowed to stale (urinate). After that, halts should be made every hour, for ten minutes. For these halts, a spot sheltered from the wind should be chosen and the horses allowed to turn their backs to the wind or driving rain. Especially on long marches, a halt of 30–60 minutes should be made about two-thirds of the way, and the horses given a drink and a small feed of corn, such halts being chosen for their closeness to a water source. During these halts girths should be loosened and the bit (but not the bridoon) removed from the horse's mouth to facilitate drinking and feed-ing. At all halts the drivers should check their horses, looking for badly fitting harness which might rub and cause galls, and for loose shoes. Section sergeants and NCOs should check that the loads are not working loose, then generally check the horses and wagons and report to their officers. In cold weather it might be wise to put rugs on the animals. Ridden horses should be unsaddled and their backs hand-rubbed to restore circulation to the areas where the rider's weight had rested.

The care of horses on the march is of prime importance, in particular avoiding unnecessary fatigue (depending on the military situation at the time) by riders dismounting at short stops and walking with their horses on steep hills, up or down. Every opportunity should be taken for the horses to drink and pick at any suitable vegetation. Wherever possible they should be ridden on soft verges rather than on hard roads, unless this will raise a dust which will show the enemy where they are. The pace should be suited to the surface, trotting on soft ground and walking on metalled roads. To quote an old saying, 'It's not the hunting on the heath that hurts the horse's hooves, it's the hammer, hammer, hammer on the hard high road.'

During these halts ridden horses should be allowed to graze. Watering should take place after a couple of hours, ideally three hours after the morning feed and then once or twice more during the day after loosening the girths and taking out the bits. Each wagon should carry a bucket for this purpose, or horses may be unhooked and led to water with an NCO in charge. If watering from streams, the first lot of horses should be taken downstream, and each subsequent group a little further upstream so as not to pollute the water for the others. Public watering troughs were not recommended. Where a column was not likely to arrive in camp before 1pm, a halt should be made at midday for the animals to be fed. Girths should be loosened and bits removed before nose-bags were put on. However, unnecessary stops, even brief ones to allow those behind to catch up, should be avoided, as it is when starting off from a halt that draught animals have to exert the greatest effort.

It is preferable that the distance should be covered fairly rapidly, as travelling too slowly means the weight is on the horse's back for longer. The speed of march by the Royal Horse Artillery, cavalry and mounted infantry is usually about 5mph, including halts; this requires a steady trot of 7–8mph with occasional walking. Field artillery moves at about 4mph, including halts, Army Service Corps at about 3mph. With a long column it is important to avoid checks caused at the front; a distance of 50–100yd should be maintained between troops and sections. The first and last half hour of a march should always be done at a slow pace. During these slow periods the men may smoke and talk, but should not be allowed to loll in the saddle as this can lead to sore backs.

When a unit or detachment was ordered to change quarters by march, the veterinary officer was to submit to the DG a marching-out report listing sick and lame horses, with a copy of the route. If accompanying the march, he should state with which detachment he would go. At the end of the march he should submit a marching-in report, with details of all the horses listed above, and including any subsequent casualties. This report should show which horses, if any, were left behind and who was caring for them. No horse should be left behind if it could possibly be moved by rail. If the veterinary officer did not accompany the march, he was to send a copy of the marching-out report to the receiving veterinary officer.[4]

Chapter Twelve

Cavalry and Artillery

Cavalry is a generic word for mounted troops. In the British Army these were dragoons (mounted infantry who rode to the battlefield and then fought dismounted), lancers (mounted troops who stayed mounted and were armed with a lance), and hussars (light cavalry); to these were added heavy cavalry, used for massed shock tactics. There are many incorrect concepts about the cavalry, most notably that their work consisted entirely of charges. It did, when necessary, but there were also other duties which were just as important.

There are two principal requirements for a major cavalry charge. The first is that the terrain should be suitable: more or less flat, solid enough to allow the horses free movement at speed, and unencumbered with rocks or debris to trip the horses, or other hazards. The second is that the enemy should first have been 'softened up' by infantry or artillery. Horses are liable to pull up or jib when faced with a square bristling with sharp weapons, but are happy to pursue a running mass of men whom their riders can then despatch with sabre or lance. There are psychological and practical issues here: first, that it is easier for the attacker to kill a man when he doesn't have to see his face and look into his eyes. This effectively turns the opponent from a fighter into prey which can be hunted down. Secondly, since the fleeing enemy carries his weapon in his right hand, he can be attacked on his left side and is unable to parry. Most of the killing done by cavalry was during such pursuits.

The obsession of cavalry officers with charging probably emanated from the 1760 Battle of Emsdorff when the 15th Light Dragoons completely routed the French infantry. The same regiment repeated this success at Villiers-en-Caudenes in 1794. As a result, all cavalry movements in the field tended to be performed at great speed, the intent being to shock the enemy. Unfortunately this tended to lead to loss of control, closely followed by the loss of the rider, as George Gleig reported: Colonel Taylor 'rode that day a horse, which was so hot that not all his exertions would suffice to control it, and he was carried headlong into the bayonets of the French infantry, a corporal of whom shot him through the heart ...'.[1]

Rifleman Harris reported another incident where dash and heroics proved fatal:

> I observed a fine gallant-looking officer leading [the charge]. He was a brave fellow, and bore himself like a hero; with his sword waving in the

air, he cheered the men on, as he went dashing on the enemy, and hewing and slashing at them in tremendous style. I watched [for] him as the dragoons came off after that charge but saw him no more; he had fallen.[2]

Galloping at the enemy tended to relieve the mounted man's anxiety, but on the other hand, as it is almost impossible to steer a galloping horse in a mass of others, it tended to break up the proper order of the troopers; either gaps were created, making the massed charge less effective, or the horses on the outside squeezed out those in the centre, who could then be left behind. When the charge was against opposing cavalry who were also charging, the resultant high-speed crash of the two forces tended to turn the whole thing into a disorganised mêlée.

The work of the cavalry was more likely to involve reconnaissance, patrols, escort duties (such as protecting the rearguard of a marching army), piquet duty, outpost duties and skirmishing. Reconnaissance usually involved a small group of men, acting as what was called 'the eyes and ears of the army'. When on the march, columns were preceded, flanked and followed by small cavalry patrols. Two men rode well in front, or 'at point', and small groups rode at the other positions. In camp, piquets or vedettes rode around, piquets close in and vedettes further out, but still close enough to ride back and give warning of approaching enemies.

When the army was static, small groups of piquets were positioned a little way outside the lines to provide an early warning system, with vedettes again placed further out, often in a curved line, to act as a screen against incoming enemy. Skirmishers moved about 200yd in front of their lines and mounted snap attacks on the enemy. They were organised into two lines with officers and sergeants in between.

In peacetime, cavalry was used for police work and to suppress civil insurrections.

The Peninsular War

Some of the most valiant cavalry work was performed in the Peninsula. During Sir John Moore's retreat to Corunna, what the eminent historian Sir Charles Oman described as 'perhaps the most brilliant exploit of the British cavalry during the whole of the [Pensinsular] war' took place at Sahagun at the end of December 1808. As Sir John Moore's army approached, they learned that 700 French cavalry were in the town. Lord Paget took two cavalry regiments and four horse artillery guns to intercept them. The regiments, the 10th and 15th Hussars, were supposed to make a pincer movement around the town but the 10th failed to arrive in time. The 15th, unsupported, galloped over a ditch and some rough ground, surprising the French, all but 200 of whom were killed or captured. Of the 15th, only two were killed and twenty-three wounded. They destroyed a crucial bridge and relieved the two French regiments of their baggage, plate and money. The hussars spent the next two days harassing the French to such an extent that Marshal Soult believed a major assault was beginning, and by the time Napoleon arrived with reinforcements the British were three marches away. For another four days Paget's five regiments fought day and night in a series of actions to keep the advancing French at bay.

At Mayorga five days later Paget, with the 10th, 15th and 18th Hussars, encountered two squadrons of Ney's 15th Chasseurs à Cheval, acting as part of the French advance guard. Paget ordered the 10th to chase the French piquets out of the town and up onto the plain behind it, where the French opened fire. The hussars charged, killing several Frenchmen and taking over a hundred prisoners. A few days later, at Benavente, where the bridge had been destroyed just before the French arrived, they took some time to find a fordable place, under constant attacks from Paget's men. General Charles Stewart and his men lured the French back into the town, where Paget was waiting with his reserves, sitting on his horse and 'twirling his moustachios'. In the ensuing fight some fifty chasseurs were killed or wounded and seventy-two taken prisoner, including two captains, and General Lefebvre-Desnouettes, who was one of Napoleon's favourites, was captured.[3]

However, not every cavalry action in the Peninsula was successful and there were some disastrous incidents, for instance at Campo Mayor. There is some controversy over the details, but what is indisputable is that when Beresford approached the town, he did so with strict instructions from Wellington to keep control of his cavalry and to keep them 'en masse'. However, Robert Ballard Long, then in control of the cavalry, sent the light cavalry on a detour round the town, scattered the retreating French dragoons and then chased them for 10 miles to the gates of Badajoz, where they had to abandon the pursuit, leaving behind the sixteen heavy guns they had taken en route. Beresford was furious, as was Wellington. Long later insisted that Beresford had approved his proposal to act, but Beresford pointed out that he had also sent an aide to Long telling him to stay close to the town, and 'if a favourable opportunity to strike should occur, to take it'. The argument went on, back and forth, as to who was to blame, but the end result was that 25 per cent of the 15th Dragoons were killed, wounded or missing, presumed taken prisoner.

The terrain in the Peninsula was not ideally suited to the classic cavalry charge; what the cavalry mainly did was patrol, gather intelligence, carry dispatches and perform reconnaissance work. Most of the country was rugged and rocky, and in Portugal there were few open plains except in the strategically unimportant south. Southern Spain was a little better, but there were places where hazards waited, such as at Talavera. The 23rd Light Dragoons (sometimes erroneously reported as the 20th) were advancing at what the historian Ian Fletcher contends could not have been more than a trot, rather than breakneck speed, when they encountered a dry watercourse some 6ft deep and 12ft wide. A combination of long grass and dust prevented their seeing this until the last minute, when it was too late either to pull up or to jump it, with the result that many of the horses tumbled into the trench or landed upside-down on the other side.[4]

Problems also arose from picquet and outpost work, including the loss of a piquet from the 11th Light Dragoons on the Guardiana, where Captain Lutyens mistook a body of French cavalry for the King's German Legion. During the resulting skirmish, all but one officer of the picquet's sixty-five officers and men were killed, wounded or captured. In another incident 125 men of the 11th Light Dragoons and 2nd Hussars were lost due to faulty disposition of a piquet. Perhaps part of the problem here was confusion over the precise purpose of these piquets: were they to just watch the enemy, or give them pause until reinforcements came up? Major Edward Cocks wrote that piquets should understand which of their two possible functions they were to fill: 'whether to watch the enemy or to check him'. The first required only a few men placed well forward, the latter should have a small group well forward but supported by several squadrons forming a reserve nearby, ready saddled and accoutred. Cocks also gave some detailed instructions for patrol work, being for reconnaissance or discovery, security or communication. This included seeking information from locals whenever possible.

Sir Charles Oman remarked, '...on the whole the outpost and reconnaissance work of the Peninsula Army seem to have been well done, though some regiments had a better reputation than others'.

Crimea

The debacle with the Light Brigade at Balaclava has tended to overshadow the cavalry work in the Crimea. That incident killed 107 men and 397 horses, as a result of inexplicit orders, and the personality conflicts between Raglan, Cardigan, Lucan and Nolan.

As in the Peninsula, the cavalry's activities in the Crimea were restricted by the terrain, with steep hills and winding valleys, but the heavy cavalry did achieve one major success. Major Thornhill, who participated in the charge, said: 'It was just like a mêlée coming in or out of a crowded theatre, jostling horse against horse, violent language, hacking and pushing, till suddenly the Russians gave way.' William Russell, correspondent for *The Times* said: 'The Heavy Brigade went through the Russians like a piece of pasteboard.'[5]

Second Boer War

The terrain in Natal was quite unsuited to horses and there were huge losses due to the fatigue of the long marches, lack of water and the poor horsemastership and riding abilities of the troops. On one day during the relief of Kimberley, for example, General French's cavalry lost 500 horses. This was more a war of guerrilla activity than of formal set-piece battles.

On another occasion, in April 1900, a number of horses were lost after a major stampede. A number of horses, only a few of them hobbled, were grazing in a field close to the camp when the whole regiment of the 17th Lancers galloped through the camp while practising an advance in line; this inevitably frightened the horses in the field and they stampeded. It took several days to track them down, and some were never found. Afterwards 180 remounts had to be sent from Bloemfontein to replace them.[6]

The First World War

Several myths have arisen about the role of the cavalry in the First World War, which largely emanated from the official historian, Sir James Edmonds. As is all too often the case, these myths were perpetuated by later writers, and it was not until recently that historians were able to discount them. The first myth was that the army high command was dominated by cavalry officers with ingrained ideas (i.e. Haig and his mutual support group); the second that machine guns will always win over horses (sometimes they did, sometimes not, and the cavalry actually had some good successes), and the third that feeding cavalry horses was a waste of resources that could have been better used elsewhere, especially in terms of shipping. This particular myth becomes obvious for what it is when it is remembered that cavalry horses formed only a small proportion of all the horses in that war.

The introduction of motor transport was used as an excuse for reducing cavalry, but ironically it was much used to take food to horses. There was a false assumption in India that each new mechanised unit should be matched with a reduction in animal units. This led to panicky reanimalisation when it was realised that this was not practical; as the RAVC fully expected, this led in turn to bad results from hastily acquired untrained animals and inexperienced personnel.

Other arguments against the use of horses included the idea that they could not negotiate the trench systems or barbed wire. Paths could always be cut through barbed wire and marked with flags, while the solution to crossing trenches was found by units of the Royal Canadian Horse Artillery (RCHA) and the Fort Garry Horse (FGH). The RCHA devised two portable bridges, one strong enough for artillery to cross, which could be assembled in less than four minutes, and one for mounted troops, which could be thrown over a trench in less than one minute. These bridges were demonstrated to Haig in May 1915 and the FGH was then designated a specialist bridging unit.

In July 1916 three cavalry divisions were allocated to the force attacking Bazentin Ridge, but they were not, in the event, used. There were also two squadrons of the FGH with their portable bridges, one with the vanguard and the other with the advanced guard. The majority of the mounted force saw little action, but those who did found that the German infantry were terrified of the cavalry, many popping up from their hiding places to surrender and some even throwing their arms around the horses' necks and begging for mercy.

It was not until 1918 that the cavalry was able to make a substantial contribution. On 24 March at Berlancourt three fifty-strong troops, one each from the 10th Hussars, the Royals and the 3rd Dragoon Guards, advanced towards the village of Villeselve, where they found German machine guns in two copses to the northeast. Formed into three lines, they attacked at full gallop with swords drawn. The last 200yd was across ploughed land which made it difficult to keep their line close, but the enemy from one copse broke and fled into the trees. The Dragoons dismounted and pursued them, killing several and capturing twelve. Meanwhile, the Royals and Hussars attacked the other copse, which contained a large concentration of Germans. They killed at least seventy (and possibly as many as a hundred), mostly with the sword, and captured ninety-four men and three machine guns.

There were some other cavalry successes after this, but the whole business was so complex, with constant reshuffles of units within divisions, that it is difficult to state firmly that the cavalry units in France in this war were generally successful, but it is certain that they played their part to the best of their ability, with a consequent loss of men and horses.[7]

Palestine

The Desert Mounted Corps consisted of some 20,000 men and horses in a composite force made up of British, Australians, New Zealanders and Indians. Of the British, only yeomanry regiments served in the Middle East, mostly taking British horses, including hackneys; the other nationalities preferred Australian Walers. In June 1917 Sir Edmund Allenby took over command of three divisions (increased to four when more troops arrived from India in early 1918). The first task was to capture the town of Beersheba, but for much of the time the ground around the town was unsuitable for mounted work, and the men dismounted and fought on foot, leaving their horses nearby in case the enemy gave way and had to be pursued.

The horses in this theatre were unusually free of disease, but in 1918 there was an outbreak of anthrax among the native horses and cattle in Palestine. Very few British horses caught it, due to a rigidly enforced scheme of avoiding camping near villages, keeping native animals away from the army animals, and labelling areas where cases were contracted as 'unclean'. There was much sand colic, however, the effects of which could be seen in the ulcerated stomachs and intestines at post mortem. Many of the horses had spent two years in the Egyptian desert. There was also a period when food was short and the horses had to be muzzled at night to prevent them gnawing at the wagon wheels to which they were tied.

Although in general it was very hot in Palestine and Syria, with dust storms and temperatures up to 110 degrees Fahrenheit in the shade, there was heavy rain for several weeks, and there were even places that endured extreme cold and heavy snow. The Australian Light Horse regiments avoided some of the worst effects of the heat by leaving their horses' manes and tails untrimmed. This not only helped the horses keep flies away, but also gave some protection from the sun.[8]

This campaign saw the last major cavalry charges, both in November 1917. Several hundred enemy were killed and over a thousand taken prisoner, for the cost of 76 British troopers killed or wounded and more than 360 horses lost.

The aftermath of this campaign saw many thousands of horses left in the Middle East and sold to the locals; this created a major scandal when Mrs Brooke, the wife of Brigadier General Brooke, discovered the appalling conditions in which these animals were kept and worked. She publicised what she saw, and founded her charity, the War Horse Fund (now known as The Brooke), to rescue them and provide veterinary treatment. The British government was so shamed by the scandal that it guaranteed that no British horses would be left in theatres of war again.[9]

During the Second World War there were a few cavalry units in the Middle East and Egypt; they suffered from the same problems in finding forage and water as those in Palestine in the First World War.

Artillery

There is little to be said about the artillery, other than to mention the numbers of horses used with different gun teams (*see* Chapter Eleven) and the fact that their job was to arrive in the designated place, unlimber and fire their guns and, if necessary, limber up again and move on.

Frederick the Great said of artillery that it 'lends dignity to what would otherwise be a vulgar brawl'. Although his comment is much loved by the artillery, it is a little strange as at that time most battles consisted of the infantry of the two opposing sides formally lining (or squaring) up opposite each other until someone 'opened the ball' with the first shot. Whether or not this then degenerated into a brawl is a matter of opinion, but it certainly involved artillery.[10]

Chapter Thirteen

Equines in Non-combatant Units

Useful figures for the numbers of equines employed by the various non-combatant units are not available, so we can only make informed guesses here.

There were several of these essential units. The largest of them, in terms of numbers of horse-drawn vehicles employed, was the Army Service Corps (later the Royal Army Service Corps and later still the Royal Logistics Corps), which started life as the Royal Corps of Waggoners in the Peninsular War. This corps dealt with most of the supplies needed, from the general to the more specific, such as clothing.

Next, possibly equal if not larger in size, was the Commissariat. Before its function was taken over by the ASC in the late 1880s, it was responsible for carrying basic foodstuffs such as biscuit, salt meat and spirits, as well as, in the Crimean War, the Soyer stove; all of this required many wagons and carts.

Commissariat and Transport Corps

Some figures are available for the number of horses used by the early Commissariat and Transport Corps during the Peninsular War. Sir John Bissett, the Commissary-General in the Peninsula for some years, made some calculations on the amount of forage needed. The official ration was 14lb of hay or straw and 12lb of oats or 10lb of Indian corn (maize). Each mounted man should carry three days' ration. Bissett based his figures on a cavalry regiment with a total strength of 407, which translated to 478 horses and mules. The mules had to carry the food for the men, as well as for themselves and the cavalry horses. The men were each entitled to 1lb of biscuit and 1lb of meat per day, and their spirit ration weighed 400lb. The fuel, corn and hay or straw added up to 11,123lb just for one day for the horses and mules. Multiplying that by the three days gives a total of 33,369lb; a mule could carry only 200lb so 167 mules were needed to carry a three-day ration for the regiment, plus more to carry the ration for the mules themselves. All this means almost two equines for each human.

Bissett extended his calculations to a brigade of cavalry, comprising three regiments (1,221 all ranks) with a troop of horse artillery, staff and Commissariat staff (total 1,430 all ranks and 1,658 equines). This made 115,818lb for three days' rations, requiring 965 Commissariat mules. Bissett actually reported 8,815 Commissariat mules with Wellington's army in June 1812, and 16,165 horses and baggage mules with the army, all for an army of 53,000 officers and other ranks.

One minor problem for administrators at this time related to the allowance of money paid in lieu of green forage. The general order stated that it was to be made for effective horses only, but some regiments claimed it was the custom to be paid for the numbers allowed on the establishment.

In the early 1880s the number of horses consisted of a peacetime establishment of 560 riding and driving horses. In India, due to the size of the territory, the numbers in use in 1879 were much larger, at 1,045 elephants, 9,227 camels, 2,080 bullocks and 3,857 mules, not to mention the horses for the officers. Building on his experience in the Afghan wars, Lieutenant General Michael Kennedy, Controller General of Supply and Transport, proposed an establishment of 16,137 mules and ponies and 4,780 carts. (Camels were not mentioned.)

When the Land Transport Corps was formed in the Crimea, it was calculated that the movement of 58,000 fighting men and 30,000 horses with all their equipment would require a transport department of 9,000 men and 12,500 animals.

In 1869 this corps was renamed the Army Service Corps (ASC).

In the 1880s some estimates were made for transportation in India for a six-day period. For a regiment of infantry 800 strong, thirty-two wagons each carrying 1,200lb would be needed; for a cavalry regiment of 400 men and 400 horses, fourteen wagons; for an artillery regiment of 200 men and 160 horses, twelve wagons; for the RE of about 400 men, sixteen wagons; for the RE's Park, where repairs were carried out, twelve wagons; and for the general's and brigade staff, twelve wagons. So for eight regiments of infantry, three of cavalry, two artillery batteries, the RE's Park, and the general's and brigade staff a total of 411 wagons were needed, plus 25 more for the Commissariat, which included butchers and bakers. Adding three days' provisions with the force, and a further three days to follow, required another 360 wagons, plus 193 wagons for casualties, breakages, etc., giving a total of 964 wagons with four horses each. In addition there were 12–20 two-horse wagons for the shoeing smiths and a forge, plus more for the carpenters and harness makers, giving a total of 96 two-horse wagons. The whole totalled 4,411 draught horses. Riding horses were also needed: 289 for the NCOs; 48 for the command officers; 18 for the senior officer and his staff; and 8 for mounted veterinary surgeons, totalling 363.

In the First World War Army Service Corps Horse Transport (ASCHT) companies were formed in several categories:

- Depot companies;
- Companies in divisional trains;

- Companies under command of higher formations;
- Reserve Park companies;
- Small-arms ammunition companies;
- Local auxiliary transport companies;
- Army auxiliary transport companies;
- Donkey companies: there were three of these with GHQ in Palestine from October 1917. The first had 762 donkeys on establishment.

ASCHT companies filled a variety of administrative, recruitment, induction, training and resupply roles. Base companies were in the UK or at the port of entry to a theatre of war. Advanced companies were located further up the lines of communication. There were several of these, based at Aldershot, Catterick, Bradford, Woolwich, Southport, Le Havre and Rouen (Regular Army). Others were formed after February 1915 at Park Royal and Black-heath, London, with base and advance depots in Egypt, Salonika and France; after November 1917 further depots in Italy and Ireland were added, along with a mule transport depot in North Russia.

In addition, each division of the army had some transport under its own command, known as the divisional train, which carried stores and supplies, providing the main supply line to the brigades of artillery, infantry and other attached units. There were 364 ASC companies of this sort. The train moved with the division.

On 1 August 1914 the Corps consisted of 498 officers and 5,933 other ranks; four years later these figures had increased to 10,477 officers and 314,693 other ranks. Specific numbers of equines in the ASC are not available, but official statistics show totals of 323,202 draught horses and 109,964 draught mules, plus 9,119 pack horses and 52,929 pack mules at 31 August 1917.

It is a reasonable assumption that in this war the ASC had most of the draught animals, plus numerous riding horses for the officers.

Medical Units

Medical officers in cavalry regiments might be provided with a horse, as might assistant surgeons, and might well carry their equipment on mules or in a horse-drawn cart. During the invasion of Oporto, Wellington told Surgeon George Guthrie to remove his two mules to the rear, but he refused on the grounds that there would soon be casualties and his equipment would be needed. Some surgeons may have been experienced riders, but even to them some of the horses could be challenging. Assistant Surgeon John Haddy James of the 1st Life Guards had some difficulties in shoeing his mare. She was 'still almost mad, and would not suffer Harper the farrier, even with the assistance of three men, to shoe her'. By the time the job was done, two hours later, the regiment had moved far ahead. The next day he found himself 'in an awkward predicament from the [fiery] temper of my mare … the regiment was ordered to trot and the noise and bustle … pretty nearly made her mad. She set off kicking to such a degree that I had the greatest difficulty in sitting her', and then she kicked off another shoe. Another surgeon was described as one 'whose seat on horseback was like to a huge pair of compasses'; when his horse was frightened by a shell 'bounding up the road', he was deposited 'on the broad of his back in the road; hard falling on stones and spent shot'.

Until the 1850s there were no dedicated ambulances, the wounded being transported on empty supply wagons. As is the case with much of the military history which involves equines, no consistent detail for numbers of ambulances or other carriers for wounded is available, but the best estimate is on the scale of four wagons for an infantry battalion of 800 men. Even when dedicated ambulances did come into use in the 1850s, their use was restricted by the terrain. Hills, ploughed or rocky ground, woods or thick brush all made it more desirable to use pack animals with cacolets or top-loaded stretchers, as were used by all the allied armies at the siege of Sebastopol. Early 'ambulances' consisted of whatever wheeled vehicles were available, but since these mostly lacked springs they did not give a comfortable ride. A simple solution to this was exhibited at the Paris Exhibition of 1878 by the French Society for the Help of the Sick and Wounded: it consisted of a coiled spring with a hook at each end to suspend stretchers. Four of these allowed a comparatively comfortable ride in a country cart.

Larger ambulances were made from four-wheeled wagons with high sides, a frame for a waterproof cover, and suspension points for stretchers. These could accommodate up to six stretchers or twelve seated patients, or a mixture of the two, with room for the attendants to move in the middle.

Camels were used, but were better for carrying cacolets than stretchers, as the camel's 'both legs on one side together' gait rocked stretchers. Elephants could carry up to six sitting patients but were generally too useful for other purposes to be used to carry wounded. In some countries, where carriage by human carriers was common, six men could carry a doolie (palaquin or litter) for up to six patients, but did need some training to ensure a comfortable ride. At a pinch, two men could carry a single stretcher. A train of these doolies needed one mounted commander and one surgeon for each forty patients.

Mobile field hospitals were necessary for active campaigns, to move forward or back with the troops, but stationed at a safe distance from the fighting. These also required numerous wagons for stores, rations, surgeons' equipment, drugs and dressings, and even a basic operating room for bone-setting or amputations. Surgeons or their assistants working among the troops giving first aid would also need horses to enable them to keep up with the fighting troops.

Royal Engineers (RE)

The Corps of Royal Engineers was formed in 1717 and reported up through the Board of Ordnance. In 1717 there were 28 officers, but by the start of the Peninsular War there were 172 and by 1813 there were 262. There were no other ranks until 1772, when a company of Soldier Artificers was formed to serve at Gibraltar. Prior to this, and often afterwards, civilians were hired for manual labour and trade work at garrisons as needed, and on campaign men were transferred from the infantry. A second company of Soldier Artificers was created in 1786 and six more in the following year, becoming known as the Corps of Military Artificers. (Four more companies were added in 1806 but all were only to serve at a specific location.) Their work ranged from digging saps and tunnels and laying mines to bring down the walls of besieged garrisons and towns, building (and blowing up) bridges, and building forts and other strongpoints, and they also built semaphore towers and other long-distance communications devices.

In the Peninsula the Royal Engineers built the Lines of Torres Vedras, a task that took over a year and involved the construction of three dams, fifteen redoubts, three roads, and eight other works of building and destruction. They ended with four lines, and a further 139 small forts, all of which involved transporting much material and tools. Given the terrain, much of this was probably carried by pack mules. Much of their work involved ropes and often chains.

One important part of their work was (and still is) providing bridges to enable the army to cross rivers. The technique for building these bridges was to use thick cables (usually 13in) to span the river; then individual pontoons/boats were attached to these, at an equal distance apart, and anchored at each end. They were then lashed to each other, and heavy baulks of timber were laid across them, parallel to the cables, and stout planks nailed across them at 90 degrees to form the road bed. Further cables could be added to create a side-barrier. More than twenty-five pontoons were often needed to make a bridge.[1]

Each pontoon, made of iron with tin-plate, with its carriage and equipment, weighed 3,086lb for the small size and 3,968lb for the large size. The small ones were 16ft by 4ft and the large ones 21ft by 5ft. Both were made to the same pattern: flat-ended and flat-bottomed, with a slope from bottom to top. They had a shallow draught and an open top and, not surprisingly, tended to sink easily. A new pattern with a closed top was created in 1814, but this came too late for use in the Peninsula. Sometimes local boats or large barrels were used instead of the purpose-built pontoons; for the crossing of the Adour, for example, over forty of these were used.

The ideal pontoon boat was thought to be 21ft long, 3ft 11in wide and 2ft 1in deep. When on the move, each pontoon's stores were carried inside it, to a usual weight of 1,200lb. This was only effective if trained men were sent with the pontoon train. It was suggested in the First World War that the General Service wagon would make a good pontoon, but one officer who tried using them remarked that his experience made him decide that he would rather swim.

Much of the engineering work in the Peninsula was carried out by the Portuguese Engineer Service and the pontoon trains were operated by Portuguese seamen. They were very resourceful; on one occasion, having been sent to repair a bridge which they judged would still be too weak for artillery, they improved the river bed of the nearest ford instead. Wellington tolerated this, but he was generally averse to anything that was not done under his specific instruction.

There was only one pontoon chain in the Peninsula, and it was lost in March 1811 when French forces, under Marshal Soult, captured Badajoz. Wellington promptly wrote home for another to be sent, followed by another letter asking for more experienced officers and ten warrant artificers to be sent out.

Although often referred to as 'the pontoon train', it was not a permanent unit, being formed when needed. In the Peninsula it was normally pulled by oxen, but in May 1813, when a bridge was urgently needed, Wellington ordered the artillery and Commissariat to give up 264 horses for a train of forty-four pontoons, telling them that they might be able to get better animals as remounts. This happened again in February 1814, and in both cases the dispossessed were not happy. Captain Cairnes of the artillery wrote to his step-father Major General Cuppage, '... the play or swing of the pontoon on the carriage when it comes over stoney or other uneven ground is so very great, that nothing but the slow steady pull of the ox prevents it from ... breaking something'. A list of personnel and animals needed for the train at that time shows 364 men and 580 oxen.

Each pontoon was carried separately on a four-wheeled cradle that was pulled by four horses; they also needed stout timber for the platforms over the pontoons, and rope and other materials to hold it all in place. The Royal Engineers also used a lot of timber to shore up the walls of trenches and tunnels and used fascines and gabbions as temporary walls. Although both could be made on the spot from material collected from nearby woods, these still had to be carried to the erection site. In addition, they also needed numerous vehicles to carry their equipment, from trench-digging tools to building and bridging materials and explosives to bring down walls or bridges. Even a simple wooden building for a secure store needed several wagon loads of timber and other materials, and brick or stone buildings required even more.

Communications

Before the advent of the electric telegraph, the only methods for long-distance communications were mounted despatch riders or line-of-sight devices built by the RE. A series of semaphore towers built around the south-east coast of England could quickly convey messages from London to the naval stations as far away as Plymouth, but these towers had to be high and could not be moved. The only mobile alternative was signal flags, operated by one man standing on a tall wagon, accompanied by at least one other to hand him the next flags, and another with a telescope to read incoming messages. The most convenient vehicle for this was the office wagon, with officers to deal with incoming messages and prepare others to go out.

The electric telegraph was invented in 1837, coincident with the development of Morse Code. When the Crimean War started in 1854, the Electric Telegraph Company donated its equipment and operators to the war effort, to the irritation of Lord Raglan, the commander-in-chief, who found himself more closely controlled by the War Office: 'the telegraph has upset everything', he complained.

The first task was cable-laying. For the Crimea, a submarine cable had to be laid from Varna to Sebastopol, a distance of some 340 miles. This was done with the aid of the Royal Navy, which, once it was obvious that such cables would be needed all over the world, adapted several redundant Napoleonic War battleships for the job, including the famous *Agamemnon*.[2] Overland cable was laid in trenches. A special plough was used for this, but in the Crimea, after a hard winter, the ground was still frozen until the spring and the trenches had to be dug by hand. To deal with this, a new unit called the Signal Service was formed within the Royal Sappers and Miners (later called the RE). In the Crimea this unit only had two telegraph office wagons, a cable cart and the trench plough, but after the American Civil War a separate signal unit was formed with its own field telegraph train and an establishment of five officers, 245 non-coms and other ranks, and 150 horses, of which 90 were for riding and the others for draught. Although they had a few wagons for carrying stores, a forge and pontoons, the wagons were mainly used to carry spools of insulated wire and the tools necessary for joining it. Each wagon carried 3 miles of cable (referred to as wire until 1884) in six drums, mounted on reels. They also carried the arms of the escort troops. Whenever possible, the cable was laid adjacent to roads; if it had to cross another road a bridge of poles was erected to carry it. The first trial of this system was made in 1871. The cable itself was made of copper wire insulated with gutta percha; this proved a very popular snack for the local mice, whose nibbling often broke the wire.

In India at this time telegraph supplies were carried in packs on mules and camels. Two short rolls of cable could be carried on one mule, while another carried the trenching tools, a third the poles and a fourth the office equipment. The poles were in three pieces and each mule carried enough to cover half a mile. In Assam and Burma elephants were used and could carry 2 miles of poles, or a large drum of wire mounted on a howdah.

By the end of the Boer War most cables were carried on tall poles rather than laid in trenches, but the work was still known as 'laying cable'. A cable-laying team consisted of a four-horse wagon, two telegraphers, three sappers on foot or riding on the wagon, a mounted commander and two mounted linesmen. These men often stood on their horses when attaching the cable to the poles, so they had to be trained to stand absolutely still.

The Royal Engineers' Signal Service was transformed into the Corps of Signals in 1920, and soon after received the addition of Royal to its title. In 1922, by which time almost all the cable was carried on poles, the team had changed to one mounted non-com officer, two signalmen and six linesmen, three of whom were mounted. The wagon had been enlarged and now required six horses, and was accompanied by a two-horse limbered wagon carrying extra cable, spares and rations. This type of vehicle remained in use until 1937.

The standing orders for signal units included a section on the care of the horses. As usually happened, these horses had numerous friends among the ranks, to the extent that when 'Nobby' retired at the age of twenty-four in 1934, his unit clubbed together and bought him. He was given the freedom of the barracks and, reported Alan Harfield, 'attended all functions such as the Sergeants' Mess Dinners, and NAAFI breaks'. Not only was he rated as 'expert' at his job, whether ridden or driven, he was also clearly expert at extracting treats from his human team-mates! Nobby was not the only old horse to end his days in this fashion. 'Old Bob' of the 11th Hussars spent twenty-five years with the regiment, surviving the Crimean War and the Charge of the Light Brigade, and was never off-duty sick. He died at the age of thirty-three and was given a splendid funeral with full military honours.

During the First World War messenger pigeons were used in sufficient numbers to require mobile lofts. As well as a few mechanised wagons, 60 horse-drawn lofts, each holding seventy-five birds, were used at first, this number increasing to 120 lofts in 1917 and again to 150 by the end of the war.

Chapter Fourteen

Other Animals

Although this book is about horses and other equines, the British Army also used other animals for draught and pack purposes. At the end of the First World War, in addition to horses and mules, there were also 56,287 camels, bullocks and donkeys in army service. During the Second World War there were some 13,000 oxen in service in India, and over 10,000 donkeys were sent to India from South Africa, many of which went on to work in Burma.

Camels

In the Afghan War of 1878–1879 numerous camels were used, at least 8,000 of them purchased and nearly 14,000 hired. Of these, 9,496 were lost due to poor selection, inadequate care, starvation, cold and overwork. In the campaign as a whole, some 26,700 camels were lost.

Full-grown camels weigh about 10cwt, their average length is 8ft nose to tail and they can carry a load of 320–450lb, according to their size and strength. The stride of a baggage camel at the walk is 6–7ft long, moving at 2–2.5mph. The riding camel, which is a different breed to the baggage camel, ambles at 4–4.5mph and jogs at up to 7mph. They also gallop, but are rarely asked to do so as this pace is very uncomfortable. These riding beasts can carry 250lb at 12mph for long periods, covering 30 miles daily.

There are several breeds of baggage camel, all of which perform best in conditions similar to those where they were bred. They can carry 250–450lb and occasionally pull carts. They should not work for more than eight hours per day, and should ideally be allowed to graze for six hours per day and given time to ruminate. If grazing is not available, they should have about 6lb of grain or ground gram (chickpeas) and 40lb forage. The grain should always be mixed well with bhoose (chaff) to prevent it being gobbled without proper mastication. Ideally all grain should be crushed. A little salt should be mixed with the feed to make it more palatable. They should be watched when feeding, as failure to eat properly is usually a sign of sickness. As far as grazing is concerned, camels like wormwood, thorn bushes, thistles and coarse, prickly and saline grasses, and they will fight for a leguminous plant called 'rtem'. They should be supervised when grazing to ensure they do not wander off or get mixed up with another herd. After a few hours they will begin to stand about or sit down; when this happens, the whole herd should be stopped from moving forward, and they will all sit and ruminate for a couple of hours. Herds should never be larger than sixty to eighty individuals.

Their watering needs depend on the breed, but range from daily to every four days. Deprived of food and water, the camel will die of exhaustion; an inexperienced handler may not recognise the symptoms of deprivation until the camel lies down and dies. Their drinking pattern is to take in a long draught, then bring their head up and stare about them for several minutes before taking another long draught. Some will do this a third time, and the inexperienced handler may think they have finished and pull them away from the water. They should be left at the water until all the group have finished drinking, as if one is taken away, the others are likely to follow before they have had enough. Like horses, they should be watered before feeding, and after unloading. When watering, the nose-rope should be removed; if he or another beast puts their foot on it he will jerk his head up and possibly damage his nose in the process.

Camels do not have a single internal 'cistern', as is sometimes suggested; they have one of about 2 pints on the right side of the stomach and another of about 1 gallon on the left. These hold a mixture of food, water and mucus. The hump is mainly adipose tissue, not a 'larder'. Its size and firmness are an indication of health and it will waste away with privation.

Camels' feet are adapted to soft sand; they do not do well on muddy or slippery ground, or on very stony ground. When the ground is slippery they are liable to strain their legs, or even fall and break bones. They also get sore chest pads when parked on stony ground. In this event, a hole should be dug and filled with soft sand for the pad to rest on. Although they swim well, they cannot cross narrow ditches and need a bridge; in terrain which is likely to include such ditches, portable bridges should be carried. Consistently wet feet are not good for them.

It has been said that the camel's temperament is 'peculiar at times'; this translates to the bad temper of a male when in musth (breeding condition). The booklet on camel management issued by the Indian government remarked hopefully:

> ... though a camel may make a fuss, and his open mouth and formidable tushes may look terrifying, in ninety-nine cases out of a hundred, there is nothing to be afraid of. All he requires, in common with other animals, is firm handling, and if this is set about in a businesslike way it is very seldom that he will try to savage his attendant.

It was felt that camels would be more even-tempered if they were gelded but they rarely were. Otherwise, they are only bad-tempered if cruelly treated, normally responding to kind treatment. When in a temper they are likely to bite each other, often on the head, feet or withers, or, when grazing, the testicles, often so badly that they have to be removed. Bites to the withers may seem to heal, but abscesses may break out a little way away from the original wound where sinuses connect to the bite.

Like other working animals, camels need to be groomed regularly. When they moult, they should not be worked hard. In summer weather, and those with short coats in winter, they should be groomed with a brush and curry comb. Coarser and shaggy-coated animals need a stiff brush. A rope quoit is also useful for grooming. With the camel sitting down, his handler brushes his back, neck and sides, then he is made to stand so the thighs, belly and legs can be thoroughly cleaned. Failure to do this can lead to sores or mange. Camels in musth or with diarrhoea should be washed. Camels are also prone to ticks, which gather in large numbers between the hind legs, and to lice, which favour the long hair on the hump and shoulder. In both cases the hair should be clipped and disinfectant washes used. Camels like being groomed, and doing it every day helps to develop a good relationship between the camel and his handler. In cold wet weather they may need to be covered with a fitted waterproof rug called a jhool.

Camels should be kept on well-drained ground (with stones removed), with shade in the summer and wind-screens in the winter. The lines should slope away a little and a drain should be dug behind them.

A healthy and well-bred camel will have a short compact skull, with a distinct 'stop' which makes the eye sockets look prominent, short lips and a short slightly arched nose. The head should be carried up with ears pricked and the neck, where it joins the skull, should be broad and strong; the eye should be clear. The forelegs should be straight with the elbows set out from the side so they do not rub on the chest pad. The body should be compact with muscular loins.

Camels are prone to sarcoptic mange. The ground on which the sufferers have been sitting should be disinfected and no other camels allowed on it, and the men handling mangey camels should not be allowed to touch other camels. Long hair should be clipped off and burned and remedies applied to the whole animal. When several camels are affected, they will need to be dipped. A trench 2ft 9in deep should be dug and filled with the dip – a mixture of freshly dug lime, sulphur and liquid creosote mixed with water. The camels are made to sit in it, and with their nose held shut the liquid is poured over them and scrubbed in. The other major disease of camels is surra, which is transmitted by flies or ticks, usually active in hot weather at sunrise or sunset. It causes intermittent fevers and severe cases will die quite quickly; others linger on for many months, becoming more and more debilitated.

Camel hospitals were allocated according to the number of camels with an army in the field. They were stationary units appropriately placed (ideally in surra-free zones). Unlike the hospitals for other animals, they did not require stables as the patients were kept in lines with mud-built feeding troughs. However, they should have wind-screens and be located where there was good shade from trees and reasonably close to good camel grazing with a water supply not used by other animals. They should be well away from cultivated land or horse hospitals, and kept meticulously free of camel dung, especially close to water troughs.[1]

Camels could be transported by train, six to a truck. There should be at least 6in of sand on the floor. They usually needed to be forced in the first time, using pulley blocks and a rope passed under the root of the tail. If they resisted, two men should take hold of the stifles of the hind legs, lift and push forward; rather than fall on its nose, the camel will step forward. Once inside, they were made to sit down until they had grown accustomed to the motion of the train, when they could be allowed to stand. They should be fitted with nets over their noses to prevent them biting each other. After their first train ride most camels will usually enter the trucks freely on their own.

Dogs

In the First World War Germany had a large force of trained dogs, but Britain, having seen their usefulness, only started training them after that war under the auspices of the RAVC. Together with the RSPCA, they made a joint appeal for suitable dogs to train for military duties and the Director General asked the civilian veterinary profession to persuade the public to donate young healthy dogs for this purpose, rather than having them put down because of the food shortage and other difficulties associated with the Blitz, as suitable dogs to train were scarce. Some 6,000 dogs were obtained through this appeal. The War Dog Training School, which was initially at Aldershot, was moved to other premises: a large greyhound kennels at Northampton and another location at Cheltenham. At the start of the war these dogs were required for guard patrols on aerodromes; later they were also used for sentry duty and as message carriers. The RE needed them for mine detection (and laying fine cable over short distances) and the Royal Army Medical Corps (RAMC) for finding wounded troops. They were also used by the Civil Defence Service to locate people buried under rubble after air raids.

The breeds wanted initially were Airedales, Alsatians, Boxers, Collies, Bull Terriers and Bull Mastiffs and crossbreeds of Dobermann Pinschers, Great Danes, Irish Terriers, Rottweilers and Malinois. Later Boxers were dropped from the list because of their aggressive temperament, while Labradors and Retrievers were added. When dogs were sent abroad, those going to hot countries were carefully selected. Long-haired Alsatians, being prone to skin diseases, were rejected, as were any dogs with a history of skin disease. Flat-faced dogs, such as Rottweilers or Boxers, tended to suffer from heat exhaustion in transit and could not be sent to tropical countries in summer.

In Belgium dogs were traditionally used to pull small carts delivering milk; this practice was adapted by the army to pull machine-gun carts. Dog-sleighs were also used in northern Russia, using local dogs and sleighs; elsewhere Alaskan Malamutes were used. With a pair of panniers, dogs can carry half their own weight, usually about 50lb.

Dogs were extensively used for guard duties at supply depots, which were viewed as prime targets by locals with what was politely described as 'pilfering proclivities'. A dog training school was started near Cairo in June 1942 and trained dogs and their handlers were posted to the Royal Military Police Dog companies. They made 3,398 arrests in the Canal Zone and recovered £94,000-worth of stolen property.

Dogs were transported by sea and air in specially built crates called shipping kennels and went on to where they were needed by lorry or other vehicle. Some were even dropped from planes by parachute. The cargo ships used to take dogs to the Middle and Far East had little space for conducting personnel, so there was one man for every ten dogs, two for up to twenty dogs. For larger numbers, three or four men were required, one of whom would be a senior NCO. Ideally there would also be a veterinary officer, otherwise the men would be given basic training in veterinary first aid and in the prevention and treatment of enteritis, diarrhoea, skin diseases, fevers and heat exhaustion. They were issued with a veterinary first aid wallet (one per ten dogs), and if the veterinary and remount services decided, with additional items, all with instructions for their use. A common ailment in dogs at sea was constipation caused by lack of exercise, so unless the weather conditions were exceptional, each dog should have ten to fifteen minutes of exercise twice a day, ideally at cooler times of day. They should also be vigorously brushed and hand massaged, to prevent the skin becoming dirty and itchy.

Other equipment issued started with one kennel per dog, leather collars at a rate of one per dog plus 50 per cent spare, halter chains, lead ropes and muzzles at a rate of one per dog plus 25 per cent spare, two bowls and a brush and comb for each dog, a 13in bucket per ten dogs, electric torches with reserve batteries, saddle soap for leather equipment and a small supply of lubricating oil for dog chains and door hinges.

The kennel crates needed to be strong enough to contain the dogs but light enough for easy handling. There had to be enough room for the dog to turn round and have adequate ventilation but still provide cover in wet weather. It should have attachment points to fix it to the deck of the ship. As the kennels were carried as deck cargo, they could not be loaded until the hatches were closed and any other deck cargo positioned. The name and army number of the dog should be stencilled on the outside of the kennel.

The kennels were to be scrubbed out and aired at least once a day, the dogs being tethered outside while this was done. They often took this opportunity to relieve themselves, and the final task when they were back in their kennels was to hose down and scrub the immediate area. Awnings should be erected to keep the kennel area cool, and the area should be frequently hosed.

If the conducting personnel had no experience of sea travel, they were issued with anti-seasickness pills in case of need. Although most ships' crews were usually helpful, they could not be expected to care for the dogs if the conducting officer was incapacitated. The conducting personnel were given a minimum of seven days before the voyage to handle and make friends with all the dogs. Documents which needed to be carried included a descriptive list of all the dogs, with health certificates, export/import licences and rabies cards where required.

At home, or on permanent bases abroad, the standard ration for dogs included fresh meat (often horsemeat), biscuits and green vegetables. On board ship the ration was usually tinned dogfood and biscuit. To ensure that neither diarrhoea nor constipation occurred on the voyage, the dogs needed to be accustomed to the tinned diet before embarkation. On board, they had 1lb of meat and 1/2lb of biscuit per day, with a 25 per cent reserve carried; they also had 2lb of straw per dog per day with a reserve of 10 per cent. In hot areas they should be fed in the cool of the evening; in cold climes twice a day. Fresh water should always be available, but some dogs needed to be watched as they either upset their water bowl, or even tried to lie in it to cool down.[2]

After the end of the Second World War the RAVC set up a quarantine unit at Chilbolton for service personnel who wished to take their dogs home. A base was set up at Milan; batches of up to twenty dogs were taken there and then on by train to Antwerp and from there to England. By the spring of 1946 over 600 dogs had gone home through that pipeline.

Elephants

Elephants can carry up to 1,200lb each and under this load can move at 3½mph. They were used to transport heavy guns and mortars and the large heavy tents which were used in India, where elephants were most commonly used. They can also carry up to six men, two on each side and one each at the front and the back. During the Afghan War of 1878–1880 they were used to move heavy batteries. Two elephants carried one gun, and there were six on the establishment of a heavy battery, but they were found to be gun-shy (and their size made them a good target for the enemy). They were kept in use for about fifteen years after 1889 but they did need a tremendous amount of food, ideally including a large quantity of greenery. When resting, they should be sheltered from the sun. They need about 30 gallons of water a day, taken in two waterings, and should also be washed twice a day, ideally (at least from their point of view) in a shallow river or stream.

Elephants were occasionally carried on ships, but then needed 4lb of grain, 20lb of rice or flour, 2½lb of salt, 175lb of hay and 40 gallons of water per day. On the Abyssinian expedition of 1868–1869 forty-four elephants were shipped in from India, to the amazement of the locals who only knew elephants of the wild and dangerous African sort.[3]

Oxen

Oxen (known as bullocks in India) tended to be used as draught rather than pack animals but were very slow, rarely moving at more than 1.5mph. They can draw heavy weights uphill, but tend to lose control of their legs going down. In the Peninsula they were thought capable of drawing three times the weight carried by three mules, but it was deemed sensible to keep the load at only two times.

On good roads, and with a two-wheeled cart, a yoked pair of oxen can draw a load of up to 960lb; teams of up to sixteen beasts could manage up to 5,000lb. Wellington used them in India to draw his artillery (but with teams of horses marching along with them in case the guns needed to move faster). In India two types of oxen were used: a large strong type bred to pull siege trains, eight bullocks to each gun, with the wheelers in harness and the others yoked; and a smaller beast for pack work. These Indian bullocks were of the type with a hump on their shoulder, and the pack saddles had to be made to accommodate this. Under packs, they can carry 150–200lb, but ideally should not be expected to carry more than the lighter load in mountainous country. They are very slow in hilly terrain.

The general rule with cattle is that they need an hour chewing the cud for every hour of grazing, ideally about six hours a day of grazing, and about eight hours' sleep. Oxen fed on corn do not require such a lengthy digestive process, but unless in a situation where they can graze, have to carry this corn or 'long' fodder (hay or straw). The corn was either crushed or soaked. During the Second Boer War many of the British officers in command, from Kitchener right down to those in command of the supply column escorts, did not understand the daily habits of cattle, or did not care. They should not work in the heat of the day but will not drink unless the sun is high. Ideally they should work from 2am to 9am, rest, drink and graze until 4pm and then work again until 9pm. If forced to work during the middle of the day they just died. On one occasion the Boers had set an ambush by some good grass, and the hungry cattle made a dash for the grass, making the Boers a gift of some 2,500 animals.

Oxen (and their cousins, yaks) were prone to the normal cattle diseases: rinderpest, anthrax, and foot and mouth. Rinderpest is also known as cattle plague and is so virulent that it kills 90 per cent of animals very quickly. The only sensible action on discovering it was to slaughter all affected animals and any which had been in contact with them. It can also affect sheep and goats, but horses are immune. Anthrax, although very rare in Europe, is widespread throughout tropical and sub-tropical countries. The spores which cause it can remain active in the ground for over ten years. It can also affect sheep, goats, pigs and horses. In horses, if the animal is not slaughtered quickly, it will eventually go into convulsions and die. It can also affect humans and thus is a notifiable disease. Foot and mouth disease is an acute feverish disease of cattle, sheep, goats and pigs, and in a milder form, sometimes humans. There are now vaccines available, and it is not necessarily fatal, but animals which have had it do not do well afterwards. It is characterised by weeping vesicles in between the toes (but not in humans) and weeping blisters in the mouth. It does not affect horses.

More than 5,160 oxen were used in the Afghan War of 1878–1879.

Pigeons

Pigeons were used as message carriers as far back as the sixth century BC, but it was not until the First World War that large numbers were used by the British Army. As each bird's range is no more than 200 miles, it was not practical to use them anywhere other than northern France, mostly close to the Channel.

The way 'pigeon post' works is that the birds want to return to their home loft, and are trained to do this by being taken away and released at progressively greater distances. This ability to 'home' is judged mainly on how quickly they do so; this is measured by the known distance and their average speed of 30mph. Male birds are better, but the best are those with a mate and a nest of chicks, as they are anxious to get back to them.

Clearly pigeons were not as fast as the telegraph, but where the lines for these had not yet been laid the birds were very useful. Units setting out for such locations were provided with the birds' food and water, and message pads.

Training flights were best conducted early in the morning, and the birds were released in pairs, as this was the procedure when carrying messages. If possible, they were gradually accustomed to gunfire. They were taken from their home lofts in baskets and could be kept in large baskets for up to seven days, or in small baskets for up to forty-eight hours. After seven days they seemed to forget where home was, and if not used in that time had to be released and a fresh batch obtained. The large baskets could be carried on a wagon or lorry, small ones on a bicycle, motorcycle or on a soldier's back.

In France there were some mobile lofts, but the birds were requisitioned under lease from private owners and remained in their home lofts until needed. The first group of seven lofts were established close to the Channel, but others were soon added further inland. These lofts were fitted with electric bells to let the owner know when the birds came back, at which the message container (leaving the message inside) would be removed and taken to the designated signal office. In some cases, when shelling was heavy, trained pigeon-handling troops were billeted nearby in case the owner wanted to leave. A bicycle was provided.

The food for these birds (wheat, maize and small dry peas) was provided by GHQ Intelligence as a bulk supply and in small packets to go with the birds when they were taken for duty. They were not to be fed immediately before flying as this slowed them down, but they needed plenty of water available at all times.

The message carrier consisted of one part which was attached to the bird's leg and a message cylinder which attached to this. Message pads were supplied in triplicate: one part remained in the pad and the other two, with perforated edges, were torn out and sent by two different birds with a time delay between them. This was for safety, in case one bird was lost en route. The message slips were very flimsy and made to fold into eight, then rolled up and put in the cylinder just before the bird was released. They could also carry microfilm. The Germans also fitted pigeons with cameras attached with a harness to their breast, presumably for aerial reconnaissance.

Pigeons were also extensively used in the Second World War, and for a few years after, operated by the Air Ministry Pigeon Section, decisions on their use being made by a Pigeon Policy Committee. It was suggested that they could be used to deliver bioweapons or small explosives but this idea was vetoed. MI5 had access to about 100 trained pigeons for intelligence work until 1950. Thirty-two pigeons have been awarded the Dickin Medal, the animal equivalent of the Victoria Cross, awarded for valour; one American pigeon, Cher Ami, was awarded the French Croix de Guerre with Palm. She returned to her loft with a crucial message after being shot in flight, blinded and with one leg shattered.

Reindeer

Reindeer were used in North Russia in 1918. Hired from their Lapp owners, they pulled sledges in teams of two with a third harnessed behind to act as a brake. With a light load they could do up to 10mph, and they could also carry a pack of 50lb. However, they could only be used in areas where there were beds of their preferred moss for them to eat.

Yaks

Yaks are an extremely hairy type of ox native to Tibet; they do best in cold weather and at high altitudes, not surviving long at altitudes of less than 8,000ft. There is a yak/ox cross called a zoom which is a little more tolerant of low altitudes. Yaks were used by the Tibetan Mission in 1904, but only

70 survived of the 1,000 they started with. They suffer from the usual cattle diseases. They are very slow and can only travel 6–8 miles a day; their response to any attempts to speed them up is to lie down and sulk. They need two days per week grazing. They were used either singly pulling a light two-wheeled cart, or driven in droves carrying packs, but would only carry 160lb each.

Human Carriers

Without any intention to suggest that human carriers are animals, and included here only because they are mentioned in many of the sources, numerous humans (often known as coolies or bearers) in some countries, including China, India and New Zealand, were used by the army to carry supplies and munitions. Some 3,000 were employed in China in 1860, being supplied with two suits of clothes, rations and monthly pay. They wore bamboo caps bearing the initials CCC (Canton Coolie Corps). They did their job, but tended to break away when possible for plundering and other mischief.

In some parts of Africa human carriers were the only form of transport available, carrying their load either on the head or back, or attached to the two ends of a flexible pole. In some cases, especially when carrying wounded, the load was suspended from a pole carried fore and aft by two men.[4]

Chapter Fifteen

Ceremonial Duties

As well as regular ceremonial duties, army horses are sometimes required for major occasions. Perhaps the greatest of these was the coronation on 2 June 1953, when senior officers of the army, navy and air force rode in the procession. Eight months before 'the day' responsibility for providing and training the 100 horses thought to be needed was given to the Veterinary and Remount Service. The officer placed in day-to-day command of the operation was Major 'Bill' Richey, at that time running the Army Equitation School at Melton Mowbray. Of the horses available at Melton Mowbray, only ten were deemed suitable. Twenty-two young horses were purchased in England, and all were given names with the initials ER: Ever Ready, Emma's Retort, etc. A further fifty horses were obtained from Army Saddle Clubs on the continent. After some training and assessment at Melton Mowbray, all the selected horses were moved to a horse camp in Hyde Park.

It transpired that many of the officers who were to ride in the procession either had no experience on horseback or had not ridden for years. The Household Cavalry closed riding school was made available for an hour each evening, during which Major Richey taught the beginners to ride and reminded the 'rusty' riders of the basics. Few of the servicemen seconded to act as grooms had any experience with horses, so they also had to learn to ride and how to handle and care for the horses. A contingent of the Royal Canadian Mounted Police was also intended to take part in the procession, but when they arrived it was found that some of them had no experience of riding anything other than a motorcycle, and so they also had to be taught how to ride a horse.

Few of the learners fell off, but there was one incident where a senior admiral, known as 'Controller', took a fall when his horse took off at a gallop and swerved into the entrance to the stables. Forunately it happened early in the morning when the press photographers had not yet arrived, so the admiral's public dignity was preserved. However, a signal was received by the First Sea Lord from the Secretary of State for War:

<u>Reference high speed trials recently carried out by Controller aboard entirely new type carrier.</u>
Much regret hear of pilot's crash landing and hope fully recovered.

Believe unwise this type carrier steam thirty knots when passing close to home port.

Hope Controller and general repute [of] carriers undamaged.

Major Richey likewise received a poem from the Board of Admiralty:

What a pity it is when the Board,
Or even just one naval Lord,
Is supplied with a charger –
Like a pony but larger,
He isn't informed
Or even forewarned
That it wheels to the right
When its stable's in sight
One blare on the horn
Is sufficient to warn
Of a turn to the right at sea.
We don't understand why
You don't modify
Your chargers accordingly.

There was one important aspect relating to riding in such a procession. In general the whole procession was kept at a walk; it was necessary to keep the royal coach moving at the same speed throughout, but in such a long procession there tends to be a 'concertina' effect when the column either comes almost to a halt or gaps open up and the horses have to trot to catch up. Novice riders find the sitting trot uncomfortable and there was insufficient time to teach them how to deal with this, so instead they were taught the rising trot, which is comparatively easy. After the fourth lesson on this all that was needed was to refine their use of the aids to enable them to maintain their dressing.

While the riders were attending the coronation service in the Abbey, grooms held their horses. It was raining and windy and the horses became excited; when remounted, they were keen to go and pranced about, but their riders were able to control them and they soon settled down when the column moved on.

As well as their basic training, the horses had to learn to remain calm when suddenly presented with a new, and potentially dangerous, situation. In such a procession there are many scary possibilities and the horses had to receive what the mounted police call 'nuisance training'. They were exposed to recordings of music and football crowds cheering, and were rewarded with oats as the volume increased. Next they were ridden (by instructors) through a lane lined with flags and bunting, and finally this was augmented by schoolchildren waving flags and yelling. The final 'dragon' was a person dashing across the lane opening and closing an umbrella, and soon even this was greeted with equanimity rather than panic.

All went well on the day, and on the following day Major Richey was supervising the break-up of the camp in Hyde Park and the return to Melton Mowbray when he received a visit from the four Sea Lords who presented him with a silver salver in appreciation of his efforts. Following this, several of the riders applied to buy the horses they had ridden in the procession; where the horses could not be absorbed into the RAVC establishment, such purchases were permitted.

In 1934, the organisers of the International Horse Show at London's Olympia decided to stage a parade of veteran war horses. It was rather short notice, but they managed to gather twenty-five horses who paraded each evening, carrying shabraques embroidered with their regiment's battle honours.

Such horses as are still in use in the army are entirely used for ceremonial purposes and belong to either the Household Cavalry or the King's Troop Royal Horse Artillery. Getting black remounts for the Household Cavalry became more and more difficult but the Dutch royal family made a gift of some, and the Royal Canadian Mounted Police deliberately chose black horses when they came to England for the Royal Military Tournament, and kindly returned home without them.

The Household Cavalry's mounted regiment carries out ceremonial duties in London, including the provision of a sovereign's escort (as seen at Trooping the Colours). They also provide the Queen's Life Guards at Horse Guards Parade.

Although most of their horses are chestnut, dark bay or brown, the King's Troop retains at least one full team of blacks and one black charger for state funerals. For state funerals in Britain, what used to be called a caisson (and still is in America) is replaced by a platform on top of the gun, and is then known as a gun carriage.

Appendix

1. Weights and Measures

As I find it cumbersome, I have not included conversions from imperial to metric in the text. For those younger readers who are not familiar with the imperial system:

1 mile   = 1.609 kilometres.
1 yard   = 0.9144 metres.
1 foot   = 0.305 metres.
1 inch   = 25.4 millimetres.
1 ton   = 2,240 lb or 1,016 kilograms (not to be confused with the metric measure of 1 tonne, which is 1,000 kilograms).
1 pound = 16 ounces (avoirdupois) or 454 grams.
1 ounce = 28.34 grams.
1 knot   = 6,082.66ft per hour (or as maritime people like to say, 'a little longer and a lot wetter than a land mile').

2. Docking Tails

The docking of horses' tails was originally done for two 'reasons': a long tail would, in muddy conditions, swish mud onto the rider and his uniform, and with carriage horses there was a risk that a long tail could get over the reins, and could only be removed by halting and physically moving it. Leaving it there was dangerous, and having to stop to move it was at best a nuisance, and at worst, in an artillery horse, impossible when in action. Tying up the hairs of the tail or plaiting it were two alternatives but this was time-consuming, so the only alternative was to cut it. The desired effect could be achieved by cutting the long hairs flush with the end of the dock (an extension of the spine), but this developed into cutting off a section of the dock, or nicking the muscles underneath the dock so the tail could not be lowered and thus was carried high, which was considered stylish. There were three 'nicking' methods for civilian horses: one nick for Thoroughbreds, two for hunters and three for Hackneys, giving rise to the expression 'cock-tailed' for horses that carried their tails like this.

Docking was done at two lengths: very short, leaving just a 2in stump, known as the Cadogan tail after Lord Cadogan, who was Quartermaster General to the Duke of Marlborough; or slightly longer, amputated at the third joint, known as a bobtail. This mutilation was of long standing and had become so fashionable that by 1796 it was difficult to buy any sort of horse that had its full tail. The problem for the horse was that it had lost its natural fly whisk, and in hot weather would be tormented by flies and other stinging insects. This tended to reduce its ability to graze in peace, to the extent that persons wanting to hire grazing for their horse had to pay more for a long-tailed horse than for one which had been docked. At least in a field they could retire to the shade of a tree, but in military horse lines they could do nothing but endure or, as often happened, break free and run off.

A further mutilation which became fashionable in military horses was cropping the tops of the ears. This was supposed to prevent their being slashed by an enemy's sword, and the practice was not abandoned until 1764, when the Earl of Pembroke, who hated the fashion for docking tails, persuaded King George III to issue an Army Order which stated:

> His Majesty having been pleased to order that all his regiments of Horse and Dragoons, except the Light Dragoons, shall be mounted only on such horses as shall have their full tails, without the least part taken from them; all breeders and dealers in horses for the service of the army are desired to take notice, that, for the future, no horses but such as shall have their full tails, without the least part taken from them, will be bought for any of the regiments of Horse and Dragoons, except the Light Dragoons.

Pembroke fixed the desirable length of a horse's tail as reaching 'halfway between the hoof and the fetterlock [sic]'. But in May 1796 the adjutant general wrote to the Board of General Officers suggesting that since there was a shortage of full-tailed horses (docking was still fashionable in the civilian world), and the 'exorbitant price demanded for them', [the use of] nag-tailed chargers should be reintroduced. The Board agreed and docking was officially reintroduced by an Army General Order of 10 August 1799: heavy cavalry (but not Life Guards or Royal Regiment of Horse Guards) to be mounted on nag-tailed horses. It was not until 1840 that the practice was finally abandoned, at least for army horses.

During the First World War the Remount Commission in the USA reported at various times that there were outbreaks of horses' tails being cut. The report did not say whether this was actual docking, or just cutting off the hair, but it was probably the latter, as the price of horse hair, especially long tail hair, was high.

3. Horse Breeds and Types

A Scottish troop of Horse Guards was raised in 1661; these were probably mounted on black horses of the heavy native Lanarkshire breed. From this

Lanarkshire horse, by the use of imported Flemish stallions, the present Clydesdale was evolved.

The Cleveland Bay is thought to have originated in a Yorkshire packhorse of medieval times, bred in the district of Cleveland, with clean legs and bay in colour. When the first coaches appeared, the strong and active Clevelands were in great demand to pull them over the shocking roads. As in the case of the Hackney, Arab blood was introduced in order to increase the pace of the Cleveland Bay. The result was an outstanding harness horse. In the nineteenth century, after the disappearance from the roads of the stage and mail coaches, large Thoroughbred stallions were mated with Cleveland Bay mares to produce big horses for private and state coaches. Known as Yorkshire Coach Horses, these beautiful animals stood at about 17hh and were in great demand, but as far as the army was concerned, they were not as suitable as the original Cleveland Bays.

In 1781 what became the Indian Army but was at that time the army of the East India Company raised its first cavalry regiments in Madras. Most of the local breeds of horse were too small; this was remedied by starting government-run horse-breeding programmes, using imported stallions, but what they did was largely based on guess-work, and the project was costly. Amongst the native breeds used were the Dekhani, the Kathiawar and the Marwari, but the best were the Arab and the Turcoman. A few English officers rode Thoroughbreds as chargers, but most of these were imported solely for stud work. The other types of horse that were imported on a large scale were the Australian Waler and the Cape Horse, until the discovery of diamonds in South Africa in 1871 made the latter too valuable to export to India. Early photographs of Indian Army officers show them mounted on slim, very long-legged horses. Whether this was a matter of choice, or all that was available is not known.

At home, at the turn of the nineteenth century the Royal Artillery changed from using two cart-horses harnessed in tandem (i.e. one in front of the other) to the heavy guns which accompanied the infantry into the field, with the drivers walking alongside, to the same system as the Royal Horse Artillery which used a team of six horses harnessed in pairs with the drivers mounted on the nearside horses. Each pair performed a role slightly different from the others: the wheelers (i.e. those next to the gun) were considered the power-house of the team, and needed to be stockier and heavier, with thicker bone, thicker rear legs and a strong neck. They could be slightly less tall than the others, at 15.1–15.2hh. The pair of leaders were the most lightly built and the tallest, at up to 16.3hh; they supplied the speed. The centre pair were slightly taller than the wheelers, at 15.2–15.3hh, and were more all-rounders than specialists. This was the position in which artillery remounts began their training. This system, which allowed the guns to move at speed when going into action, required more lightly built horses than those needed for the tandem system; they could not only trot fast but also, if required, gallop to keep up with the cavalry.

The Remount Department's 1906 instructions on the desirability of types of horse started with the class of horses wanted, their size, age (between five and nine years) and gender (geldings and mares not in foal), and commented that they should be in 'fair flesh and condition' and able to carry up to 15 stone (210lb) under active service conditions. They should be 'sound in action, wind and eyes, strong and active with fair riding shoulders, strong quarters and loins, with short well-shaped backs and legs, roomy, well-ribbed, with good, clear, straight action, strong, clean legs and feet ... quiet, without vice, well-broken and mouthed. Their teeth should be complete, well shaped and not tampered with.'

Horses for the Household Regiments had to be well-bred but able to carry weight. As their work was mainly escort duties in London, they also had to be good-looking. At age five they should be 16hh. The price paid for them was considerably higher than that for other troop horses, which did not have to be so tall, at 15.2 or 15.3hh. The quality differential was also imposed on horses for the artillery: those for the Royal Horse Artillery needing to be better-looking than those for the Royal Field Artillery. Both should be of the weight-carrying hunter type and close to 15.3hh. For the Royal Engineers and Army Service Corps, draught horses of the 'Parcel Vanner' type were preferred, of close to 16hh and able to trot with a good load behind them. For Mounted Infantry, cobs or galloways were wanted, quick and active and able to gallop fast for a short distance; polo ponies were ideal. They should be at least five years old when bought.

By the start of the First World War the light draught horse of the best type had become hard to find, owing to their progressive displacement by mechanical power, especially the English coach horse which could trot with a substantial load on good roads at 8mph for long distances. Most of the light draught horses used in the First World War were crosses between Shires or Clydesdales and Hackneys; these were called on to do the hardest work in the field artillery and other branches of the army, and they 'contributed more than their fair proportion of wastage from sickness and mortality'.

Many heavy draught horses died from pneumonia in the first year of the war, both in Britain and on landing in France, to the extent that it was queried whether any more should be bought. Veterinary officers with experience of these heavy horses had warned of their weakness for military purposes, not only from their high susceptibility to disease and inability to tolerate forced marches, but also from their large requirements for food and water.

However, two good heavy horses such as Shires, Clydesdales, Suffolk Punches or Percherons could do the work of four mules or light draught horses, provided they were not asked to go above a steady walk. This meant less equipment, shoeing, attendants and stabling. But the vets had another objection to the Shires and Clydesdales, in that their hairy legs and feet made it difficult to get them dry in wet and muddy conditions, leading to various skin complaints. Suffolk Punches and Percherons do not have feathered legs and so are not prone to such problems.

4. Colours and Markings

In general, the army has always preferred dark-coloured horses; in the early days black was the preferred colour, but by the third quarter of the eighteenth century the difficulty in obtaining sufficient black horses had resulted in different regiments using horses of different colours.

In the 1780s an order was given for the colours of horses to be used by the light dragoons: General Elliot's troop horses should be mostly chestnut, with one grey; Lieutenant Colonel Ainslie's troop should be mostly bay, with one grey; Major Elliott's troop should be all black, except one brown; Captain Bain's troop should be mostly bay; and Captain Churchill's troop should be mostly brown. Where one horse was to be of a different colour from the rest, this animal was usually used as a drumhorse or by a trumpeter. The Scots Greys were, of course, all grey.

In 1796 a Board of General Officers remarked on the scarcity of black horses suitable for mounted regiments, and soon after this the rigid colour schemes for different regiments was abandoned. However, in 1811 the 3rd Dragoons were still mounted entirely on black horses and took them out to the Peninsula.

The Remount Department's 1906 instructions stated that their colour should not be white or very light grey. Colours should not be 'washy' coloured or very light, and white or grey horses were only needed for particular purposes and were always specially ordered. The only white or grey horses (apart from those of the Scots Greys) were those serving in medical units and administrative work on lines of communication. The reason for this colour rule was that very pale-coloured animals are more easily seen at a distance than darker ones. (Their hairs are also more conspicuous on clothing.) With the exception of drumhorses or trumpeter's horses, two-coloured horses were not used. Horses for the Household Regiments were still required to be black.

The rule on not buying pale-coated horses applied to mules as well, but many mules bought in Iraq and Persia were grey. There was some disagreement over their visibility in daylight, but this was later found not to matter. Until then, a brown dye was used; this lasted about three months, but later batches of the dye proved less effective.

The colours of horses are as follows:

- Black – black, with a black muzzle.
- Bay – varying shades of brown (often quite dark) or chestnut, with black mane and tail and in some cases, black points (the lower legs from the knee or hock down).
- Chestnut – a rich reddish colour, varying from light to quite dark, in which case it is known as a liver chestnut.
- Brown – darker than chestnut, but not as dark as black.
- White – horsey people maintain that there is no such thing as a white horse: they are actually very pale grey, and become paler as they age. They have a white muzzle.
- Grey – variations on the grey theme. All these horses are born very dark brown and become paler as they mature. Many are dappled, like an old-fashioned rocking horse. Some are dark with black points and are called steel grey.
- Roan – the colour is made up of an even mixture of individual white hairs and individual hairs of another colour: black, chestnut or brown. A blue roan is made up of white and blue-black hairs with a black muzzle, mane, tail and points; a strawberry roan is made up of white, black and chestnut hairs with a light muzzle and chestnut mane and tail.
- Dun – a pale-ish coat, ranging from mid-grey (known as mouse-dun, or grulla in America), through dark cream to dull gold. They have a black stripe running down their backbone from the withers to the root of the tail, and black points.
- Piebald and skewbald – basically white, with large irregular patches of black (piebald) or chestnut/brown (skewbald). These are unacceptable in the army, except as drumhorses or trumpeter's horses. They are considered by most of the horsey establishment to be rather common.
- Palomino – gold coat, with white mane and tail. Considered by most of the horsey establishment to be over-showy, and not used in the British Army.
- Appaloosa – there are two types: either white all over with black spots, or strawberry roan at the front with white spotted quarters. The latter tend to have very sparse tails. They were not used by the British Army.

Horses also have what are known as markings; these are white or black patches on the legs and white patches on the face. On the legs white points are known as stockings (where the white extends from close to the knees or hocks down) or socks (shorter white parts of the leg, from the fetlock down). They may be on one or more legs, and have long been considered a sign of temperament, hence the saying, 'One sock, try him; two socks buy him, three socks suspect him, four socks reject him.'

White face markings range from white-face, where the white covers both eyes and much of the cheeks, to a star, where there is just a small white patch on the forehead, or a blaze, which is a long white stripe from the forehead or between the eyes down to the nose.

Small white marks elsewhere on the coat are a sign of a healed injury, when the colour of the hair is lost. They are most common on the lower legs or around the withers, where saddles have rubbed sore patches.

5. Telling Age by the Teeth

It is well known that you can tell the age of a horse by his teeth, but few people, other than the deeply horsey, know how to do it. It depends on the number of permanent teeth in the mouth, or, once all the permanent teeth are through, by changes in the appearance of the front teeth in the lower jaw.

Horses have three kinds of teeth: front teeth or incisors, back teeth or molars, and canine teeth or tushes. The part of the gums between the tushes and the back teeth is known as the bars of the mouth, and it is here that the bit goes. The whole of a horse's dentition is called his 'mouth'.

The tushes (two in the top and two in the bottom jaws), which are rarely found in mares, are permanent teeth, which do not come through until the horse is mature at about four-and-a-half years old. On the bottom jaw they sit about ½in behind the corner front teeth, and about 1½in behind the corner front teeth on the top jaw.

The incisors and molars start as temporary or milk teeth, and are gradually replaced by permanent teeth as the horse grows up. A foal, in his first month, has sixteen teeth: one front and three back on each side. By six weeks old he has four more front teeth, and between six and nine months another four front teeth develop. At twelve months he has one permanent molar on each side, top and bottom, as well as the three milk teeth. Between two-and-a-half and three years old an additional four permanent molars appear at the back of each jaw, and the first and second temporary molars have been replaced by permanent teeth. By three-and-a-half years old a fifth permanent molar has come through and the last of the temporary molars have been replaced, as have the 'next to the centre' incisors.

By four-and-a-half the last four molars (the sixth) have come through, and the outer incisors have also been replaced. A five-year-old horse is said to have a full mouth: twelve front teeth, twenty-four back teeth, and (in males) four tushes, making a total of forty (or thirty-six for mares).

The front teeth should meet flat against each other (this is known as the table), and are used to nip and pull off vegetation, usually with an alternate sideways motion, left to right then right to left. For efficient grazing they require the grass to have a little length (as opposed to sheep, which nibble short grass even shorter, leaving a lawn-like surface; cows require longer grass as they wrap their tongue round it and pull it off). The horse, having pulled/ bitten off a bunch of grass (or leaves, if browsing, or even flowers, if a visitor is rash enough to carry a bunch), passes it back to the molars which grind it up with a lateral movement. The back teeth do not meet flat on, but at an angle of about 25 degrees, those on the lower jaw sloping upwards and inwards, and those on the upper jaw sloping downwards and outwards. Older horses some- times develop sharp edges on these teeth which can discourage them from eating; these have to be ground down with a special rasp.

After five years the age of the horse can be seen in his front teeth as they push up and are worn down. At six years the upper corner teeth, looked at from the side with the mouth closed, are a little longer front to back on their table surface. By seven years this difference will have developed into a notch or hook at the back of the teeth, known as 'the seven year hook', which protrudes back and downwards. Unscrupulous dealers often rasped these down flat to make the horse look younger. At ten years old a groove called Galvayne's Groove appears on the top centre of the corner teeth, and works its way down; by fifteen years it reaches half-way down the teeth, and by twenty will have reached the bottom; at twenty-five it is half grown out and at thirty it is completely grown out and cannot be seen any more.

After seven years old it is extremely difficult to age a horse accurately by his teeth, and he is just referred to as 'aged'. However, as the front teeth continue to grow, they project forward rather than meeting perpendicularly; the longer the teeth, the more acute the angle, but they still function perfectly well.

6. Hiring Horses to Officers[1]

Between the wars (and after the Second World War Two) officers whose rank entitled them to a horse but who did not need one for military purposes could hire one from the Remount Department for general purposes, including ordinary hacking, hunting, polo, show-jumping, National Hunt racing or other competitive use. Officers issued with a horse for military purposes could also 'hire' it for these non-military activities. They could also allow their family (those living with them) to use it, or lend it to another officer.

Hiring fees at home in 1930 were £3.5s per quarter for Household Cavalry chargers, £3 for other chargers and £2.2s.6d for cobs; abroad, the fees were £2.2s.6d for both chargers and cobs. By 1939 these charges had fallen to £1.1s.8d and £1 for chargers at home and 14s.2d for chargers abroad. Further instructions were issued in 1954 and 1966, but these do not state the amounts involved. It was also possible for officers to buy their chargers on a hire- purchase basis. If the hirer took the horse away from his unit, he was respon- sible for veterinary costs, and any costs of keeping the horse away from its unit (stabling, rail charges, grooms, etc.). Wherever the horse was situated, the officer had to pay for it to be shod monthly.

There were some restrictions on the use of these horses. Those used for hunting were not to be used for polo as well without special permission; those for polo were not to be used more than three days a week, nor for more than two chukkas on any single day. Those horses which were hunted should not go out more than three days a fortnight, or two days a week if used exclusively for drag hunting.

7. Syllabus of Officer Courses at the Army Veterinary College

- Introduction – Explanation of the general nature of the course. Outline of the various subjects and suggestions for useful books, etc.
- Conformation – Minute description of the various 'points' of the animals, describing perfection, true and faulty shapes; how to detect a lame limb; various external seats of disease; lessons in horse judging and selection of remounts, chargers, etc.; practical demonstrations on living animals.
- Construction of stables – True and faulty constructions; situation; aspect; light; ventilation; drainage; mangers and bails; headcollars; chains; logs; surcingles, prevention of disease due to bad management; sanitary laws.
- Stable management – Structure and functions of the skin; theory of grooming. General routines of stable duties and how they should be performed; precautions to be observed; evils to be avoided; management of remounts. Causes, prevention and treatment of sore backs (in barracks, on the line of march, in camp and on service). Fitting of saddlery with reference to conformation, structure and function of the back, structure of the saddle; loss of condition; stuffing panels, and remedies to prevent collar and girth galls; numnahs and blankets. Principles of watering and feeding and varieties of bedding.
- Forage and dietetics – Situation, structure and functions of digestive organs; course of the food, digestion, nutrition. Description of the various grasses found in hay; their relative value (specimens of each shown); how to distinguish the different qualities of hay (good, indifferent and bad); various qualities and relative nutritive value of oats, beans, peas and other kinds of grain, roots, hay, etc. (specimens of each shown). Proportions of flesh-forming and heat-giving constituents; damaged grains; weights of different qualities and how to detect impositions practised; chaff cutting; oat crushing; patent and compressed foods; nose-bag feeding; service rations; green forage, roots, mashes, gruels, food and feeding in different countries.
- Embarkation and management of horses on board ship – Various methods of embarking. Precautions to be observed; securing, slinging, dietetics and general stable management on board; ventilation and sanitary measures to be observed; daily routines; and practical suggestions on landing.

- Management of horses in line of march and in camp – Rations; water and watering; watering from rivers and ponds, barrels, troughs, etc. Picketing (various methods); prevention of accidents, picketing of wind-suckers, kickers and biters; sanitation of standings, disposal of manure; blankets, surcingles, eye-fringes, etc.; change of ground, preventing waste of forage; care of feet, preventing line-gear injuries; grazing, knee haltering; clearance of encamping grounds of bottles, etc.; levelling unseen parts; causes of and prevention of stampedes; nose-bags; heel ropes; head rope and picket-line galls; tails to be allowed to grow; grooming, etc.
- The foot – Situation and function of its various structures. How to examine for and to detect foot lameness generally. Minor diseases of the foot, their varieties, causes, symptoms, treatment and prevention. Corn; nailbound; puncture or pricked foot; contusion, foot congestion; thrush, sand crack and seedy toe. Also cutting or brushing, overreach, speedycut and treads.
- Principles of shoeing – Precautions to be observed in preparing the foot for the shoe, and the evils to be avoided. Careless fitting, paring, rasping, etc., and how to detect (given in detail). Shoeing for defective conformation. Description of service regulation, and also ordinary, special and machine-made shoes (specimens exhibited); shoeing for frost; various descriptions of nails, etc.; shoeing tools; loose and lost shoes; care of feet in and out of stables; frog pressure; picked up nails and stones; interchange of shoes; store shoes and nails; shoe cases; forging or clicking; foot contraction and causes.
- Diseases and injuries – Elementary description of the situation, structure and function of the heart, lungs and air passages, circulation of the blood, pulse, etc.; general outlines of disease and lameness; the causes, symptoms and treatment of ordinary cases met with in barracks, camp and on service; detection of glanders and farcy, and how to act in emergency. Varieties of diet for sick horses, good nursing and general hospital management. Causes, symptoms and popular treatment of various wounds, scalds, burns, sprains, windgalls, cracked heels, mud fever, ringworm, mange, prevention of fractures, catarrh, strangles, colic, diarrhoea, exhaustion, indigestion, hidebound or swelled legs. Various methods of arresting haemorrhage, bandaging, sick nursing, etc.
- The teeth and age – Outlines of the structure of the teeth. Dentition; how to detect age by the teeth, and the changes that take place from birth to extreme age (specimens exhibited); impositions practised [by those who wish to make old horses look younger].[2]

8. Syllabus of the Course of Instruction in Shoeing

- The easiest and safest method of seizing, lifting and holding the horse's front and hind feet, as in the operation of shoeing. NB: this operation should be carried out on old steady horses and particular care should be observed in showing how the shoer is to manage the restless or vicious horse, and the precautions to guard himself from injury. Patient and gentle treatment should be inculcated. How to shoe troublesome horses with the wide-line on the hind leg is also to be taught.

- The best and most expeditious way to take off fore and hind shoes. NB: completely cut off all clenches, insert pincers between shoe and hoof, towards the extremity of inside heel, prise steadily and firmly downwards and across the foot to start heel nails and withdraw these; then apply pincers to outside heel in the same manner, withdrawing nails, and go on until the shoe is off. Show how to remove broken nails from the hoof when the shoe is off; and also how to take off shoes from a painful foot, by driving the nails downwards from the front of the hoof and withdrawing them one by one.

- How to handle the rasp, and reduce the wall of the hoof properly to its normal dimensions. NB: the proper length and natural slope of the wall are to be shown, and the method of obtaining these in an overgrown hoof demonstrated. This is important. Hoof to be made quite level on the ground surface, which should have a wide and solid bearing for the shoe to rest upon. The sides of the hoof should be equal in height, so as to keep leg and foot in a straight direction. Toe of hoof well shortened; heels not too much lowered. Sole and frog to remain strong and unpared, loose fragments only being removed. Edge of the wall to be rounded.

- How to fit a shoe properly and quickly. NB: as it is not possible to provide shoes to fit all hoofs exactly – these varying greatly in size and form – the number of the size required should be explained, and if alteration in length or shape is needed, how this should be effected – making the shape narrower or wider, more elongated or more circular, as the shape of the hoof may demand. The shoe should fit the full outline of the hoof. A small portion of the horn must be removed at the toe of the fore foot, sides of toe of hind foot, to effect this and to lodge the clip. If the alteration is made on the anvil it should be by a series of firm, steady and not too heavy blows of the hammer. When altered to the proper shape, the shoe should be made perfectly level by hammering it lightly on the surface; this also makes it wear better. Instruct how to alter shoes without an anvil, as on the tyre or nave of a cartwheel, stone, etc. Nail-holes to be easy for the neck of nails; if too tight, widen from the fuller surface, not the back of the shoe. With holes too tight, the nails break at the neck. Show how to narrow or close fuller, so as to allow smaller nails to be used in case of necessity. There should be solid and close co-adaptation between the surface of hoof and shoe, to ensure the latter being well retained. Shoe to rest on the entire width of the wall and margin of sole. All but the hind shoes with calkins can be altered in a cold state, as a rule; and these can also be altered to some extent without heating them, when alteration is necessary.

- How to nail a shoe safely and securely. NB: the shape of the nails to be explained and the reasons for the bevel at the point insisted upon in order to prevent the nail from entering the sensitive parts of the foot. The mode of driving the nails; height to which they should be driven in the horn; their direction – toe-nails slightly forward so as to include more of the fibre of the wall; when all are inserted, how they should be driven home and drawn up at ends (with the forefeet toe-nails first and firmly; heel nails last and lightly).

- How to finish shoeing. NB: laying down and embedding the ends of the nails, or 'clenching' to be taught; and the necessity for the clenches being strong, and projecting as little as possible beyond the wall, especially on the inside of the hoof. The surface of the wall not to be rasped except round the edges between it and the shoe.

It is desirable, if possible, to acquaint the men under instruction with the structure of the horse's foot, even should the instruction be very elementary, the hoof being the chief subject for consideration.

How to fasten a loose shoe; how to make a hind shoe fit a front foot, and vice versa, on an emergency; how to remedy too fine or too coarse nail-holes; and how to act when a nail has been accidentally driven into, or too near, the quick, should also be taught.

Notes

Introduction
1. William Napier, *The Life and Opinions of General Sir Charles Napier* (London, 1857).
2. Statistics of the Military Effort of the British Empire during the Great War 1914–1920 (HMSO, 1922).
3. Philip Haythornthwaite, *The British Cavalryman, 1792–1815* (Oxford, 1989).

Chapter 1: The Nature of the Beast
1. Philip Warner (ed.), *A Cavalryman in the Crimea: the letters of Temple Goodman, 5th Dragoon Guards* (London, 1977).
2. Countess of Ranfurly, *To War With Whitaker* (London, 1994).
3. Alexander Dickson, *The Dickson Manuscripts*; John Edgecombe Daniel, *Portugal to Waterloo with Wellington: Journal of a British Commissariat Officer in the Peninsular War and the Campaign of 1815* (London, 2012); Dick Tennant, in *First Empire* (Jul./Aug. 2010).

Chapter 2: Getting the Horses
1. Piers Mackesy, *British Victory in Egypt* (London, 1995); Janet Macdonald, *Sir John Moore, the making of a controversial hero* (Barnsley, 2016).
2. Report of the Committee of Enquiry into the Army in the Crimea (1855).
3. TNA WO 33/42.
4. TNA WO 32/8758.
5. TNA WO 33/242.
6. TNA WO 107/16.
7. TNA WO 163/21
8. The Impressment of Horses and Horse-drawn Vehicles in Time of National Emergency (London, 1924).
9. Remount Manual (War) (London, 1937).
10. For details of this, see Chapter 3.
11. For reasons contributing to this wastage, see Chapter 6.
12. Statistics of the Military Effort of the British Empire during the Great War 1914–1920 (HMSO, 1922).
13. Other sources consulted include: Army Remount Dept, Minutes of Evidence …; R.J. Moore-Collyer, 'Horse Supply and the British Cavalry: a Review 1066–1900', *Journal of Army Historical Research* (Winter 1992, vol. LXX, no. 284); Types of horses suitable for army remounts (London, War Office, 1927); J.H. Wilkins, 'Conformation of the horse & purchasing of Army Horses', *Journal of the Royal Army Veterinary Corps* (Spring 1966); H.C. Wylly (ed.), *Memoirs of Lieutenant General Sir Joseph Thackwell* (London, 1908); The Trial at large of Lieutenant General Whitelock, late commander of the forces in South America (London, 1808); S. Galtry, *Horses and the War* (London, 1983), G. Tylden, *Horses and Saddlery* (London, 1965); L.E. Nolan, *Cavalry: its History and Tactics* (London, 1853); R. Hume, *The Story of the Remount Department* (Unpublished, 2010); Alan Moorhead, *The Blue Nile* (London, 1962); TNA WO 33/608, 463, 44; WO 32 8757, 8759, 8761, WO 95/69.

Chapter 3: Remount Department Administration

1. Report of the Committee on the Supply of Remounts (1902); Report on the purchase of horses and mules by the British Remount Commission in Canada and the USA, 1914–1919.
2. TNA WO 32/8757.
3. Remount Manual (War) (London, 1937).

Chapter 4: Transporting Horses by Land and Air

1. Notes on March Discipline, Entraining, Slinging and Care of Animals at Sea (Aldershot, undated but probably in the First World War).
2. J. Wortley Axe, *The Horse, its treatment in health and disease*, vol. 9 (London, 1905).
3. Transport of Horses by Rail and Sea.
4. Report on the formation and despatch to Palestine of the Cavalry Division September 1939–March 1940.
5. Remount Manual (London, 1906).
6. *Animal Transport*, part III. RASC Training Manual (London, 1922).

Chapter 5: Transporting Horses by Sea

1. James Tomkinson (ed.), *Diary of a Cavalry Officer in the Peninsular War and Waterloo Campaign 1809–1815* (London, 1894).
2. Augustus Schaumann, *On the Road With Wellington* (London, 1999).
3. Moore to Gordon, BL Add. Mss 49482, 28 October 1808.
4. R.K. Sutcliffe, *British Expeditionary Warfare and the Defeat of Napoleon* (Woodbridge, 2016).
5. Warner, *A Cavalryman in the Crimea*.
6. Major General Sir Frederick Smith, *A History of the Royal Army Veterinary Corps, 1796–1919* (London, 1927), p. 139.
7. Army Remount Department ...; Ann Hyland, *The Warhorse in the Modern Era* (London, 2015); Statistics of the Military Effort ....
8. M.H. Hayes, *Horses on Board Ship; a guide to their management* (London, 1902).
9. W.G. Bligh, 'Across the Atlantic in a Horse Transport', *The Canadian Magazine* (Nov. 1922).
10. Other works consulted include G.A. Furse, *Military Transport* (London, 1882); TNA WO 6/159; R. Glover, *Wellington as Military Commander* (London, 1968); Wylly, *Sir Joseph Thackwell*; Notes on March Discipline ...; Army Remount Dept, *Minutes of evidence*; Movement of animals by sea (c.1960).

Chapter 6: Horse Care

1. For instance: *Manual of Horse and Stable Management* (London, 1904); Catchism of Animal Management (undated); Notes on Horse Management in the Field (undated); Animal Management (London, 1908); Farriery, Patent Application no. 17805, for 'New or Improved Apparatus for use in Instructing Persons in the Art of Farriery (1915).
2. Tomkinson, *Diary of a Cavalry Officer*.
3. R. Blakeney, *A Boy in the Peninsular War* (London, 1899); C. Hibbert, *Corunna* (London, 1961); Ian Fletcher, *Galloping at Everything: the British cavalry in the Peninsular War and at Waterloo, 1808–15* (Staplehurst, 1999).
4. Annual Return for Sick and Lame Horses, 1882; Annual Statistical Report of the Veterinary Department for 1884, ditto 1886, ditto 1889. The syllabus for farrier training is given in Appendix 8; Report of the Committee of Enquiry [sic] into the Army in the Crimea (1855).

Chapter 7: Veterinary Matters

1. Annual Return of Sick and Lame Horses, 1882; Annual Statistical report of the Veterinary Department for 1884, ditto 1886, ditto 1889.

2. Handbook on Contagious & Infectious Diseases in Animals (Calcutta, 1945).

3. Captain M.R. Robson, 'Some Common Skin Conditions of Military Horses', *Chiron Calling* (Winter 2000/01).

4. The author has not been able to find references to the use of antibiotics in horses in the First World War.

5. *Black's Veterinary Dictionary* (London, 1979); Sharon Cregier, *Alleviating Surface Transit Stress on Horses* (Unpublished PhD dissertation, Walden University, 1980).

6. Douw G. Steyn, 'Animals and Poison Gas Warfare' (*Journal of the SAVMA*, 1940); Report of investigation into effects produced on horses' feet by traversing ground contaminated by mustard gas (1926), Instructions for the use of the oxygen administration apparatus for horses (1957), Chemical warfare & animals (Symptoms and treatment) (London, 1945); Regulations for the Veterinary Department of Her Majesty's Army (1882); Regulations for Army Veterinary Services (1900, 1932).

7. Other sources for this chapter included M.H. Hayes, *Veterinary Notes for Horse Owners* (London, 1884), and the www.merckvetmanual.com website.

Chapter 8: Veterinary Administration

1. Smith, *History of the Royal Army Veterinary Corps, 1796–1919*; Clabby, *History of the Royal Army Veterinary Corps, 1919–1961*.

2. Sir J. Moore, *Army Veterinary Service in War* (London, 1921).

3. It is almost impossible to heal broken bones in the horse, especially the long bones of the legs, as the animal cannot be immobilised as humans can; it is only worth trying for animals with valuable breeding potential.

4. *Army Veterinary Department Reorganisation* (War Office Selected Papers No. 62, 1910); L.J. Blenkinsop & J.W. Rainey (eds), *Army Veterinary Services in the First World War* [in *History of the Great War based on official documents*] (London, HMSO, 1925).

5. Regulations for Admission to Commissioned Rank in the Royal Army Veterinary Corps (London, 1933).

6. These diaries for the First World War are kept at the National Archives under WO 95. Unfortunately they are not numbered consecutively but can be found via the catalogue.

7. George Barnett, 'The Indian Army Veterinary Corps Centre December 1st 1942–July 16th 1946', in *The Journal of the Remount and Veterinary Corps*.

8. Other sources for this chapter include Regulations for the Veterinary Department of Her Majesty's Army (London, 1882); Regulations for Army Veterinary Services (London, 1900 and 1923); Vocabulary of Army Veterinary Stores and price supplement (1963); Dangerous Drugs Act 1951; Pharmacy and Poisons Act 1933 (amended as Pharmacy Act 1953); Therapeutic Substances Act 1956, Methylated Spirits Regulations 1952.

Chapter 9: Training Horses and Riders

1. H.C.B. Rogers, *The Mounted Troops of the British Army 1066–1945* (London, 1959).

2. Pembroke, Henry, Earl of, *Military Equitation: A Method of Breaking Horses and Teaching Soldiers to Ride* (London 1761).

3. J.G. Le Marchant, *Rules and Regulations for the Sword Exercise of the Cavalry* (London, 1796).

4. L.E. Nolan, *The Training of Cavalry Remount Horses, a new system* (London, 1852); David Kenyon, *Horsemen in No Man's Land: British cavalry and trench warfare 1914–1918* (Barnsley, 2012); Haythornthwaite, *British Cavalryman 1792–1815*; Fletcher, *Galloping at Everything*; Instructions and Regulations for the Formation and Movements of the Cavalry (London, 1796); Marquess of Anglesey, *A History of the British Cavalry 1816–1919* (London, 1973); James Fillis, *Breaking and Riding with Military Commentaries*, trans. M.H. Hayes (London, 1902).

Chapter 10: Saddlery, Accoutrements and Horse Clothing
1. TNA WO 3/29 and WO 30/13A.
2. F. Smith, Manual of Saddles and Sore Backs (Aldershot, 1891).
3. Janet Macdonald, *Riding Side-saddle* (London, 1995).
4. Tylden, *Horses and Saddlery*, p. 207, quoting an article in the *Carriage Builders and Harness Makers Art Journal* of c.1870.
5. Papers relating to a uniform horse equipment for the Cavalry (London, War Department, 1855).
6. S.G.P. Ward, *Wellington's Headquarters* (London, 1957).
7. *Harness in use in the Army Service Corps, 1917* (Aldershot).

Chapter 11: Harness, Wagons and Order of March
1. In America, this is known as the singletree.
2. Instructions relating to the baggage and marches of the army, issued by Wm Fawcett, Adjutant general, 2 November 1797.
3. Notes on March Discipline ...
4. *Animal Transport*, part III. RASC Training Manual.

Chapter 12: Cavalry and Artillery
1. George Gleig, *The Hussar* (London, 1837).
2. Edward Curling (ed.), *Recollections of Rifleman Harris* (London, 1929).
3. Macdonald, *Sir John Moore*; Sir Charles Oman, *History of the Pensinsular War* (Oxford, 1902).
4. Fletcher, *Galloping at Everything*.
5. Trevor Royle, *Crimea* (London, 1999).
6. Henry Blackburne Hamilton, *Historical Record of the 14th (King's Own) Hussars from 1715 to 1900* (London, 1900).
7. Kenyon, *Horsemen in No Man's Land*.
8. R.M.P. Preston, *The Desert Mounted Corps* (London, 1921).
9. J.M. Brereton, *The Horse in War* (Newton Abbot, 1976).
10. Other sources consulted for this chapter include: Anglesey, *History of the British Cavalry 1816–1919*; Instructions and Regulations for the Formation and Movements of the Cavalry; Haythornthwaite, *British Cavalryman 1792–1815*; Nick Lipscombe, *Wellington's Guns* (London, 2013).

Chapter 13: Equines in Non-combatant Units
1. Mark S. Thompson, *Wellington's Engineers: Military Engineering in the Peninsular War 1808–1814* (Barnsley, 2015).
2. Simon Winchester, *Krakatoa* (London, 2003).

Chapter 14: Transporting Horses by Land and Air
1. *Notes on Camel Management* (Calcutta, 1926); Veterinary Manual for War (London, 1923).
2. *Movement of Animals by Sea* (RAVC, undated but probably about 1935).
3. Moorhead, *The Blue Nile*.
4. Furse, *Military Transport*.

Appendix
1. Regulations governing the use of chargers and troop horses for general purposes 1930, ditto 1937; ditto 1954.
2. Regulations for Army Veterinary Services (London, 1900).

Bibliography

Official Pamphlets, Reports and War Office Documents

Army Remount Dept, Minutes of evidence, Court of Enquiry on the, 1/3/1902–12/6/1902.

Anti-gas cover for horses, 2/1940.

Animal management (London, 1908).

Animal Transport, Royal Army Service Corps training manual (London, 1922).

Annual Return for Sick and Lame Horses,1882.

Annual Statistical Report of the Veterinary Department for 1884, ditto 1886, ditto 1889.

Army Veterinary Department reorganisation, 1910.

Army Veterinary and Remount Services, 1939–1945 (HMSO, 1961).

Army Veterinary Service, Report on Veterinary Reconnaissance with BEF, 26/11/39–7/12/39.

Army Veterinary & Remount Services in the 1939–45 war.

Camel Management, Notes on (Calcutta, 1926).

Carrier pigeons, Memo on the use and training of.

Catechism of Animal Management (undated).

Chemical warfare & animals (Symptoms and treatment) (London, 1945).

Farriery, Patent Application no. 17805, for 'New or Improved Apparatus for use in Instructing Persons in the Art of Farriery' (1915).

Gas protection for horses, 1931 (Patent).

Handbook of Contagious & Infectious Diseases in Animals (Calcutta, 1945).

Harness in use in the Army Service Corps (Aldershot, 1917).

Horse Management in the Field, notes on (War Office, 1919).

Horses' feet and mustard gas and HS [gas] ointments.

Horse leggings, anti-mustard gas.

The Impressment of Horses and Horse-drawn Vehicles in Time of National Emergency (London, 1924).

Instructions governing use of army horses hired for non-military purposes, 1966.

Instructions relating to the baggage and marches of the army, issued by Wm Fawcett, Adjutant general, 2 November 1797.

Instructions for the use of the oxygen administration apparatus for horses (1957).

Instructions and Regulations for the Formation and Movements of the Cavalry (London, 1796).

Manual of Horse and Stable Management (London, 1904).

F. Smith, Manual of saddles and sore backs (Aldershot, 1891).

March Discipline, Entraining, Slinging and Care of Animals at Sea, Notes on (Aldershot, undated but probably in the First World War).

Methylated Spirits Regulations, 1952.

Movement of animals by sea (RAVC, undated but probably about 1935).

Oxygen administration for horses (Instructions on use of German captured equipt, 1944).

Pack Transportation (US Army War Dept, 1944).

Papers relating to a uniform horse equipment for the Cavalry (London, War Department, 1855).

Pharmacy and Poisons Act 1933 (amended as Pharmacy Act 1953).
Register of Royal Army Veterinary Corps contractors.
Regulations for Army Veterinary Services (London, 1900, 1923, 1932).
Regulations for Admission to Commissioned Rank in the Royal Army Veterinary Corps (London, 1933).
Regulations governing the use of chargers and troop horses for general purposes, 1930, 1937, 1954.
Regulations for the Veterinary Department of Her Majesty's Army (London, 1882).
Remount Manual (London, 1906).
Remount Manual (War), 1937.
Report on the Census of Horses [in GB], 1934.
Report of the Committee of Enquiry [sic] into the Army in the Crimea (1855).
Report of the Committee on the Supply of Remounts for the Army, 1902.
Report on the formation and despatch to Palestine of the Cavalry Division, September 1939–March 1940.
Report of investigation into effects produced on horses' feet by traversing ground contaminated by mustard gas (1926).
Report on the purchase of horses and mules by the British Remount Commission in Canada and the USA, 1914–1919.
Report on veterinary arrangements of the cavalry concentration at Gargaon [Simla].
Royal Wagon Train, Establishment of, 1802.
Statistics of the Military Effort of the British Empire during the Great War 1914–1920 (HMSO, 1922).
Standing orders for the Royal Army Veterinary Corps, 1960.
Training of war dogs, 1952.
Types of horses suitable for army remounts (London, War Office, 1908, 1912, 1927).
Uniform equipment for the cavalry, 1855.
Unit Animal and Animal Ration accountancy, 1953.
Veterinary Manual for War (London, 1923).
Vocabulary of Army Veterinary Stores and price supplement, 1963.
Warrant for raising a corps of wagoners by George III, 1794.
TNA: WO 33/608, 463, 44, 42; WO 32/8757, 8758, 8759, 8761; WO 33/242; WO 95/69; WO 107/16; WO 163/21; WO 95.

Books, Theses, Journal Articles
Anglesey, Marquess of, *A History of the British Cavalry 1816–1919* (London, 1973).
'Army Equitation School', in *Stable Management* (Oct./Nov. 1965).
Axe, J. Wortley, *The Horse, its treatment in health and disease*, vol. 9 (London, 1905).
Badsey, Stephen, *Doctrine and Reform in the British Cavalry* (Aldershot, 2008).
Barnett, George, 'The Indian Army Veterinary Corps Centre December 1st 1942–July 16th 1946', in *Journal of the Remount and Veterinary Corps*.
Blackburne-Hamilton, Henry, *Historical Record of the 14th (King's) Hussars, from AD 1715 to AD 1900* (London, 1925).
Black's Veterinary Dictionary (London, 1979).
Blakeney, R., *A Boy in the Peninsular War* (London, 1899).
Blenkinsopp, L.J. & Rainey, J.W., *Army Veterinary Services in the First World War* [*in Official History of the War*] (HMSO, 1925).
Bligh, W.G., 'Across the Atlantic in a Horse Transport', *The Canadian Magazine* (Nov. 1922).
Brereton, J.M., *The Horse in War* (Newton Abbot, 1976).
Brett-Smith, R., *The 11th Hussars (Prince Albert's Own)* (London, 1969).

Clabby, J., *A History of the Royal Army Veterinary Corps 1919–1961* (J.A. Allen, 1963).

Coronation Horses, 1953 (unattributed).

Corvi, Steven J., 'Men of Mercy: The evolution of the Royal Army Veterinary Corps and the soldier-horse bond during the Great War', *Journal of Army Historical Research* (Winter 1998, vol. LXXVI, no. 308).

Cregier, Sharon, *Alleviating Surface Transit Stress on Horses* (Unpublished PhD dissertation, Walden University, 1980).

Curling, Edward (ed.), *Recollections of Rifleman Harris* (London, 1929).

Daniel, John Edgecombe, *Portugal to Waterloo with Wellington: the Journal of a British Commissariat Officer in the Peninsular War and the Campaign of 1815* (London, 2012).

Dickson, Alexander, *The Dickson Manuscripts*.

Fillis, James, *Breaking and Riding with Military Commentaries*, trans. M.H. Hayes (London, 1902).

Fitz Wygram, F., *Horses and Stables* (London, 1869).

Fletcher, Ian, *Galloping at Everything: the British cavalry in the Peninsular War and at Waterloo 1808–15* (Staplehurst, 1999).

Furse, G.A., *Military Transport* (London, 1882).

Galtrey, Sidney, *Horses and the War* (London, 1983).

Gleig, George, *The Hussar* (London, 1837).

Glover, R., *Wellington as Military Commander* (London, 1968).

Hamilton, Henry Blackburne, *Historical Record of the 14th (King's Own) Hussars from 1715 to 1900* (London, 1900).

Harfield, Alan, *Pigeon to Packhorse* (Chippenham, 1989).

Hayes, M.H., *Horses on Board Ship; a guide to their management* (London, 1902) Hayes, M.H., *Veterinary Notes for Horse Owners* (London, 1884).

Haythornthwaite, Philip, *The British Cavalryman, 1792–1815* (Oxford, 1989).

Hibbert, C., *Corunna* (London, 1961).

Smith, Major General Sir Frederick, *A History of the Royal Army Veterinary Corps 1796–1919* (London, 1927).

Holdsworth & Pugsley, *Sandhurst: A tradition of leadership* (London, no date).

Hyland, Ann, *The Warhorse in the Modern Era* (London, 2015).

Kenyon, David, *Horsemen in No Man's Land: British cavalry and trench warfare, 1914–1918* (Barnsley, 2012).

Le Marchant, J.G., *Rules and Regulations for the Sword Exercise of the Cavalry* (London, 1796).

Lipscombe, Nick, *Wellington's Guns* (London, 2013).

Macdonald, Janet, *Riding Side-saddle* (London, 1995).

Macdonald, Janet, *Sir John Moore: the making of a controversial soldier* (Barnsley, 2016).

Mackesy, Piers, *British Victory in Egypt* (London, 1995).

Moore, Sir John, *Army Veterinary Service in War* (London, 1921).

Moore-Collyer, R.J., 'Horse Supply and the British Cavalry: a Review 1066–1900', *Journal of Army Historical Research* (Winter 1992, vol. LXX, no. 284).

Moorhead, Alan, *The Blue Nile* (London, 1962).

Napier, William, *The Life and Opinions of General Sir Charles Napier* (London, 1857).

Nolan, L.E., *The Training of Cavalry Remount Horses, a new system* (1852).

Nolan, L.E., *Cavalry: Its History and Tactics* (London, 1853).

Oman, Sir Charles, *History of the Peninsular War* (Oxford, 1902).

Pembroke, Henry, Earl of, *Military Equitation: A Method of Breaking Horses and Teaching Soldiers to Ride* (London, 1761).

Preston, R.M.P., *The Desert Mounted Corps* (London, 1921).

Ranfurly, Countess of, *To War With Whitaker* (London, 1994).

Robson, M.R., 'Some Common Skin Conditions of Military Horses', *Chiron Calling* (Winter 2000/01).

Rogers, H.C.B., *The Mounted Troops of the British Army: 1066–1945* (London, 1959).

Royle, Trevor, *Crimea* (London, 1999).

Schaumann, Augustus, *On the Road With Wellington* (London, 1999).

Steyn, Douw G., 'Animals and Poison Gas Warfare', *Journal of the SAVMA* (1940).

Sutcliffe, R.K., *British Expeditionary Warfare and the Defeat of Napoleon* (Woodbridge, 2016).

Sutton, John & Walker, John, *From Horse to Helicopter 1648–1989* (London, 1990).

Tennant, Dick, in *First Empire* (Jul./Aug. 2010).

Thompson, Mark S., *Wellington's Engineers: Military Engineering in the Peninsular War 1808–1814* (Barnsley, 2015).

Tomkinson, James (ed.), *Diary of a Cavalry Officer in the Peninsular War and Waterloo Campaign 1809–1815* (London, 1894).

Tylden, G., *Horses and Saddlery* (London, 1965).

Ward, S.G.P., *Wellington's Headquarters* (London, 1957).

Warner, Philip (ed.), *A Cavalryman in the Crimea: the letters of Temple Goodman, 5th Dragoon Guards* (London, 1977).

Wilkins, J.H., 'Conformation of the Horse & purchasing of Army Horses', *Journal of the Royal Army Veterinary Corps* (Spring, 1966).

Winchester, Simon, *Krakatoa* (London, 2003).

Winton, G., *Theirs Not to Reason Why: Horsing the British Army 1875–1925* (Solihull, 2013).

Wylly, H.C. (ed.), *Memoirs of Lieutenant General Sir Joseph Thackwell* (London, 1908).

Website

www.merckvetmanual.com

Index